ROCKY MOUNTAIN BISON

LOCHLAINN SEABROOK WRITES IN THE FOLLOWING GENRES

American Civil War
American History
American Politics
American South
Ancient History
Biography
Coffee Table
Cooking
Diet and Nutrition
Education
Ethnic Studies
Etymology
European History
Family Histories
Film
Genealogy
Ghost Stories
Health and Fitness
Humor
Law of Attraction
Life After Death
Men
Military History
Mysteries and Enigmas
Natural Health
Natural History
Onomastics
Paranormal
Philosophy
Photography
Poetry
Politics
Presidential History
Quiz Books
Reference
Religion and Spirituality
Revolutionary Period
Science
Self-help
UFOs and Extraterrestrials
Victorian Period
Wildlife
Women
World History

For more information visit our Website

This volume is part of

LOCHLAINN SEABROOK'S AMERICAN WEST NATURE SERIES

which includes fine art photography coffee table books on Rocky Mountain

BIGHORN SHEEP
EQUINES
LANDSCAPES
MULE DEER
SEASONS
WATERWAYS
WILDLFLOWERS
WILDLIFE
WILD HORSES

and more

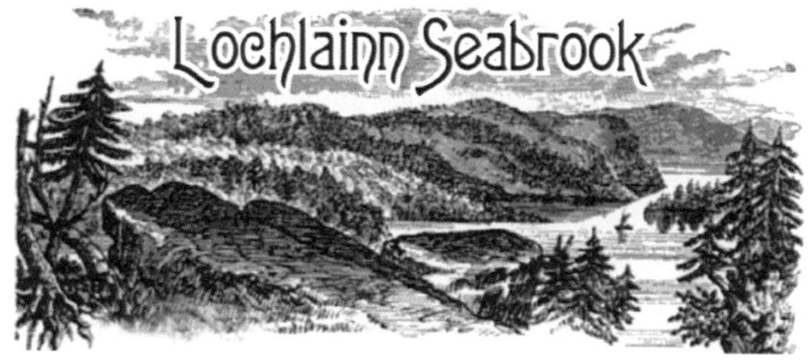

Warning:
SEA RAVEN PRESS
BOOKS WILL EXPAND
YOUR MIND!

ROCKY MOUNTAIN BISON

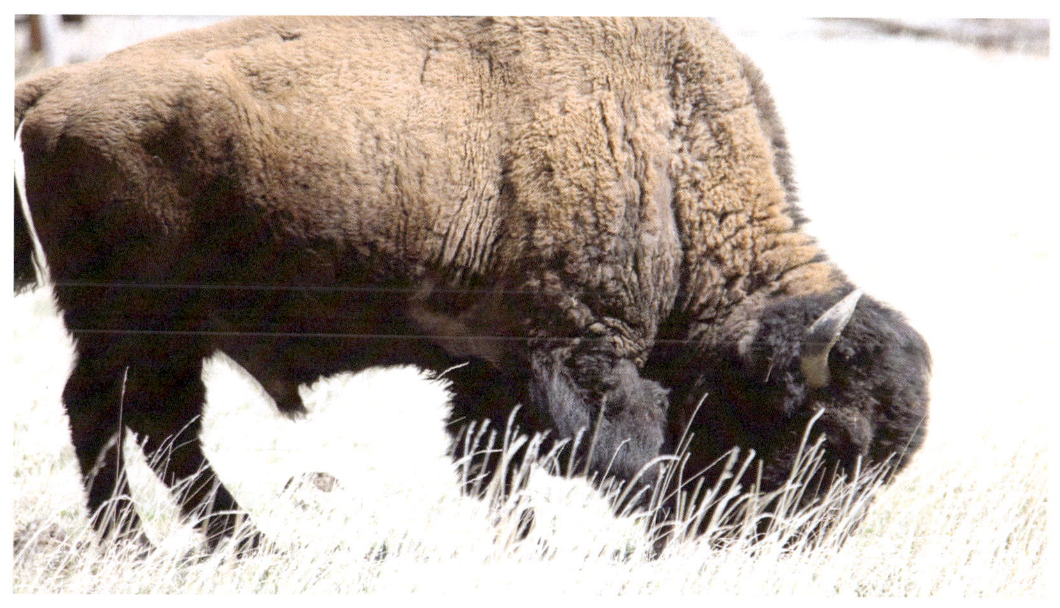

A Photographic Collection of Bison of the American West

AMERICAN WEST NATURE SERIES

LOCHLAINN SEABROOK

NATURE, WILDLIFE, AND LANDSCAPE PHOTOGRAPHER AND AWARD WINNING AUTHOR

2024

Sea Raven Press, Park County, Wyoming USA

ROCKY MOUNTAIN BISON

Published by
Sea Raven Press, LLC, Cassidy Ravensdale, President
Park County, Wyoming, USA
SeaRavenPress.com

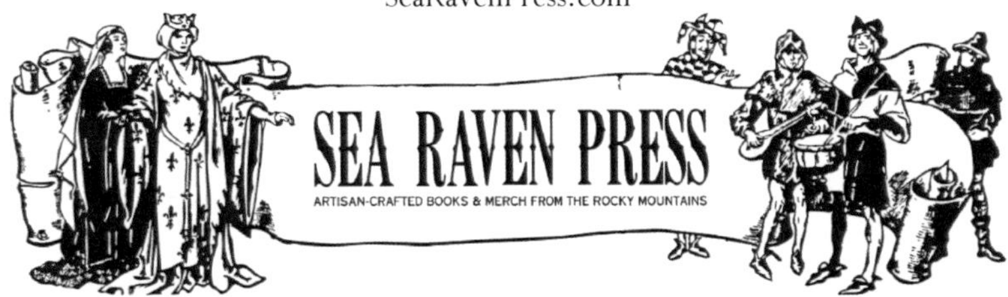

PRINTING HISTORY
1st SRP paperback edition, 1st printing, April 2025 • ISBN: 978-1-955351-55-3
1st SRP hardcover edition, 1st printing, July 2024 • ISBN: 978-1-955351-49-2

ISBN: 978-1-955351-55-3 (paperback)
Library of Congress Control Number: 2024940594

Rocky Mountain Bison: A Photographic Collection of Bison of the American West (American West Nature Series), by Lochlainn Seabrook. Includes an introduction, illustrations, photographs, captions, and a bibliography.

ARTWORK
Front and back cover design and art, book design, layout, font selection, and interior art by Lochlainn Seabrook
All images, image captions, graphic design, and graphic art copyright © Lochlainn Seabrook
All images photographed, selected, placed, manipulated, cleaned, colored, tinted, and/or created by Lochlainn Seabrook
Cover photo: "Rocky Mountain Bison," Image 7X8A7861, by Lochlainn Seabrook
Title page photo: Image 7X8A6902, by Lochlainn Seabrook

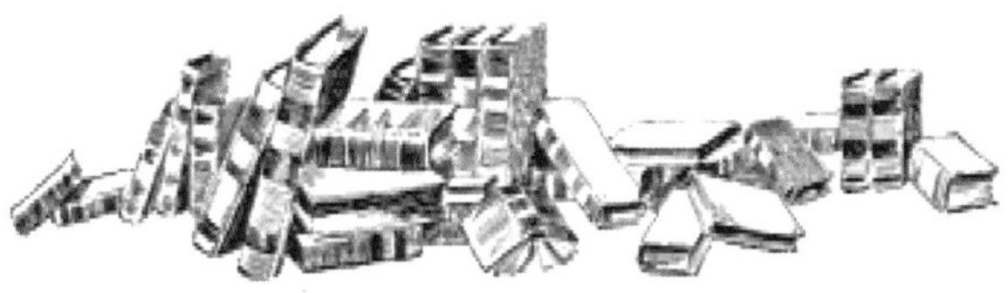

Lochlainn Seabrook does not author books for fame and glory, but for the love of writing and sharing his knowledge and art.

WRITTEN, DESIGNED, PUBLISHED IN THE UNITED STATES OF AMERICA, LAND OF THE FREE, HOME OF THE BRAVE

DEDICATION

To the noble North American bison, which, according to early explorers and settlers, once numbered some 50 million individuals and populated the entire U.S., from Alaska to New England, south to Florida, with great herds occurring throughout the Midwest, Southern states, and Rocky Mountains, all the way to California.

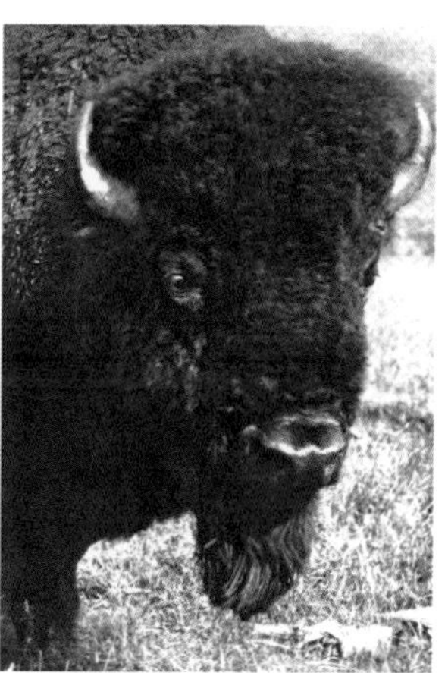

EPIGRAPH

"The following account, by Dr. Richardson, affords an instance of the danger to be apprehended from these powerful animals, when wounded, and not disabled: 'Mr. Finnan McDonald, one of the Hudson's Bay Company's clerks was descending the Saskatchewan [River] in a boat; and one evening, having pitched his tent for the night, he went out in the dusk to look for game. It had become nearly dark when he fired at a Bison bull, which was galloping over an eminence; and as he was hastening forward to see if this shot had taken effect, the wounded beast made a rush at him. He had the presence of mind to seize the animal by the long hair on the forehead, as it struck him on the side with its horn, and being a remarkably tall and powerful man, a struggle ensued, which continued until his wrist was severely sprained, and his arm was rendered powerless; he then fell, and after receiving two or three blows, became senseless. Shortly afterwards he was found by his companions . . . being gored in several places, and the Bison was couched beside him, apparently waiting to renew the attack, had he shown any signs of life. Mr. McDonald recovered from the immediate effects of the injuries, but he died a few months afterwards. Many instances might be mentioned of the tenaciousness with which this animal pursues its revenge; and I have been told of a hunter being detained for many hours in a tree, by an old bull, which had taken its post below, to watch him.'"

George Vasey, 1851

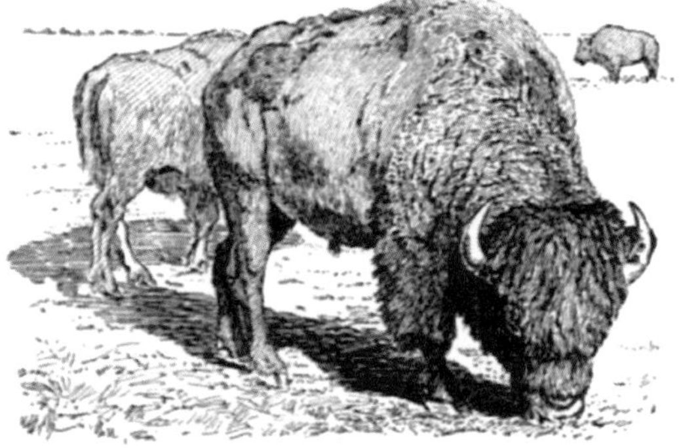

CONTENTS

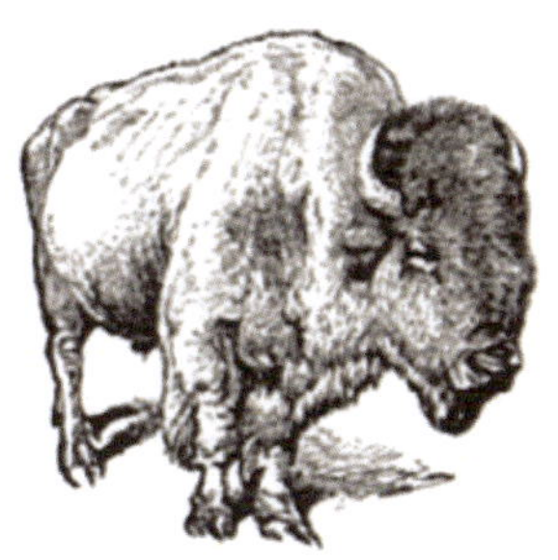

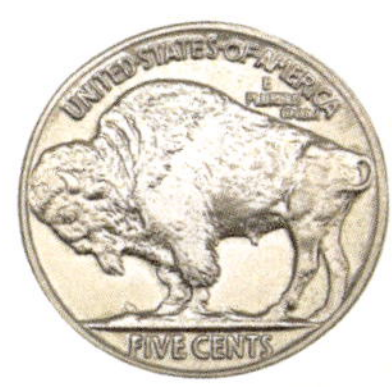

SEA RAVEN PRESS

was founded for the express purpose of publishing and circulating such books as are calculated to store the mind with useful knowledge. We therefore publish only books of a high moral tone and tendency—such works as will be welcomed in every home and at every fireside as valuable family treasures.

L. Seabrook

FINE ART PHOTOGRAPHY PRINTS
by Lochlainn Seabrook

The photos in this book can be purchased as frameable, high-resolution fine art prints through my publisher Sea Raven Press. For more information visit SeaRavenPress.com, and click on "Merch."

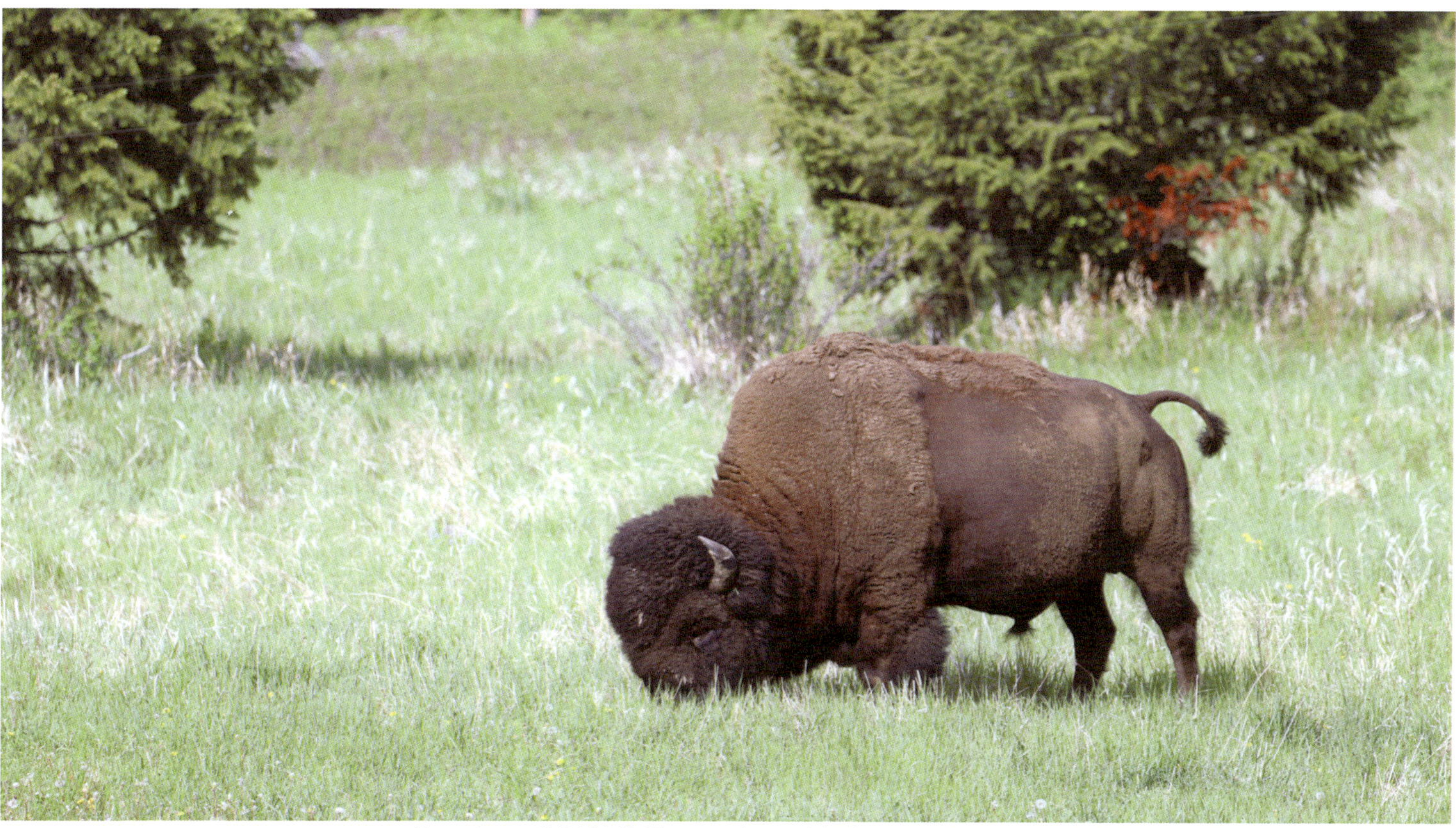

Above: Image 7X8A0463. Photograph copyright © Lochlainn Seabrook.

NOTES TO THE READER

1) In order to most accurately convey the true nature of bison as seen through my camera lenses, in this book I have included a wide cross-section of photos, from closeups to long shots, from sharply focused shots to out of focus images, from the ordinary to the exceptional, from a vintage style to a modern one. This approach derives from my own personal artistic sensibility, and is therefore not accidental, but intentional.

2) While photography is itself a science, as a wildlife photographer I rely on many other scientific disciplines, including biology, zoology, climatology, geology, mammalogy, optics, botany, physics, hydrology, ecology, paleontology, and dendrology, among others. However, the purpose of this book is to showcase my art, and so the focus here—as in the other coffee table books from my American West Nature Series—will be on my photos. Thus I have done away with photo captions, itemized photography equipment, and lists of camera settings, lenses, locations, dates, etc., preferring that my images be enjoyed and interpreted by my readers without any interferences. As I am not in competition with other photographers and shoot my own style regardless of current photography trends, I find that this policy works best for my particular approach to both art and science. L.S.

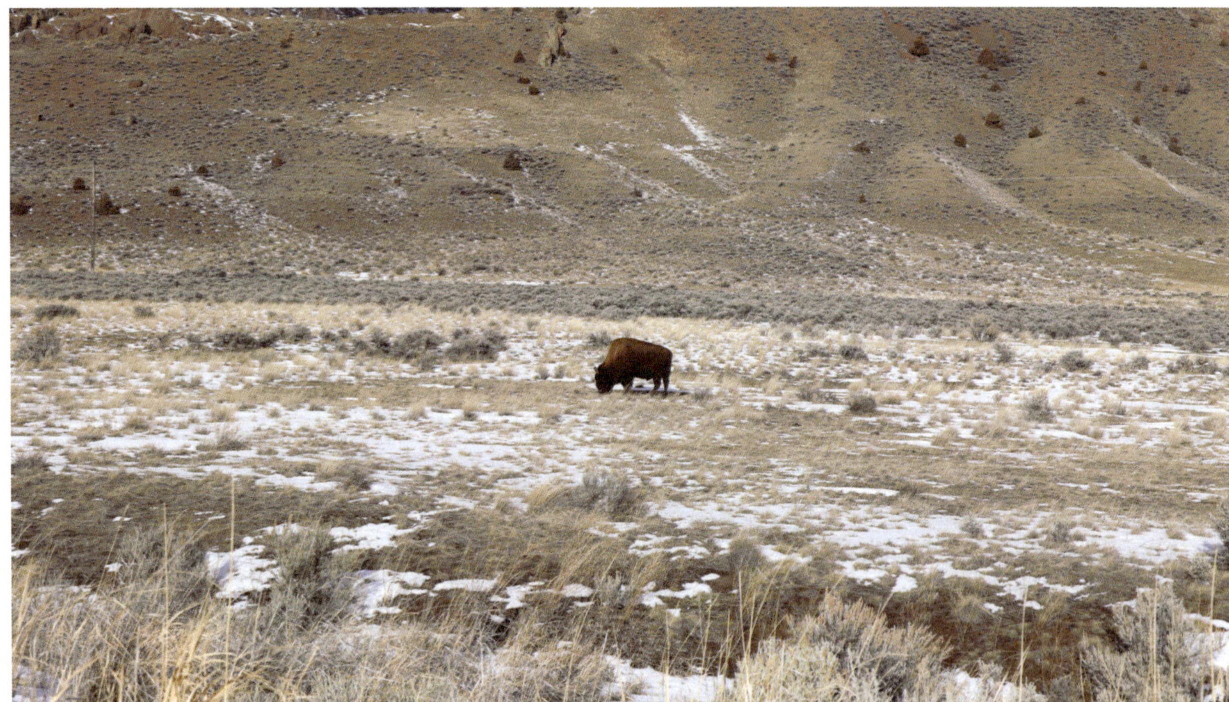

Above: Image 7X8A4478. Photograph copyright © Lochlainn Seabrook.

INTRODUCTION

OF THE APPROXIMATELY 450 SPECIES of mammals in North America, the bison ranks high among my most admired, which is why I have spent several years photographing it and included a detailed entry on it in my popular encyclopedia *North America's Amazing Mammals*. I am now devoting an entire book to this magnificent bovid, which centers around samples from my personal bison photography collection, filmed across Montana, Wyoming, and Idaho, during all four seasons, over every type of terrain, and from low to high elevations. The American plains bison, the photographic subject of this book and known scientifically as *Bison bison bison* (genus, *Bison*; species, *bison*; subspecies, *bison*), is one of two North American bison subspecies. Currently the plains bison can be found in all 50 U.S. states, while the second, the wild American wood bison (*Bison bison athabascae*), is distributed throughout Canada—primarily British Columbia, Alberta, Yukon, Manitoba, and Northwest Territories. Overall it is thought that a total of between 300,000 and 500,000 wild and semi-domesticated bison now exist (the latter group mainly as livestock on beef ranches) across North America.

The plains bison, a member of the Bovidae family (cattle, sheep, goats, water buffalo, etc.), has a truly ancient heritage, with bovine ancestors that trace back to over 1 million years, while even-toed hoofed mammals, the artiodactyls, the scientific order to which it belongs, are at least 45 million years old. Bison played a prominent role in the lives of prehistoric humans, who left sophisticated artistic renderings of them on cave walls some 15,000 years ago (examples can still be seen at such places as Spain's Altamira Cave).

Bison cave art from the Upper Paleolithic.

Our American bison originally migrated east from Asia several hundred thousand years ago, eventually numbering an estimated 50 million, creating enormous herds that blanketed the great plains "from horizon to horizon" in a sea of brown. Due to thoughtless hunting practices this number was reduced to as few as around 300 individuals by 1890, with complete extinction seeming inevitable. Dedicated conservationists, however, were eventually able to save it, bringing its current wild numbers in North America back up to approximately 30,000 individuals (20,000 plains bison, 10,000 wood bison).

Though our bison are often referred to as "buffalo," true buffalo—that is, the water buffalo (*Bubalus bubalis*) and the cape buffalo (*Syncerus caffer*)—inhabit only Africa and Asia, while true *bison* (the Latin word for "wild ox") live only in Europe and North America. The misnomer "buffalo" no doubt originated in the French word for "beef": *boeuf*.

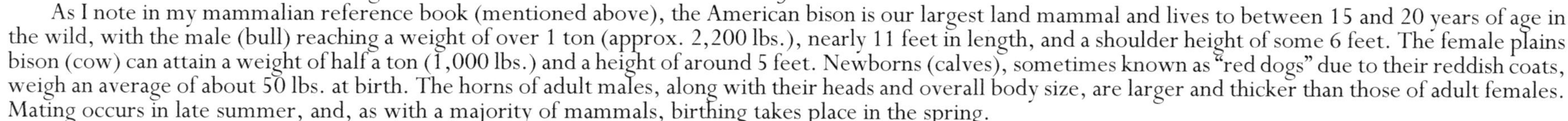

As I note in my mammalian reference book (mentioned above), the American bison is our largest land mammal and lives to between 15 and 20 years of age in the wild, with the male (bull) reaching a weight of over 1 ton (approx. 2,200 lbs.), nearly 11 feet in length, and a shoulder height of some 6 feet. The female plains bison (cow) can attain a weight of half a ton (1,000 lbs.) and a height of around 5 feet. Newborns (calves), sometimes known as "red dogs" due to their reddish coats, weigh an average of about 50 lbs. at birth. The horns of adult males, along with their heads and overall body size, are larger and thicker than those of adult females. Mating occurs in late summer, and, as with a majority of mammals, birthing takes place in the spring.

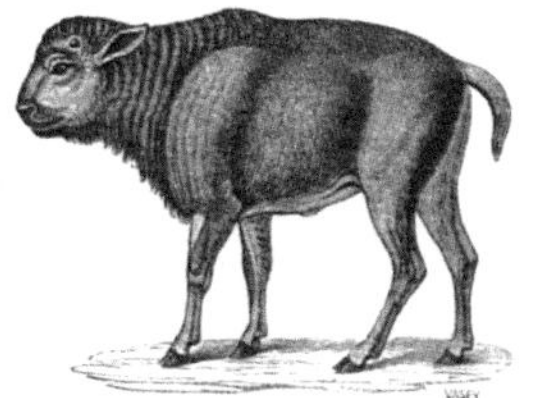

Three-week old "red dog" calf.

While 17th-, 18th-, and 19th-Century Americans, primarily professional "buffalo-hunters," often labeled the plains bison "dull, sluggish, and stupid," my own personal interactions with *Bison bison* have revealed something quite different: a gentle, patient, and inoffensive herbivore of inscrutable intelligence, sensitivity, and awareness; one that will, under normal circumstances, respect and tolerate a human's presence if he or she respects and tolerates it in return. Indeed, some of my close encounters with bison could rightly be described as "transcendental," the opposite of those described by early sportsmen. Despite this, it must be remembered that the massively muscled, nearly indestructible horned bison is an always potentially dangerous and nimble ungulate that can turn on a dime, jump six feet in the air, and run nearly 40 mph—meaning that an adult male can cover almost 60 feet in one second. Thus when filming bison I use a variety of telephoto lenses and maintain the recommended safe distance of 100 yards (the length of an American football field). Yet, in some cases bison have ignored my rigorous safety protocols: seeking me out, they approach me in an easygoing manner, their large brown eyes studying me and my camera equipment with intense curiosity. Once I am thoroughly scrutinized and accepted, such individuals usually calmly return to their favorite past time, grazing, often mere feet from me. Some centuries-old myths die hard.

May *Rocky Mountain Bison* inspire present and future generations to carry on with the preservation and protection of this treasured native species; a robust, handsome, thickly-maned beast with a large shoulder hump, luxuriant brown wooly coat, long beard, and black nose; a beloved ruminant that has become an iconic American symbol of overcoming adversity, well-earning its place as the national mammal of the United States.

Lochlainn Seabrook, Park County, Wyoming USA, July 2024

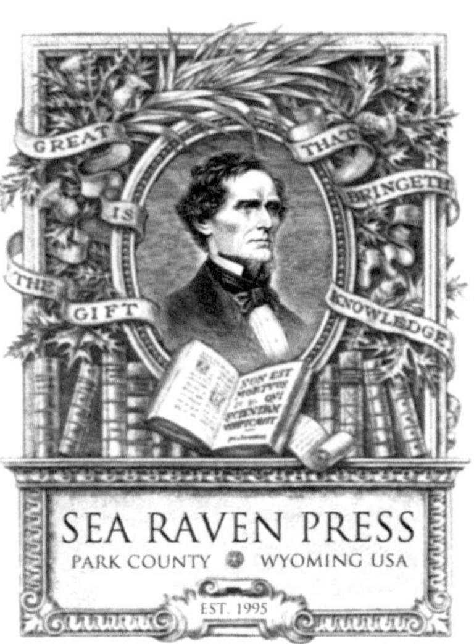

"Books invite all; they constrain none."
Hartley Burr Alexander (1873-1939)

ROCKY MOUNTAIN BISON

Lochlainn Seabrook's Fine Art Photos

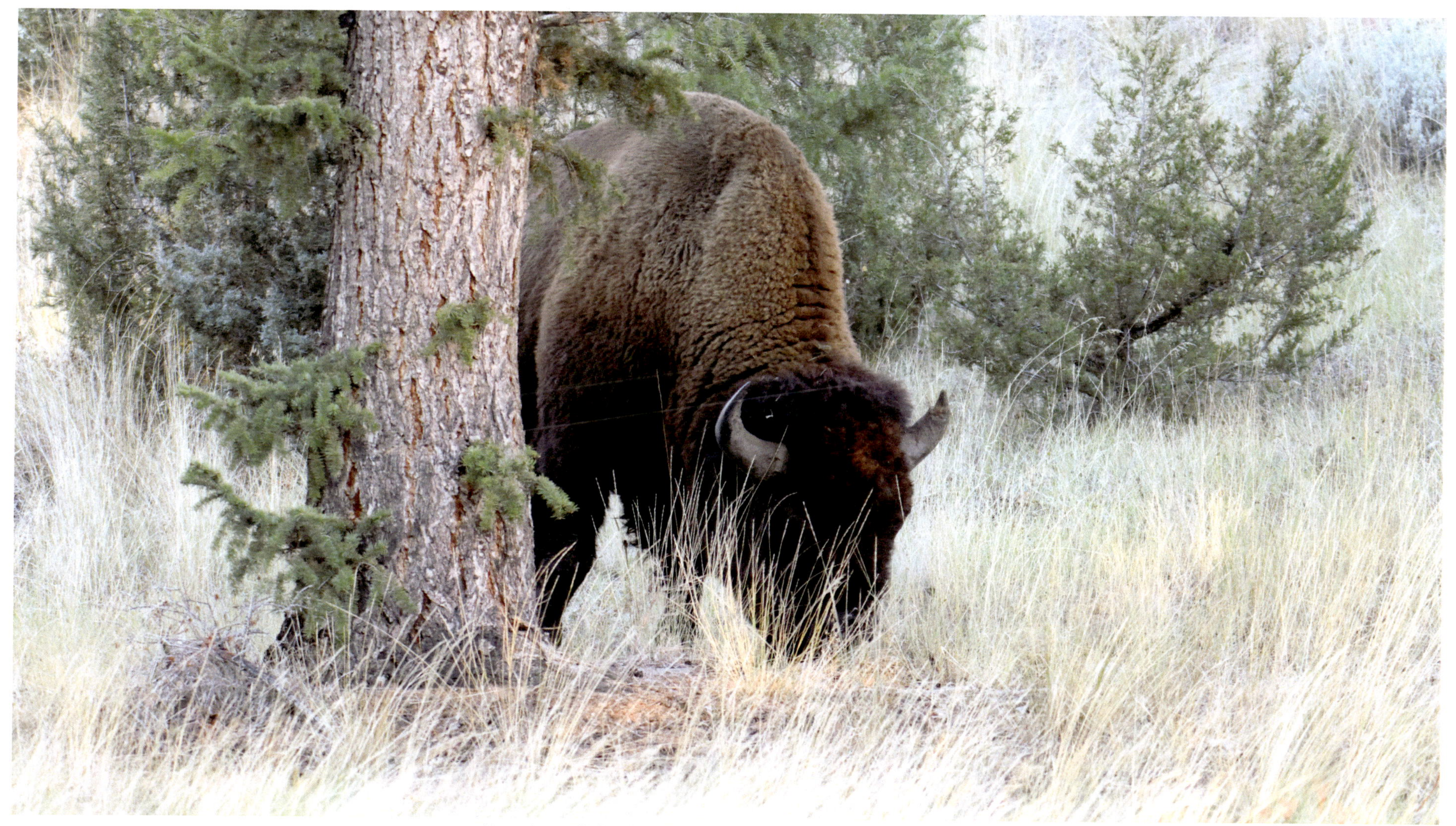

Above: Image 7X8A1084. Photograph copyright © Lochlainn Seabrook.

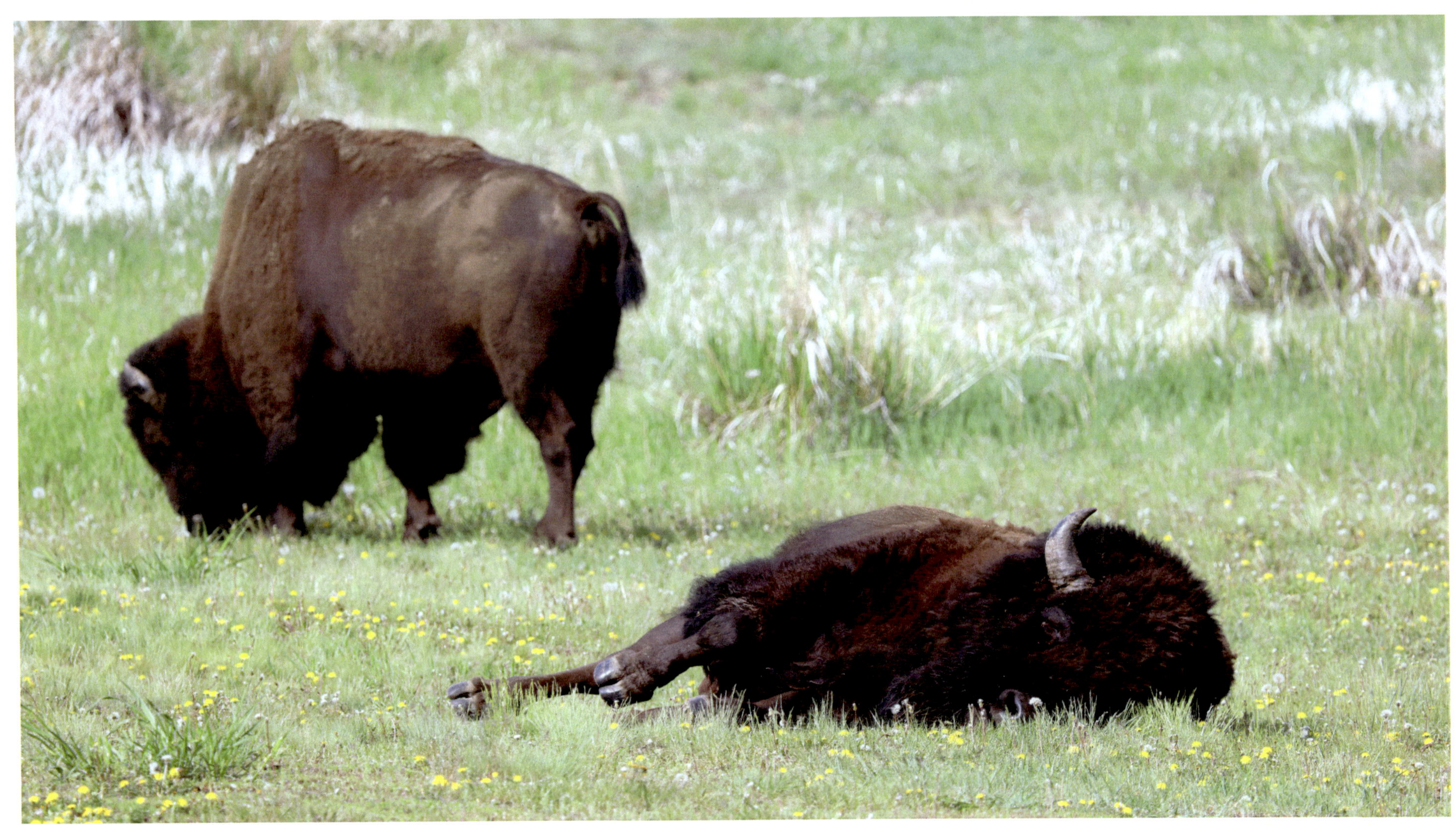

Above: Image 7X8A0486. Photograph copyright © Lochlainn Seabrook.

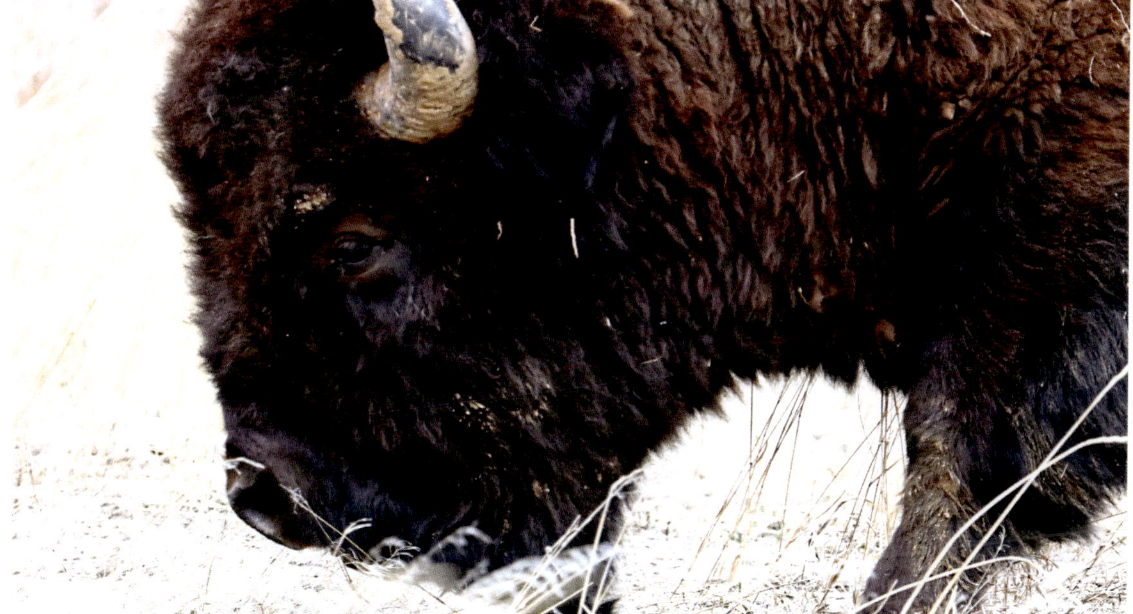

Left: Image IMG_4991. Photograph copyright © Lochlainn Seabrook.

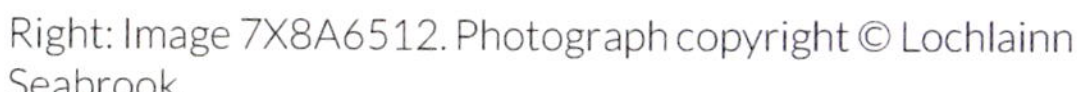

Right: Image 7X8A6512. Photograph copyright © Lochlainn Seabrook.

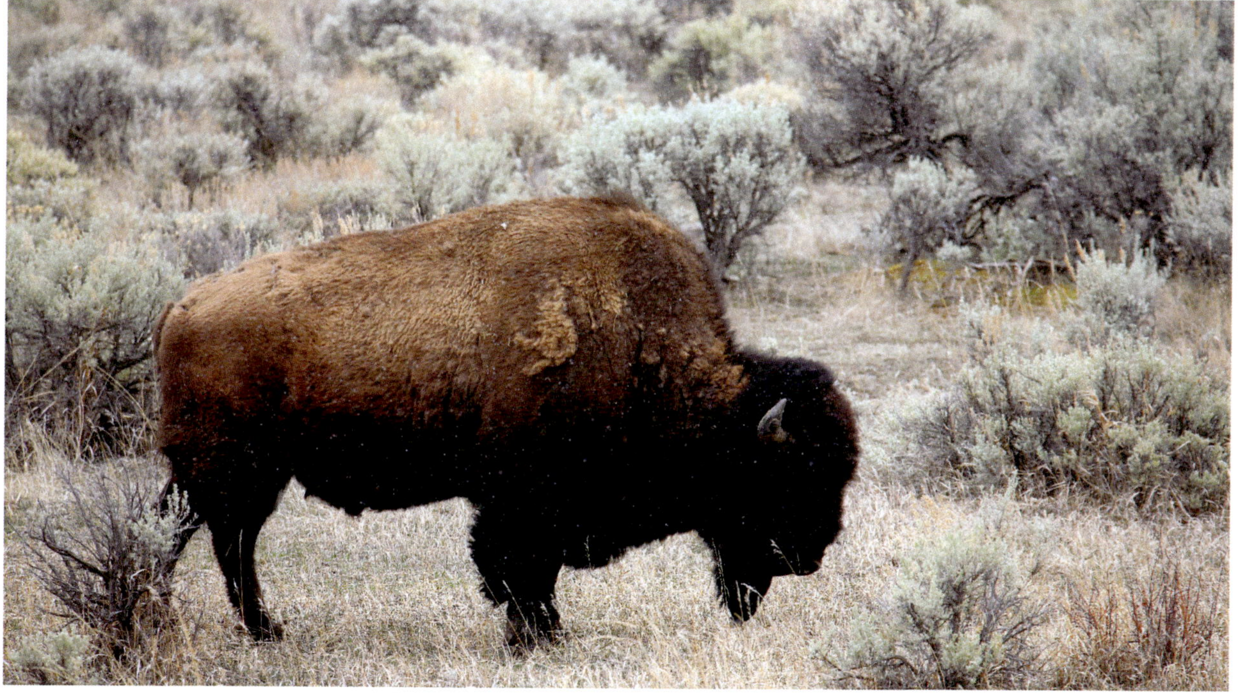

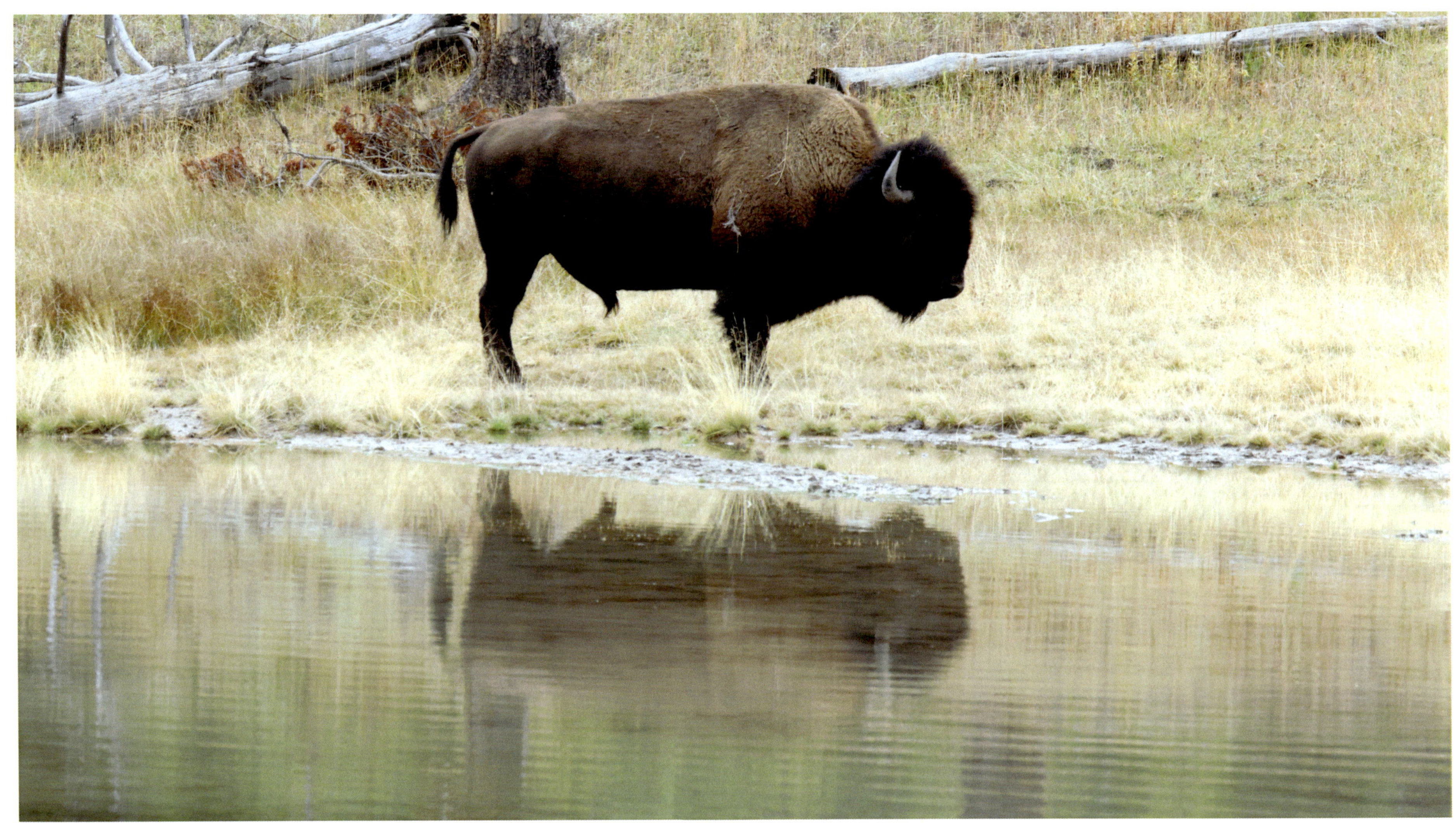

Above: Image 7X8A1476. Photograph copyright © Lochlainn Seabrook.

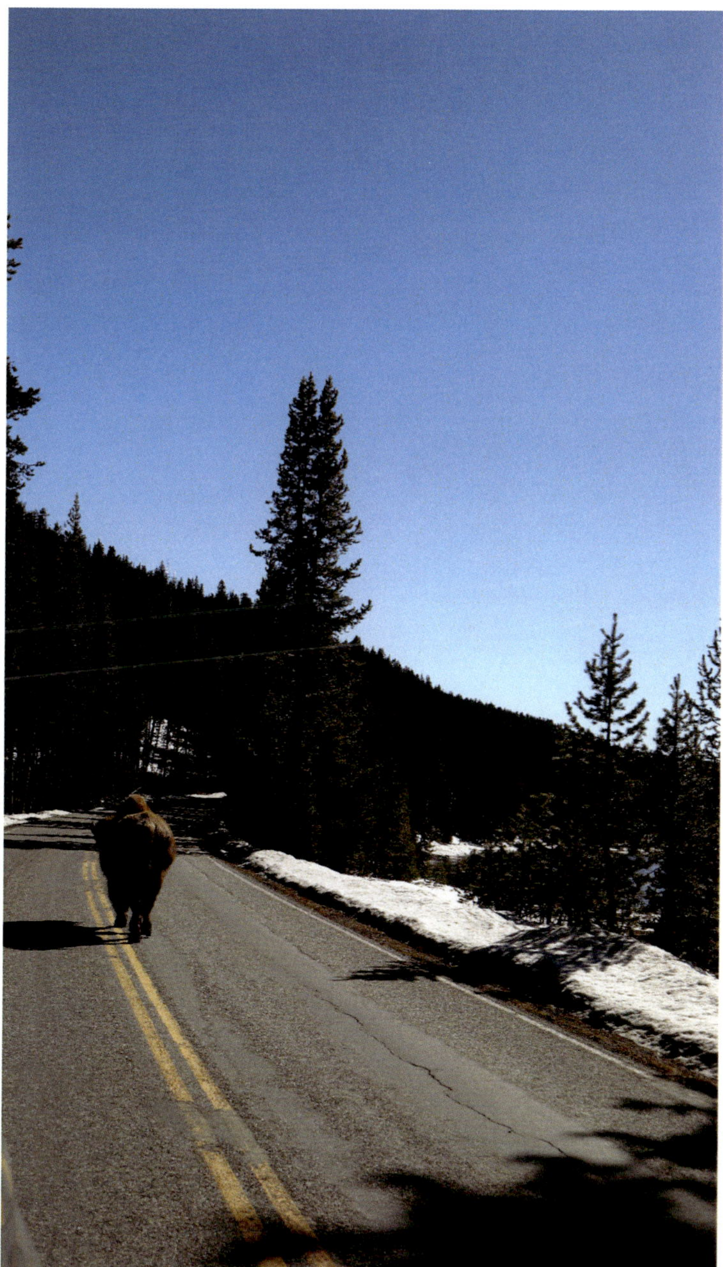

Above: Image IMG_5445. Photograph copyright © Lochlainn Seabrook.

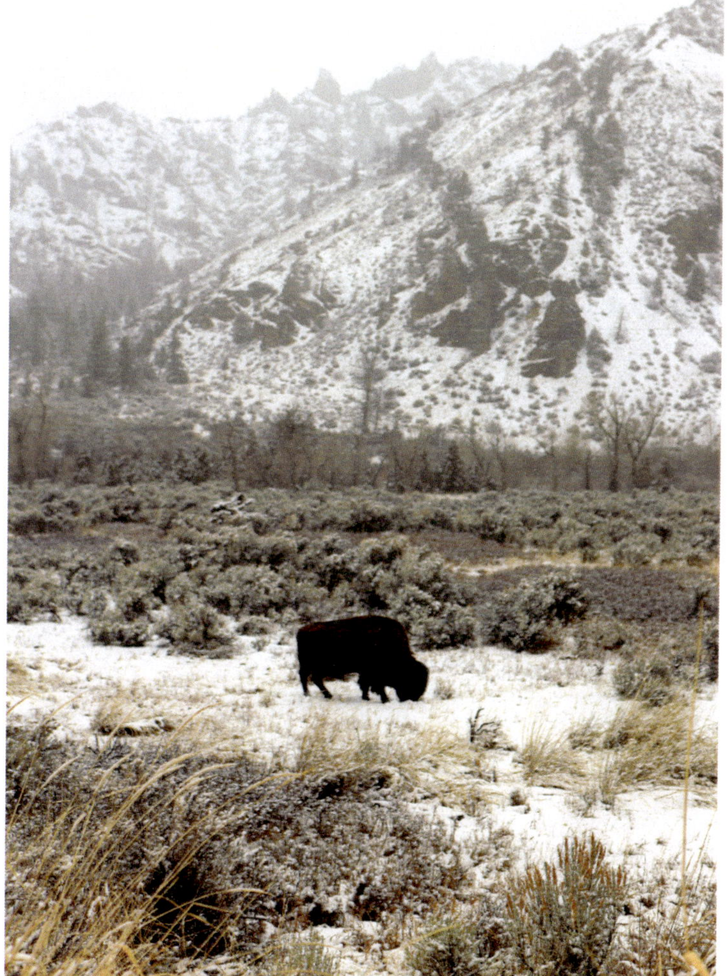

Above: Image 7X8A4605. Photograph copyright © Lochlainn Seabrook.

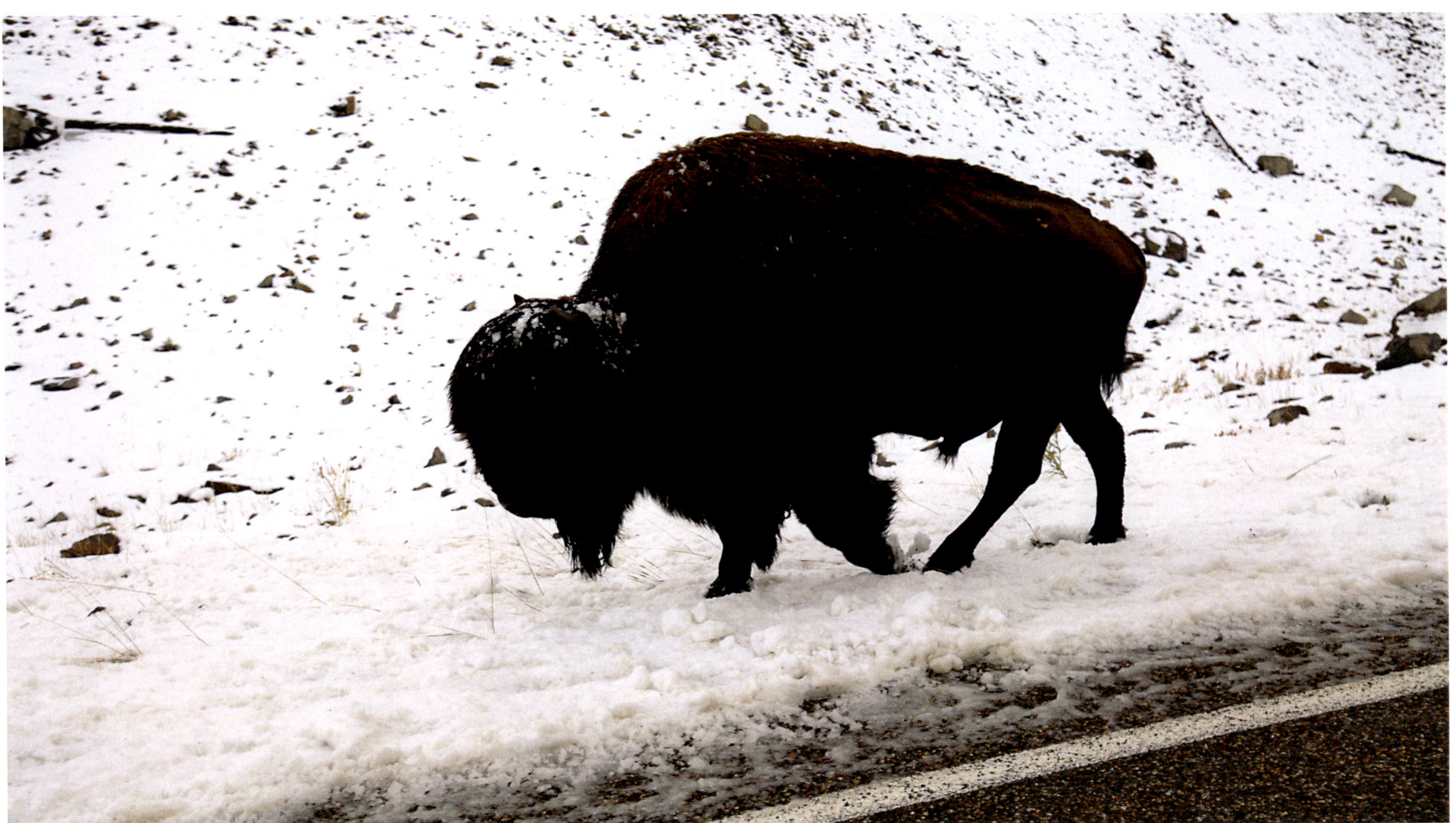

Above: Image 7X8A0855. Photograph copyright © Lochlainn Seabrook.

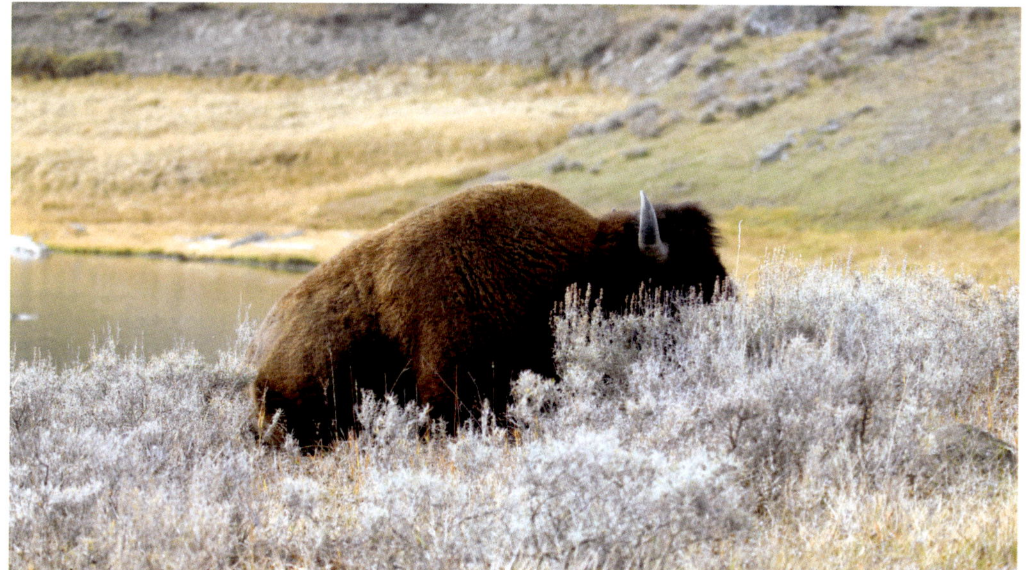

Left: Image 7X8A1820. Photograph copyright © Lochlainn Seabrook.

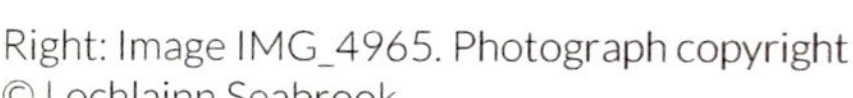

Right: Image IMG_4965. Photograph copyright © Lochlainn Seabrook.

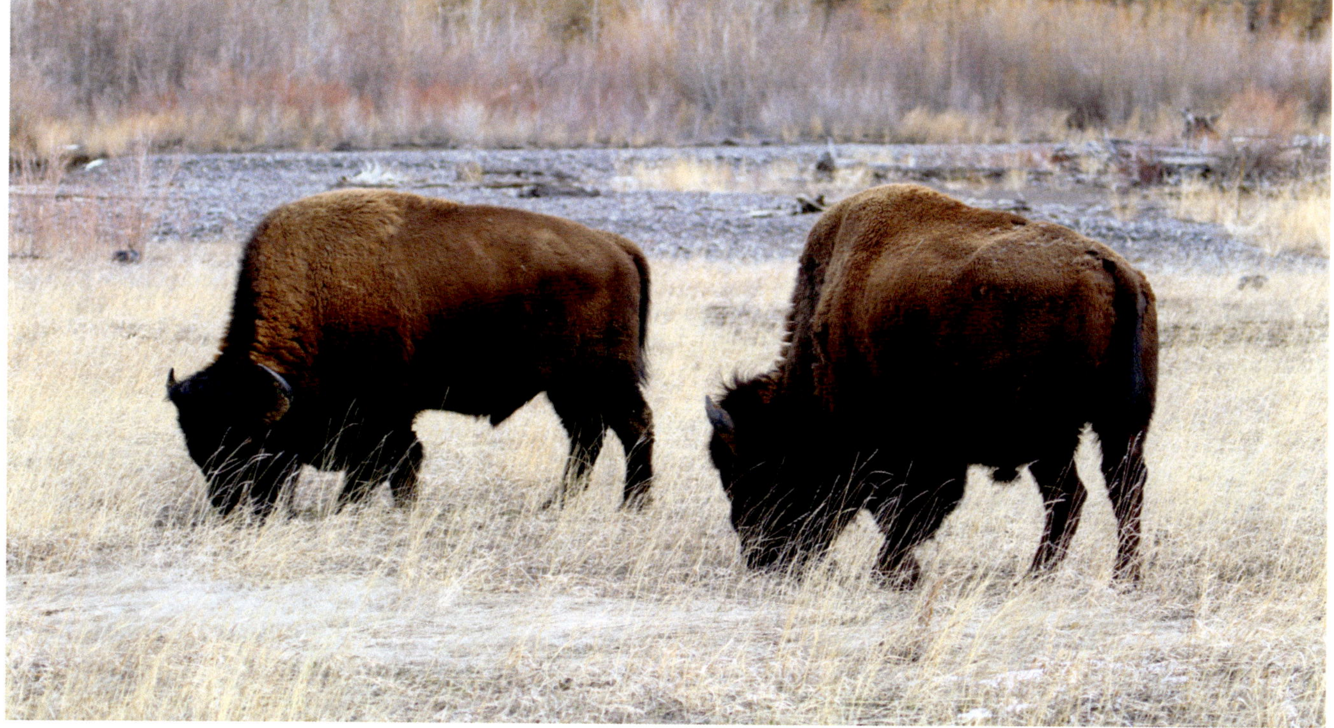

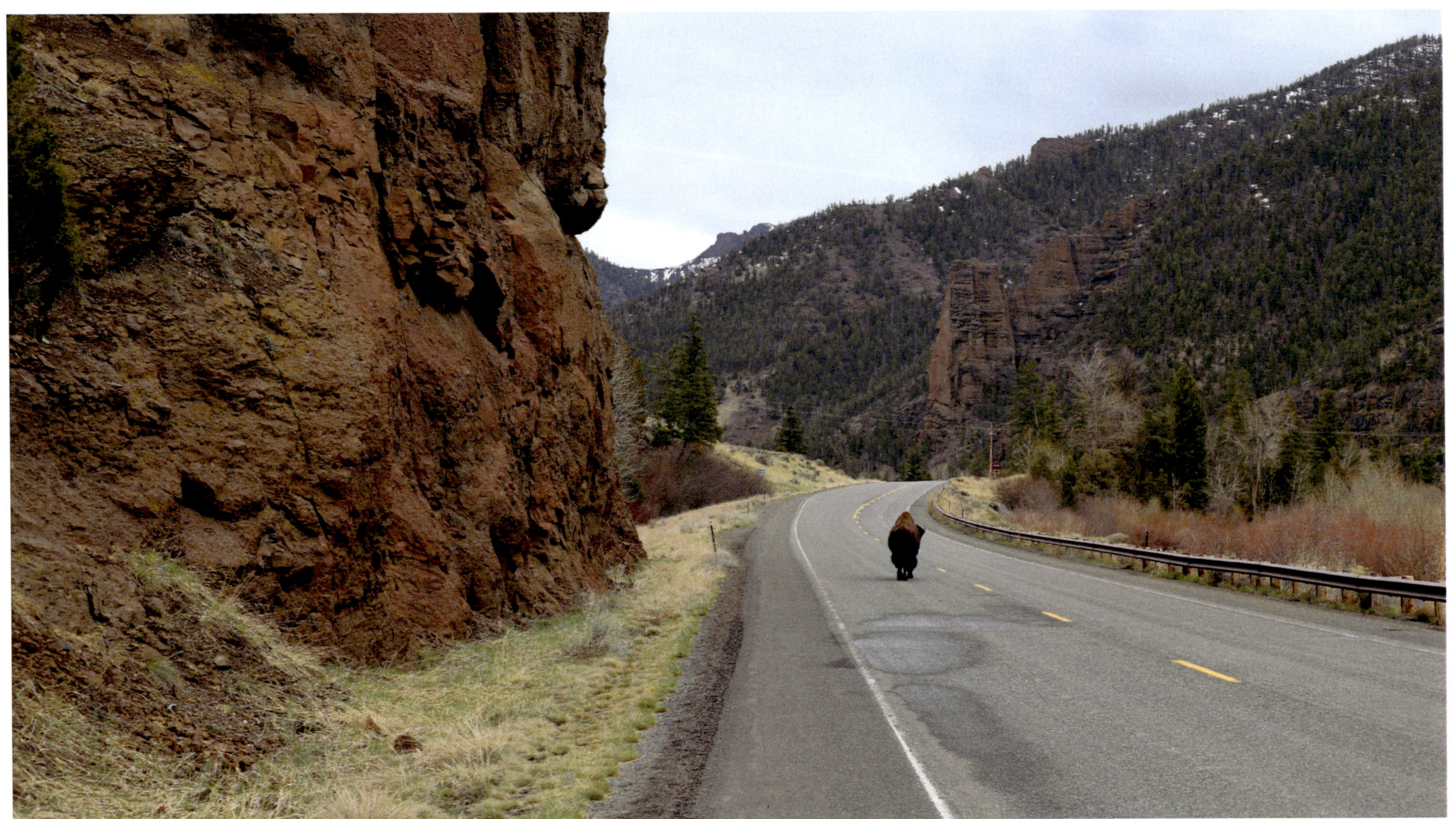

Above: Image 7X8A7845. Photograph copyright © Lochlainn Seabrook.

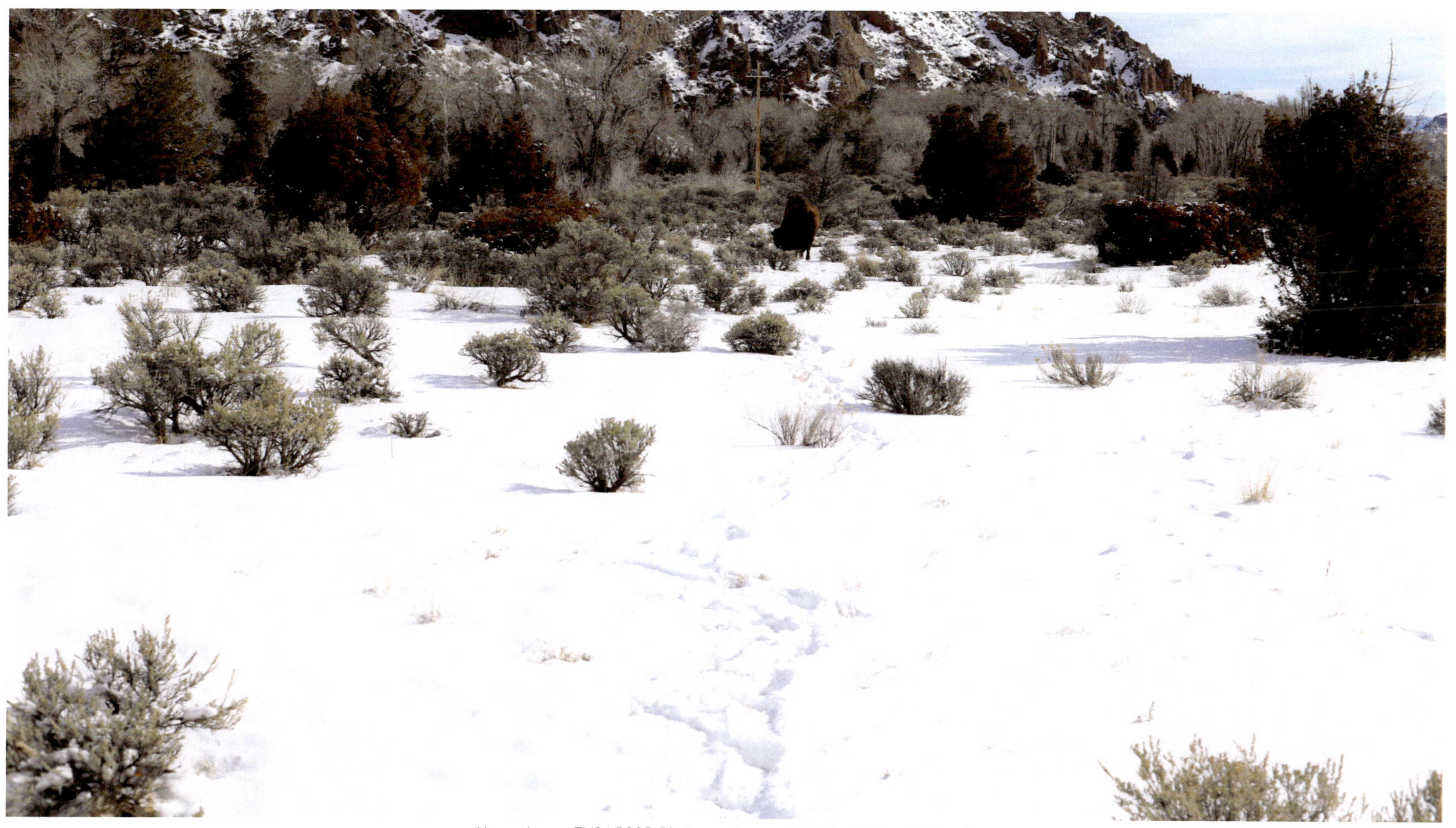

Above: Image 7X8A5295. Photograph copyright © Lochlainn Seabrook.

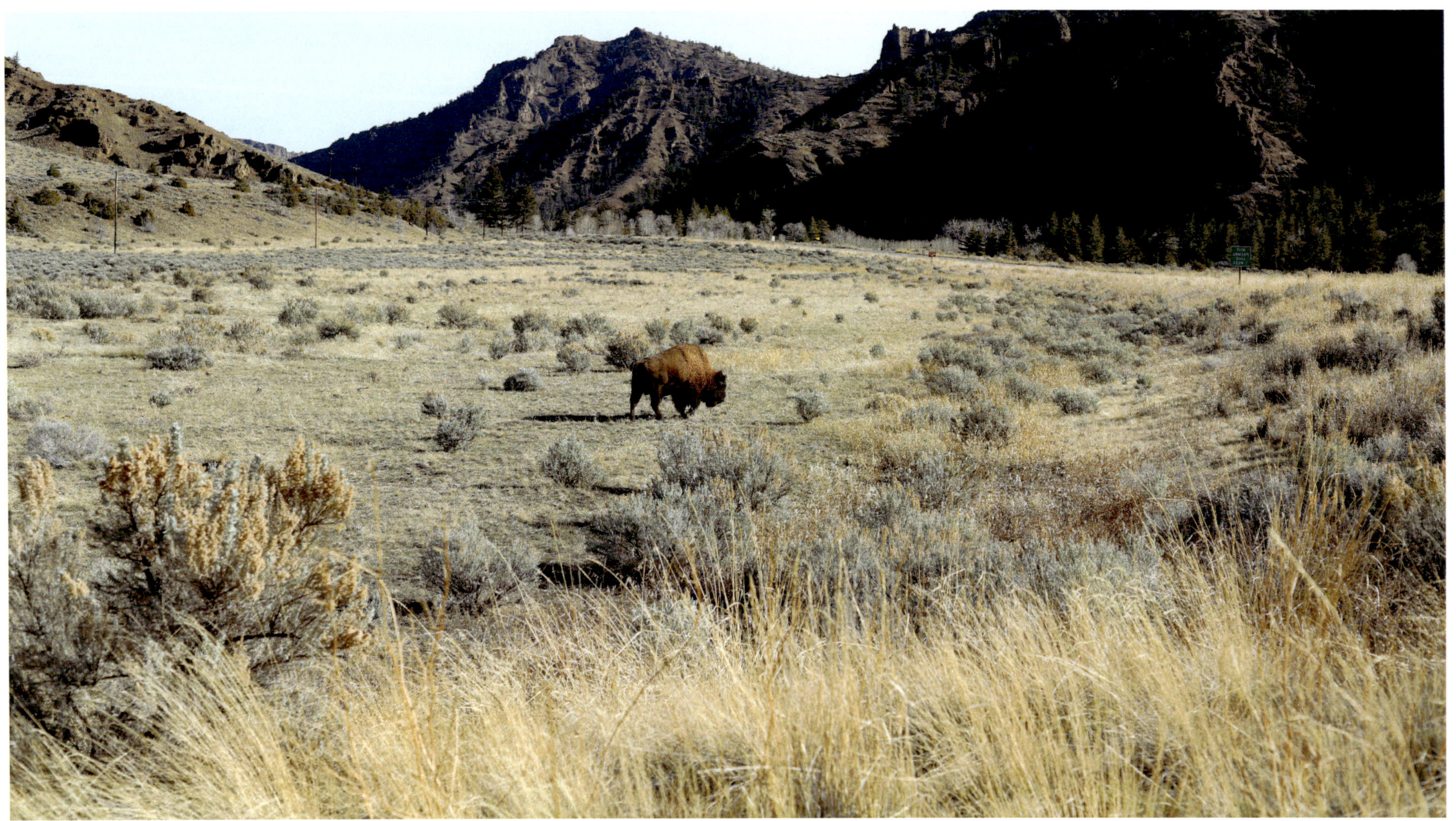

Above: Image 7X8A2589. Photograph copyright © Lochlainn Seabrook.

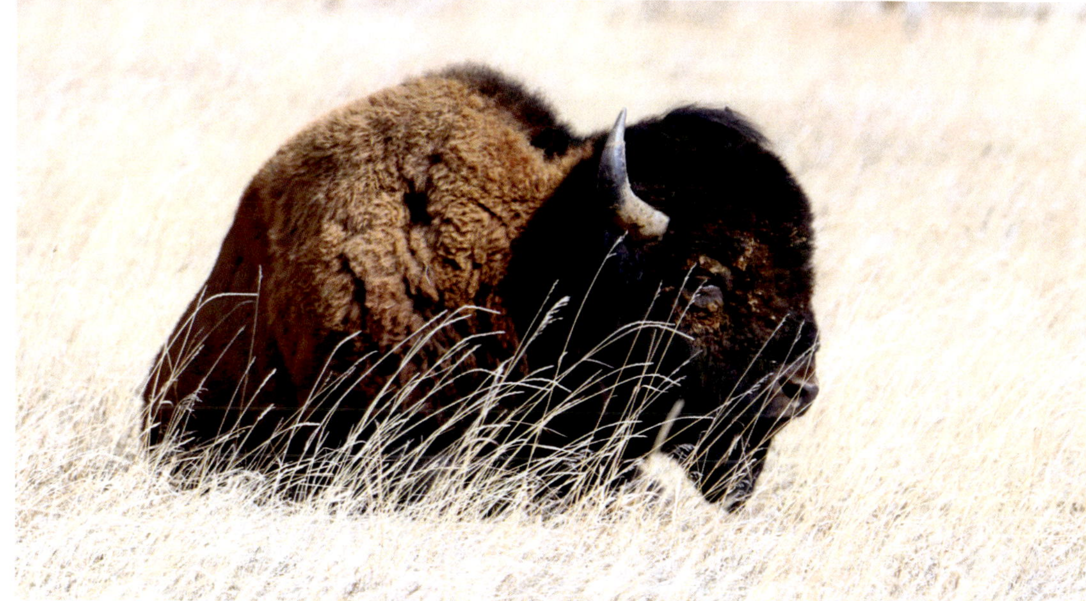

Left: Image IMG_5040. Photograph copyright © Lochlainn Seabrook.

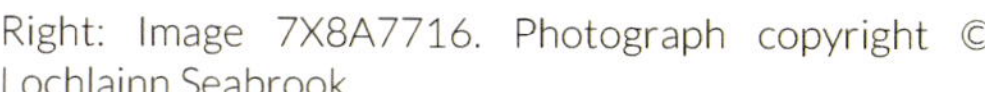

Right: Image 7X8A7716. Photograph copyright © Lochlainn Seabrook.

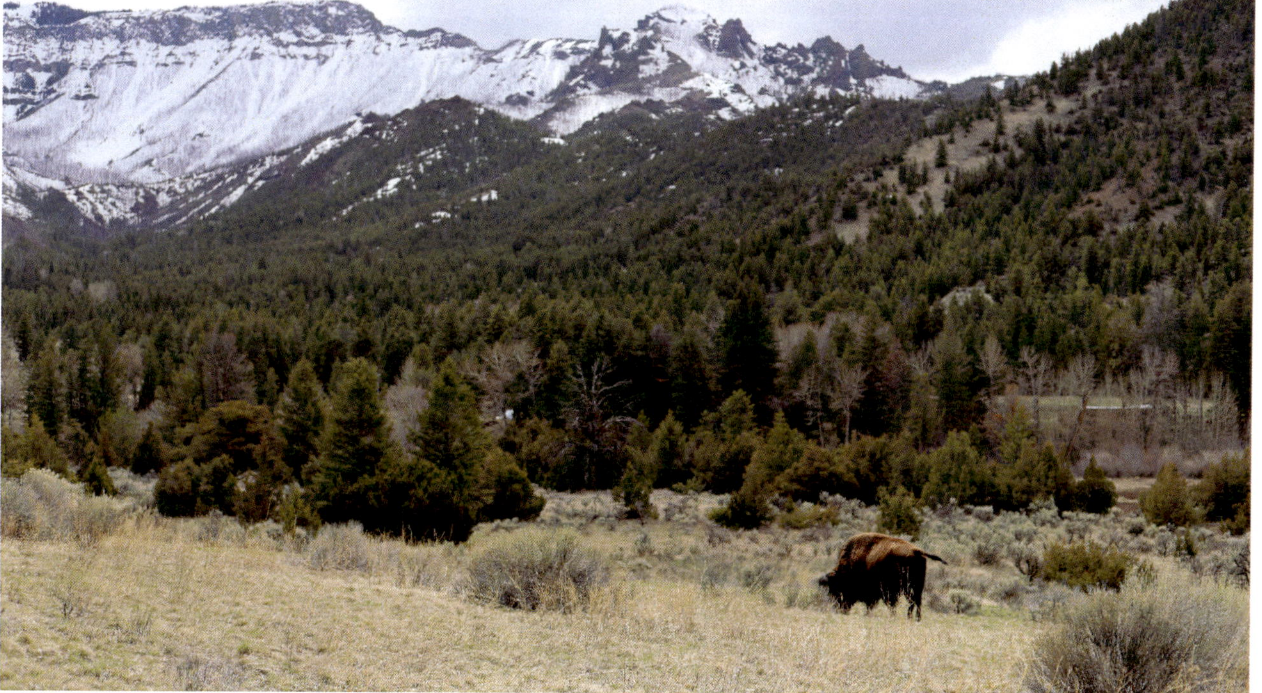

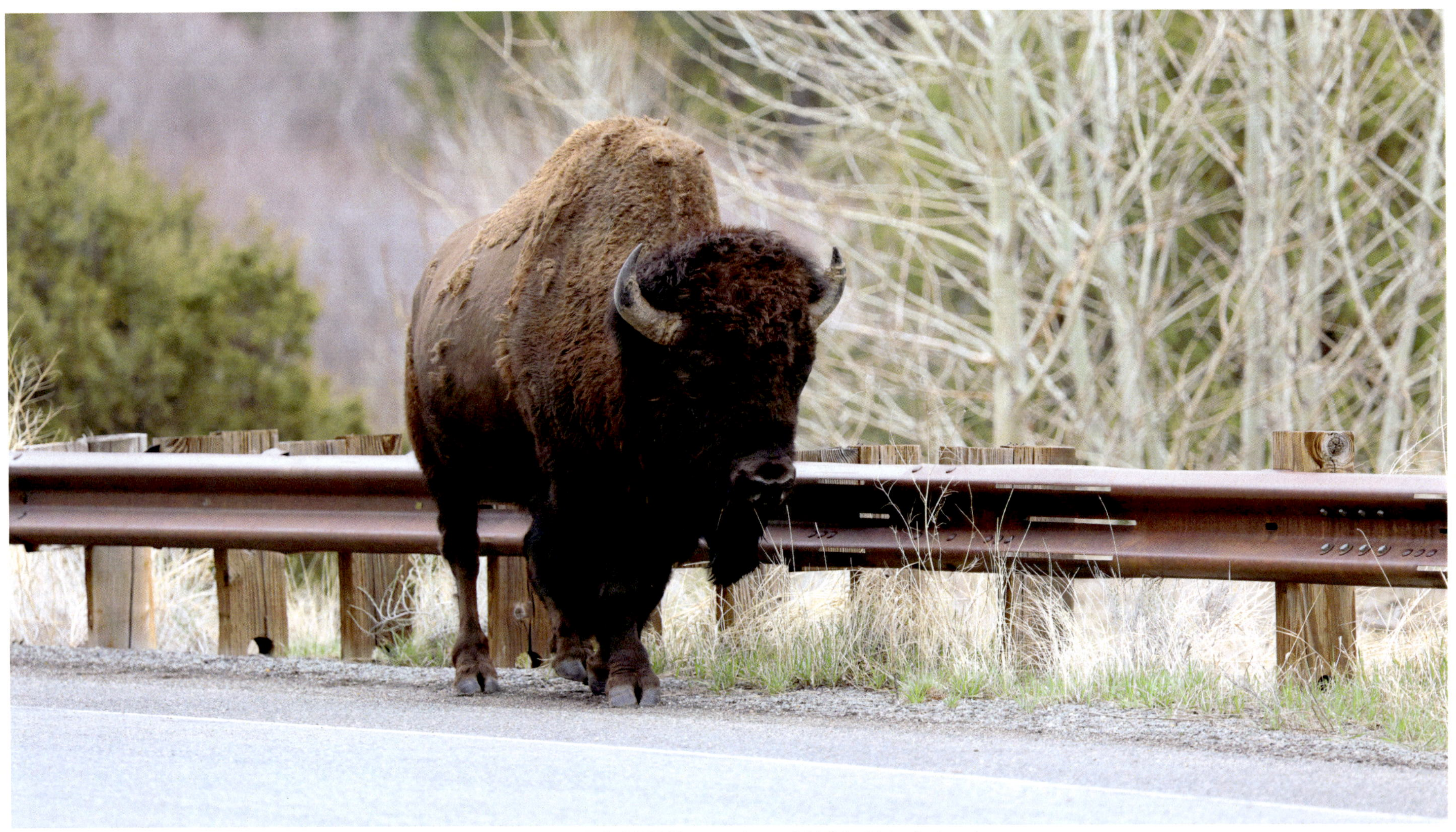

Above: Image 7X8A7857. Photograph copyright © Lochlainn Seabrook.

Right: Image 7X8A3302. Photograph copyright © Lochlainn Seabrook.

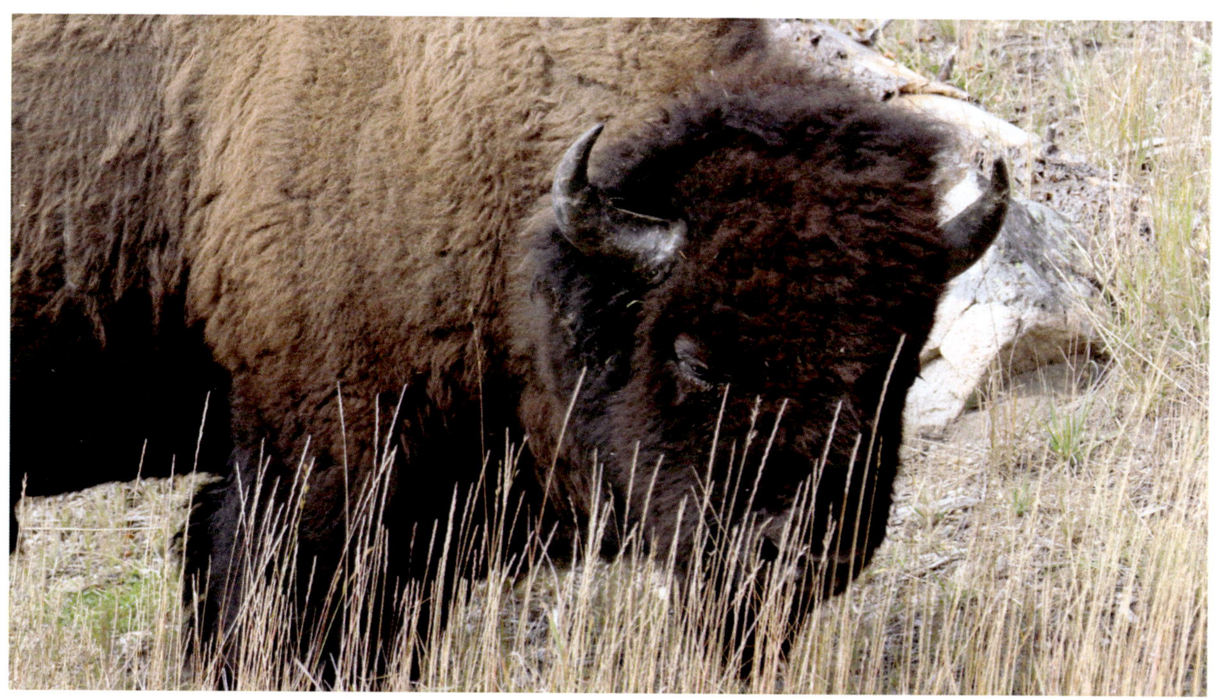

Left: Image 7X8A1000. Photograph copyright © Lochlainn Seabrook.

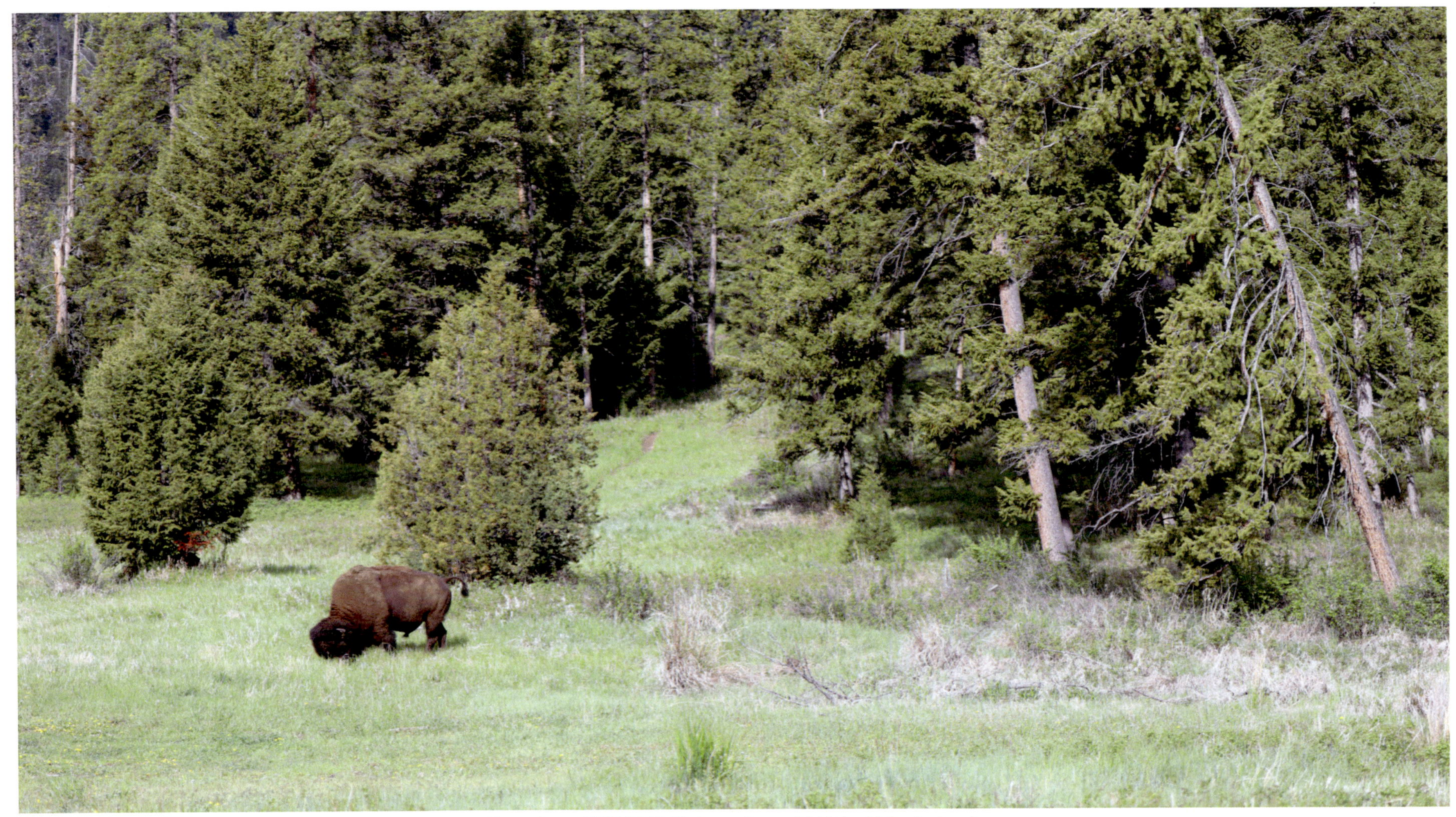

Above: Image 7X8A0462. Photograph copyright © Lochlainn Seabrook.

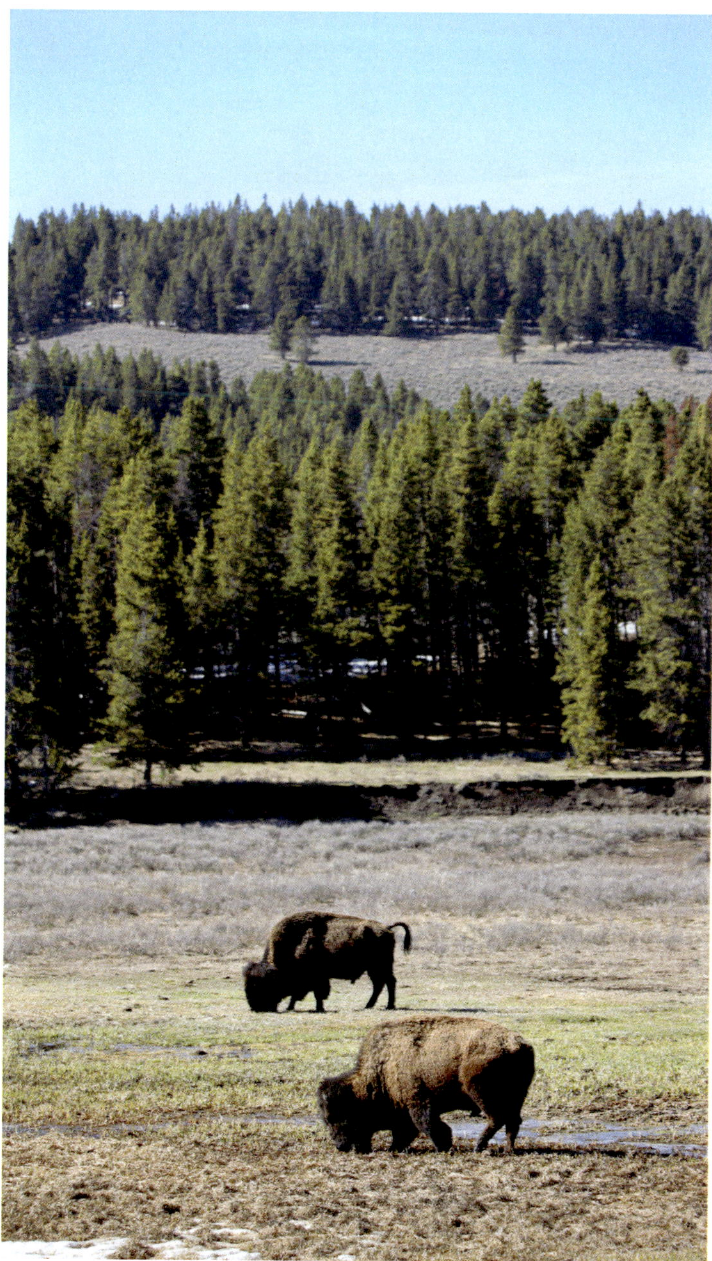

Above: Image 7X8A8973. Photograph copyright © Lochlainn Seabrook.

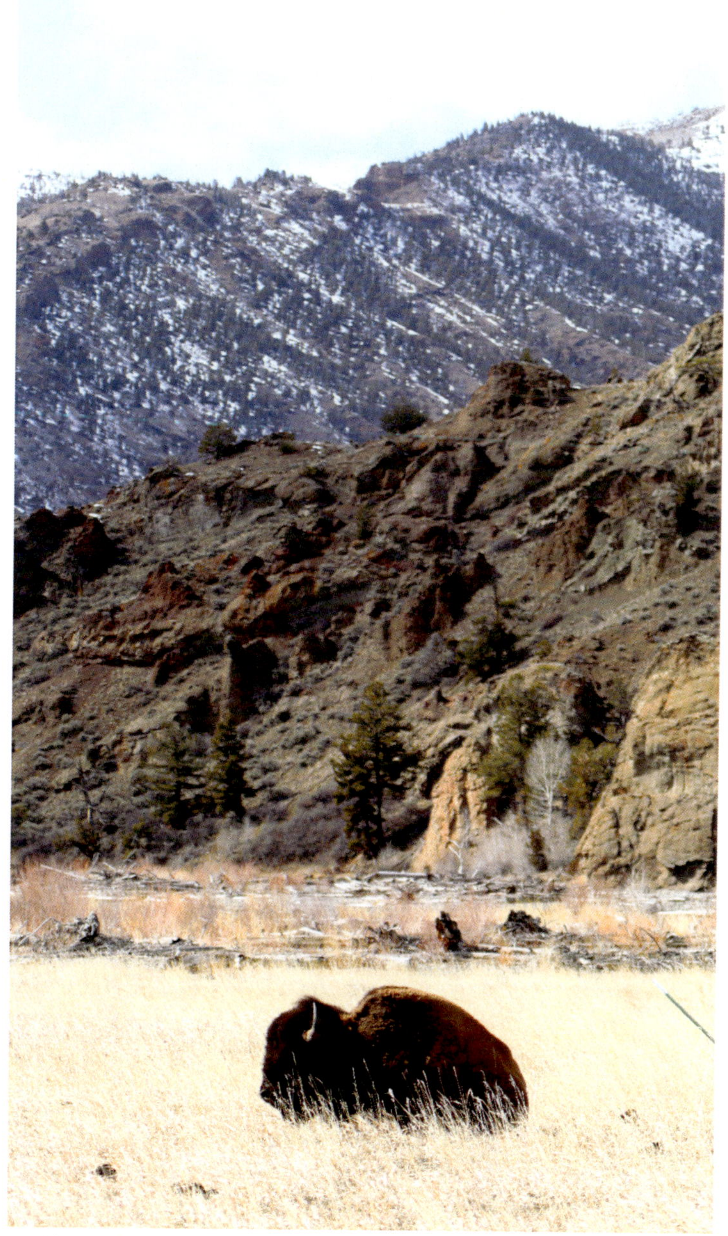

Above: Image IMG_5043. Photograph copyright © Lochlainn Seabrook.

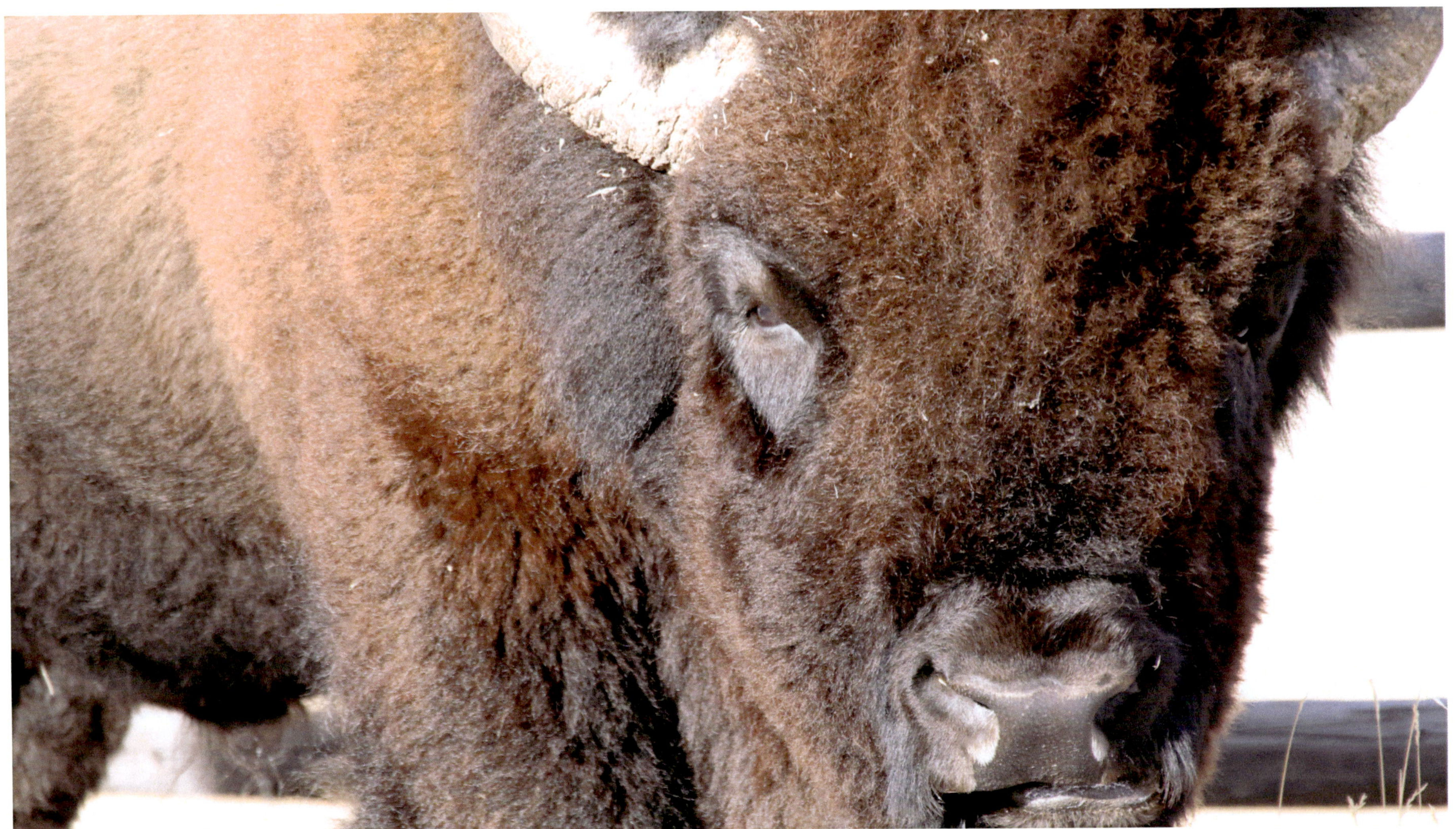

Above: Image 7X8A3392. Photograph copyright © Lochlainn Seabrook.

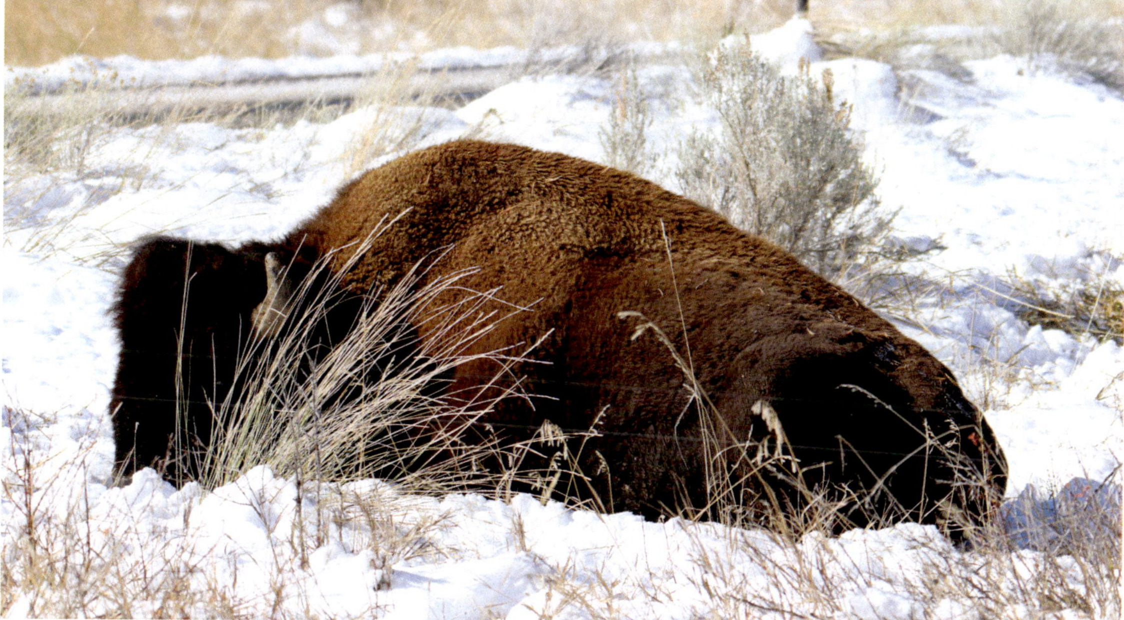

Right: Image 7X8A2206. Photograph copyright © Lochlainn Seabrook.

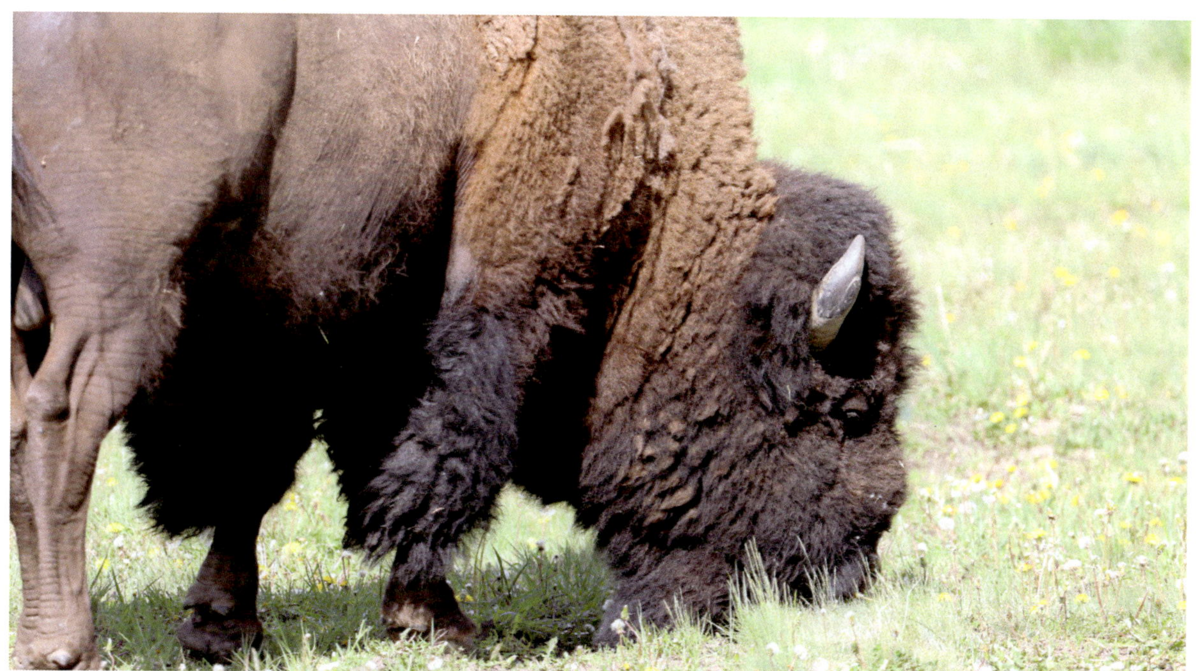

Left: Image 7X8A0533. Photograph copyright © Lochlainn Seabrook.

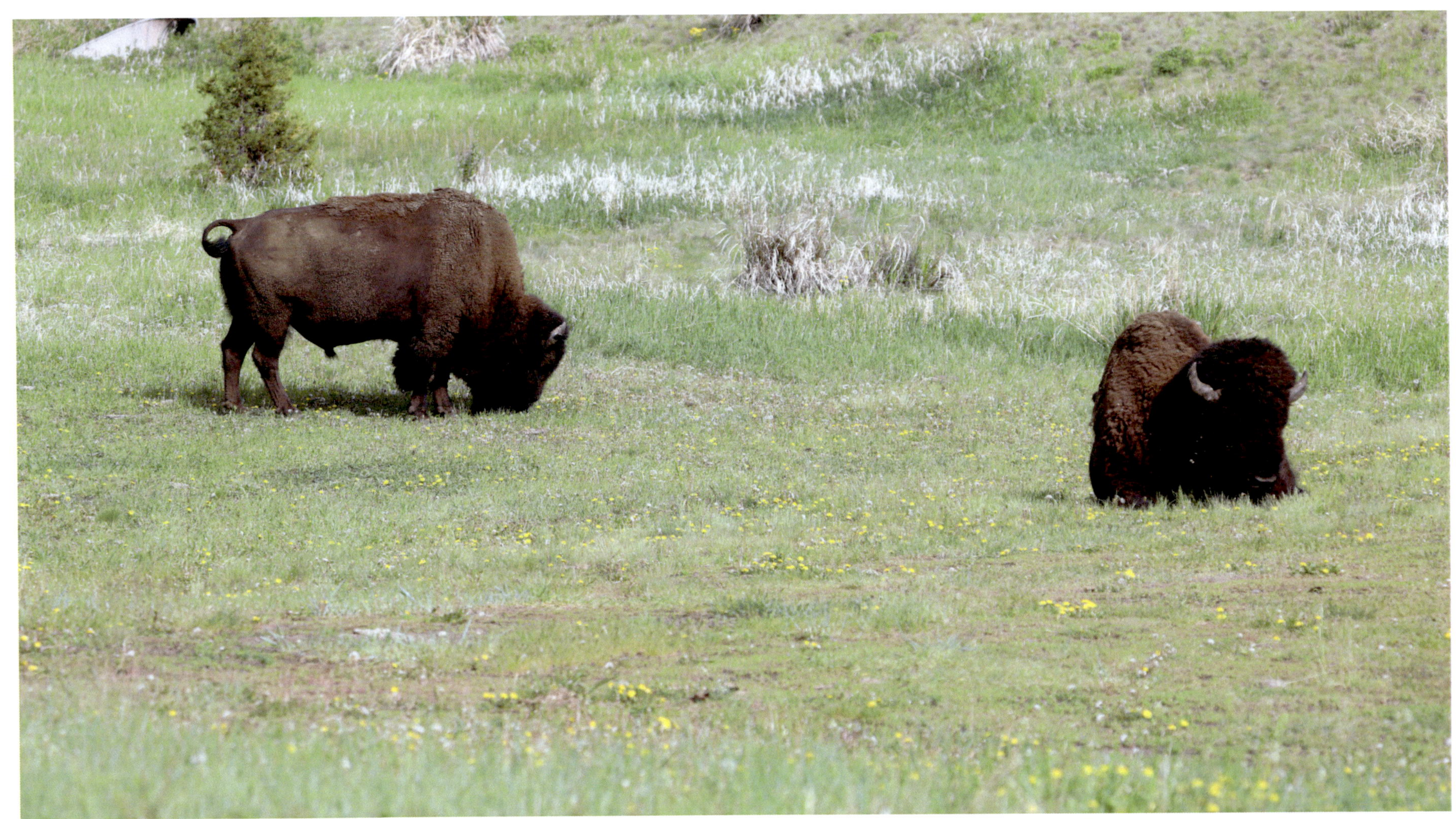

Above: Image 7X8A0469. Photograph copyright © Lochlainn Seabrook.

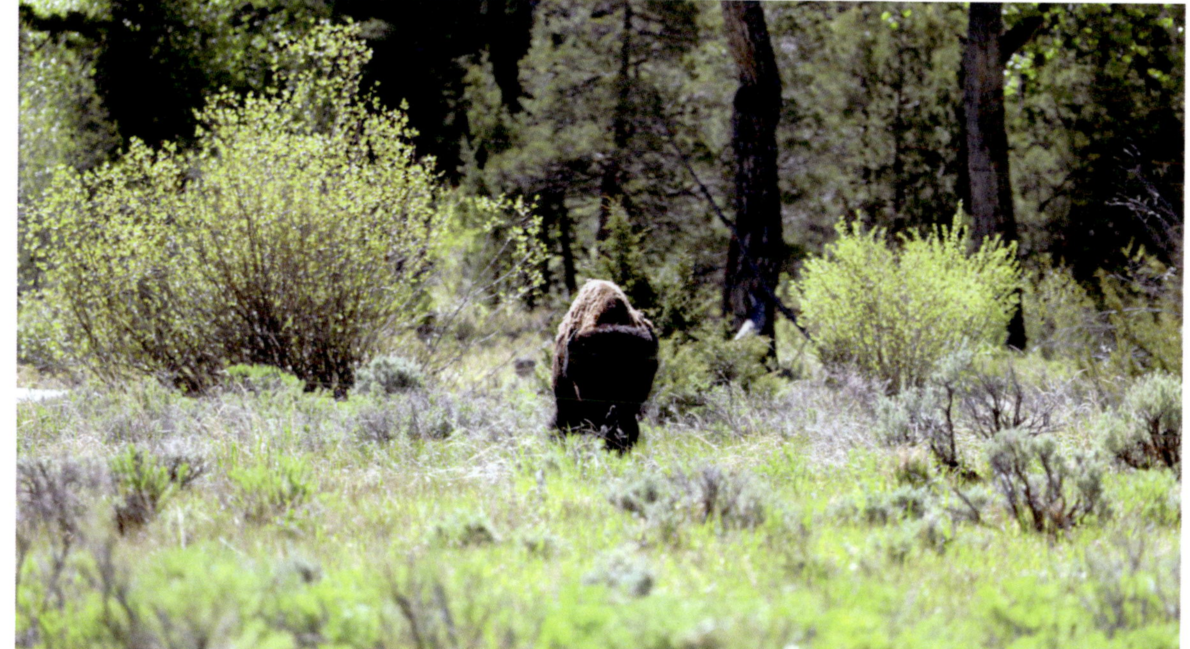

Left: Image 7X8A0260. Photograph copyright © Lochlainn Seabrook.

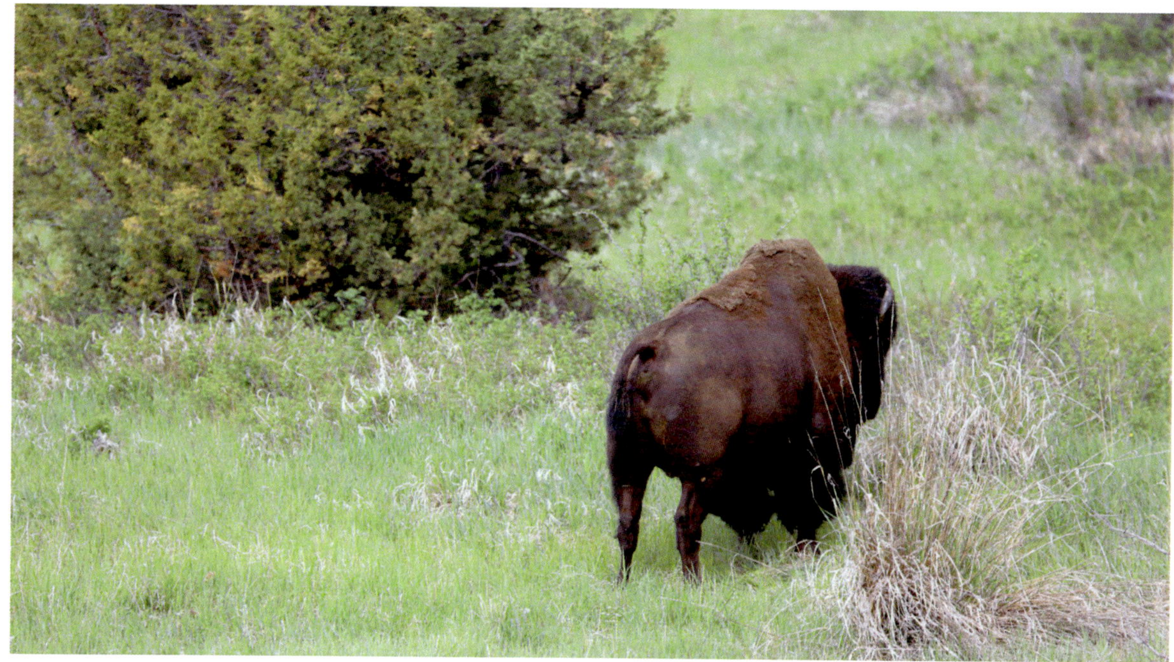

Right: Image 7X8A0451. Photograph copyright © Lochlainn Seabrook.

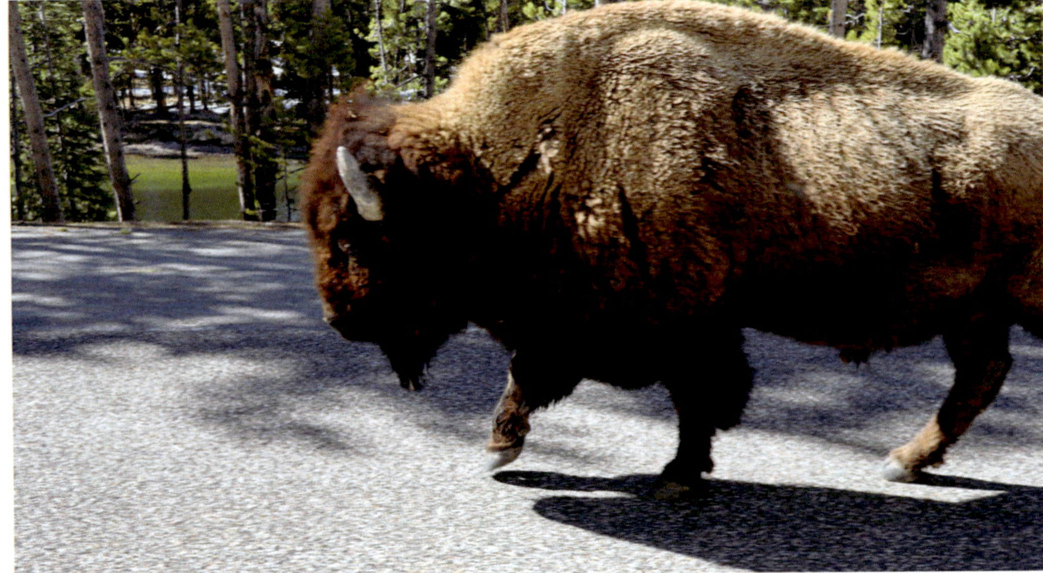

Right: Image IMG_5455. Photograph copyright © Lochlainn Seabrook.

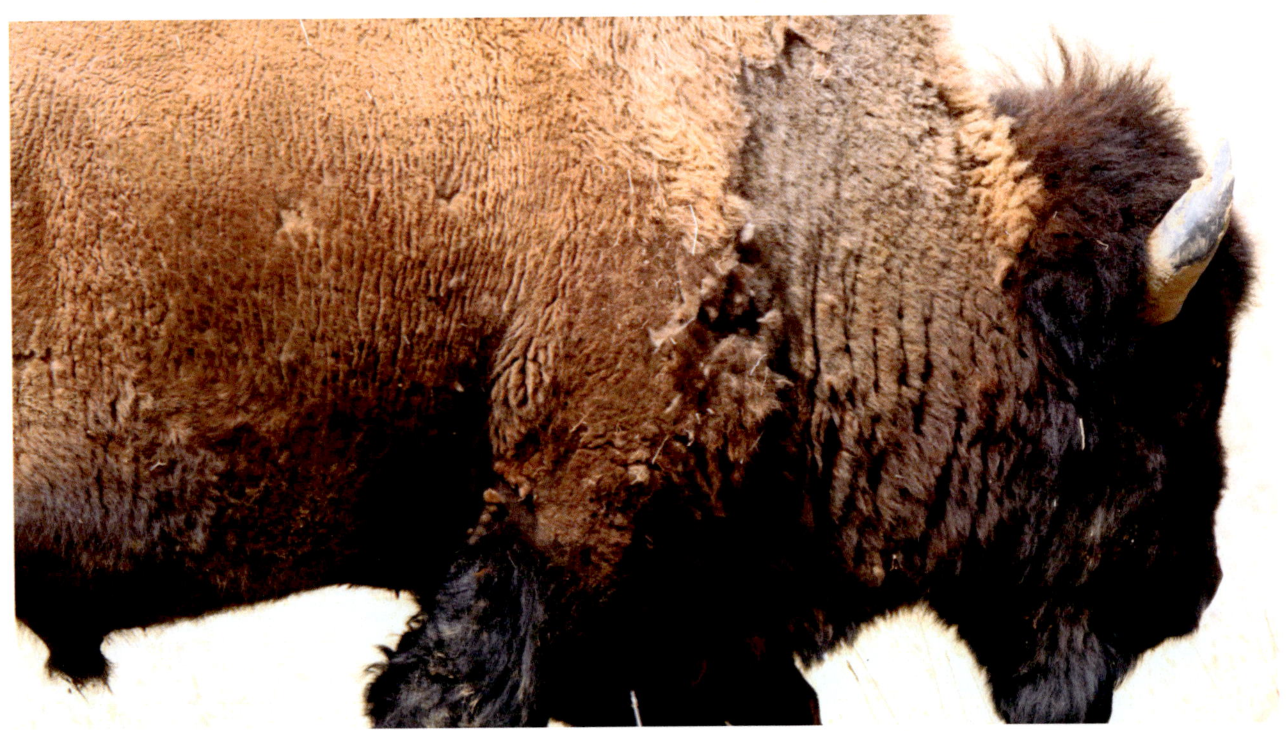

Left: Image IMG_4978. Photograph copyright © Lochlainn Seabrook.

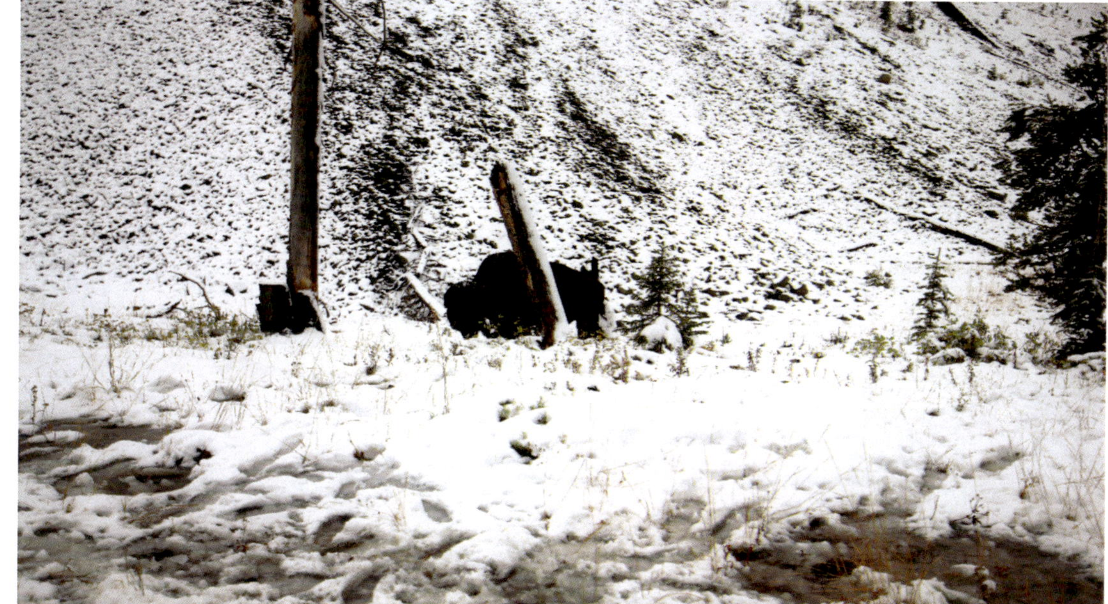

Left: Image 7X8A0849. Photograph copyright © Lochlainn Seabrook.

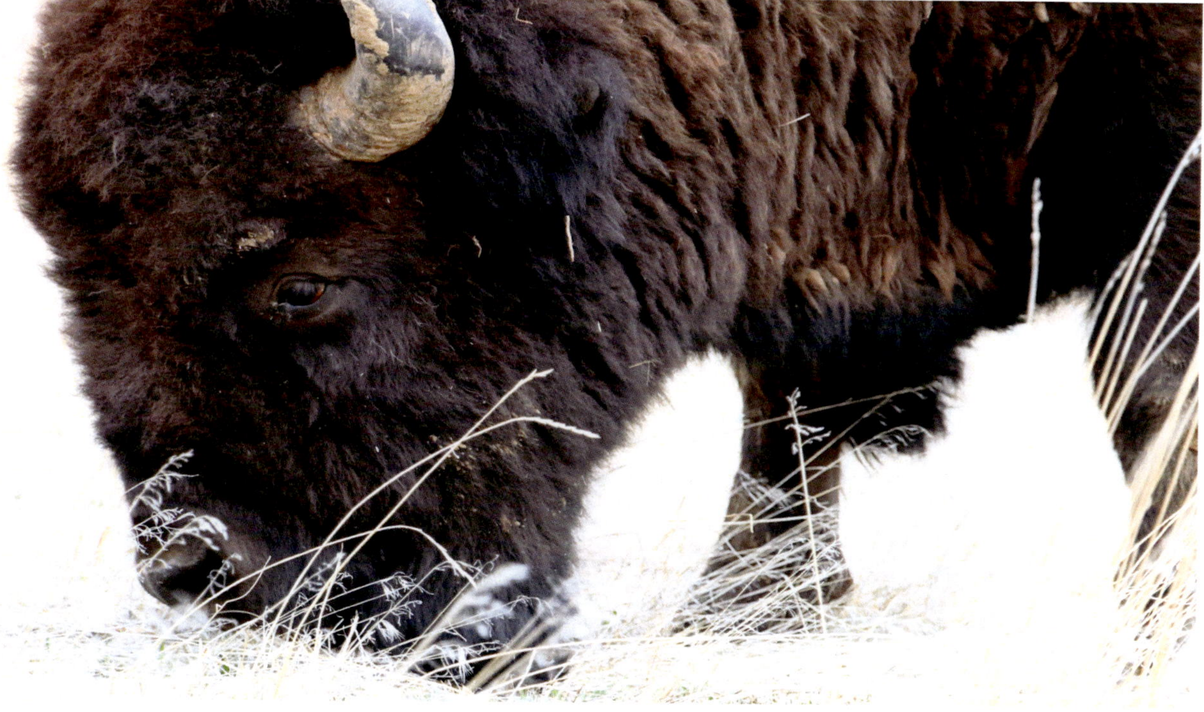

Right: Image IMG_4990. Photograph copyright © Lochlainn Seabrook.

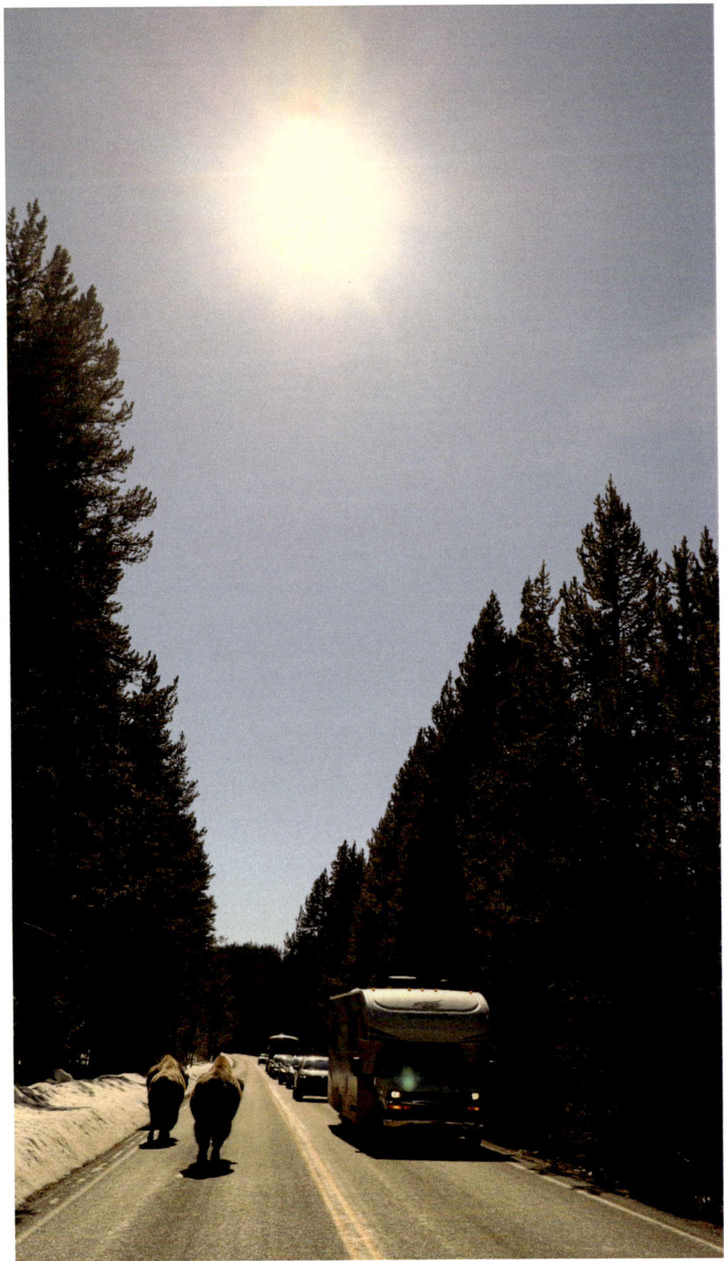

Above: Image IMG_5465. Photograph copyright © Lochlainn Seabrook.

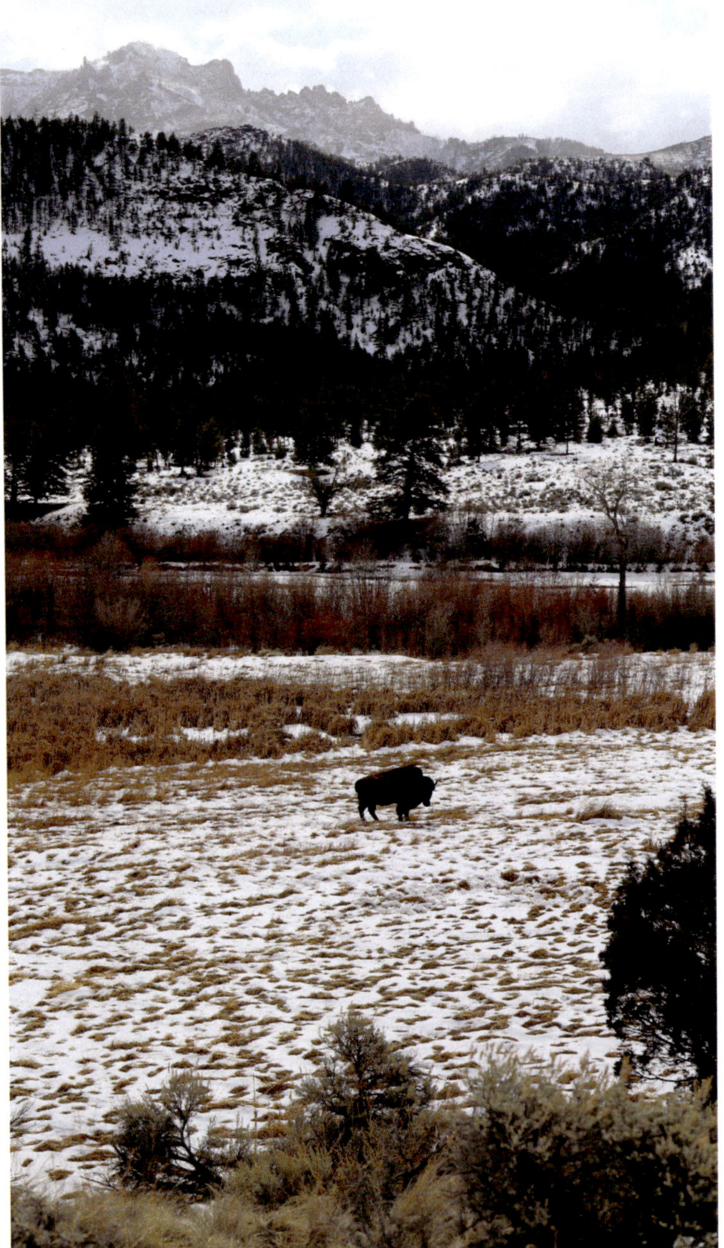

Above: Image 7X8A5144. Photograph copyright © Lochlainn Seabrook.

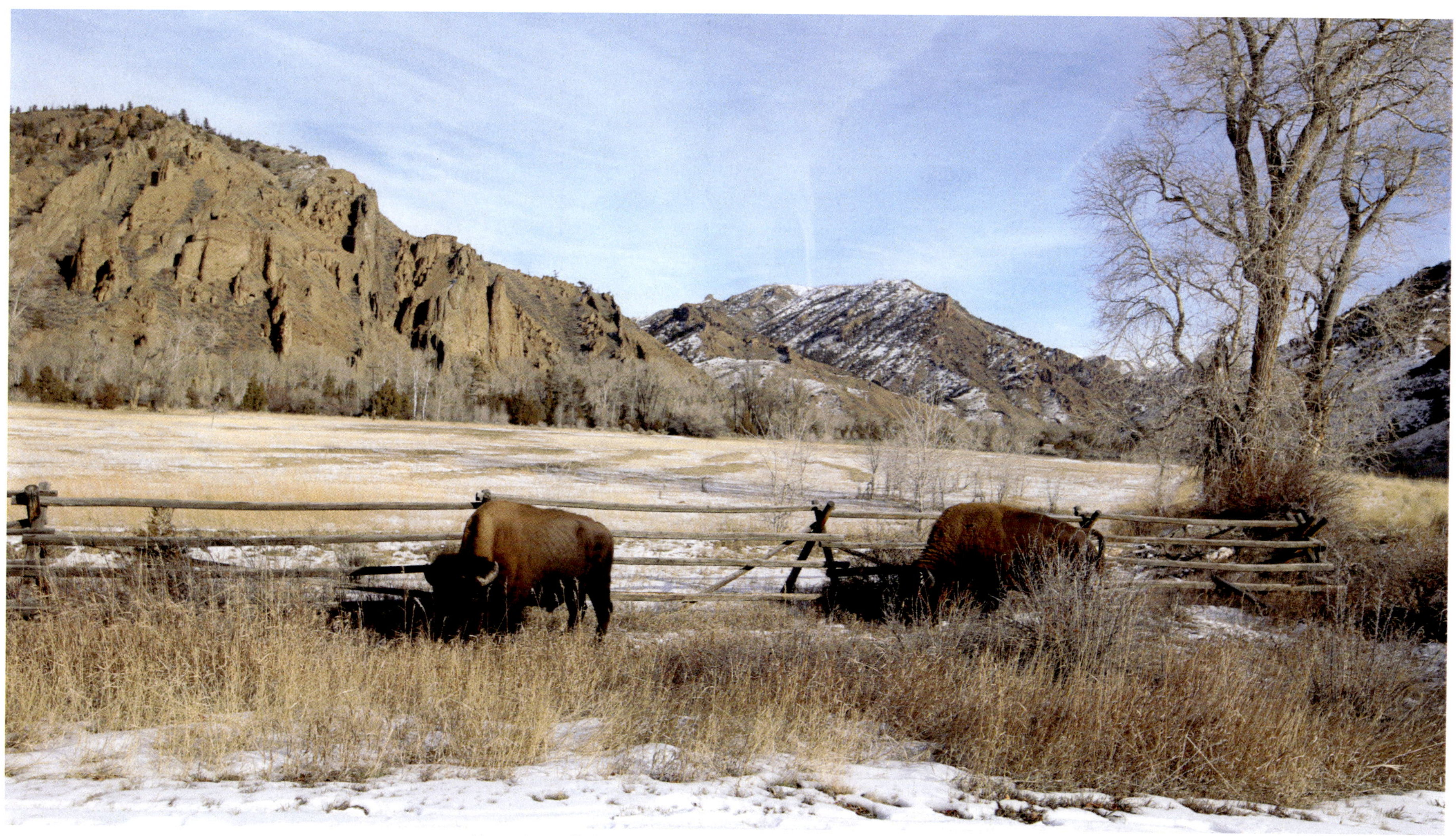

Above: Image 7X8A3320. Photograph copyright © Lochlainn Seabrook.

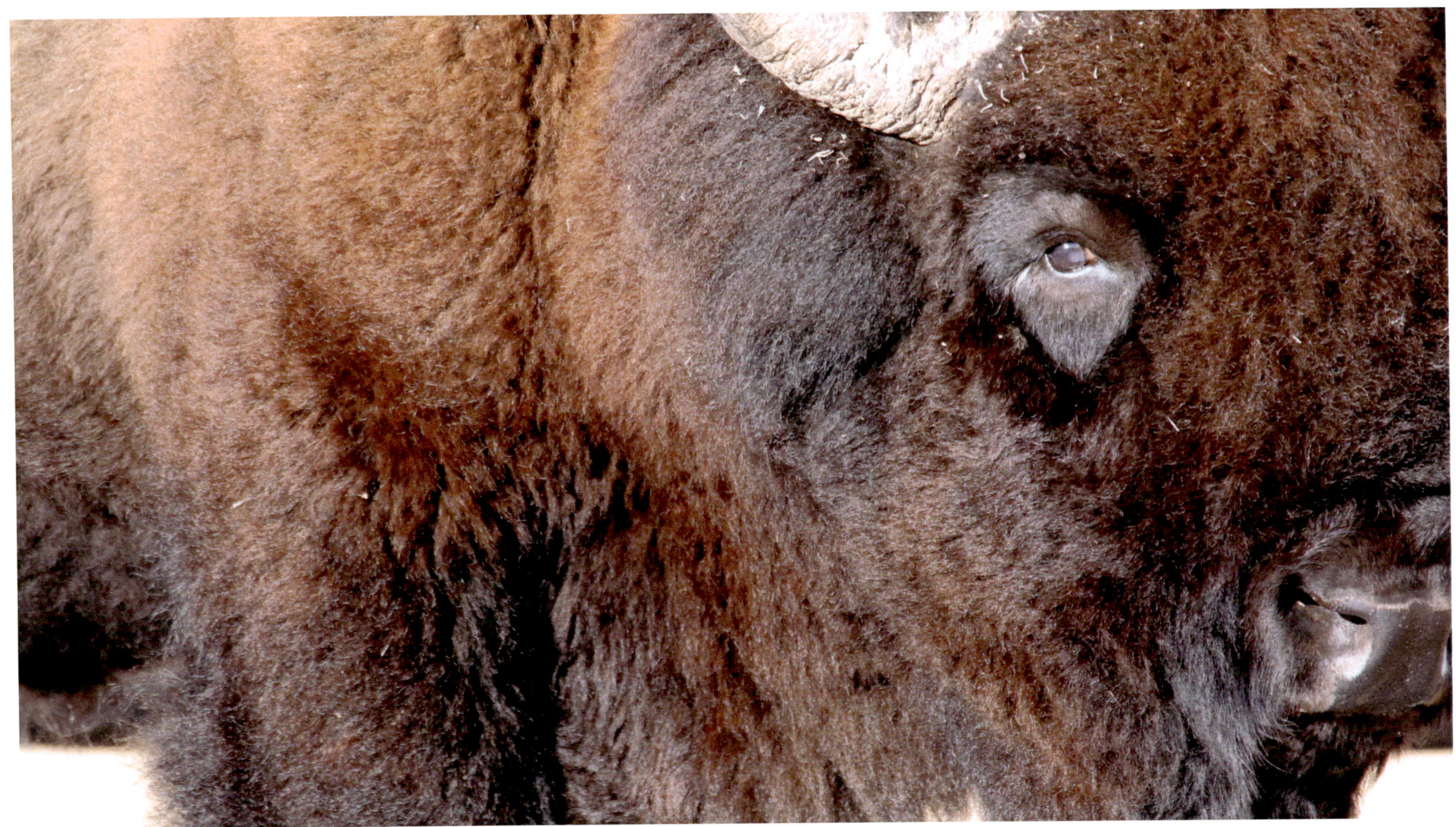

Above: Image 7X8A3389. Photograph copyright © Lochlainn Seabrook.

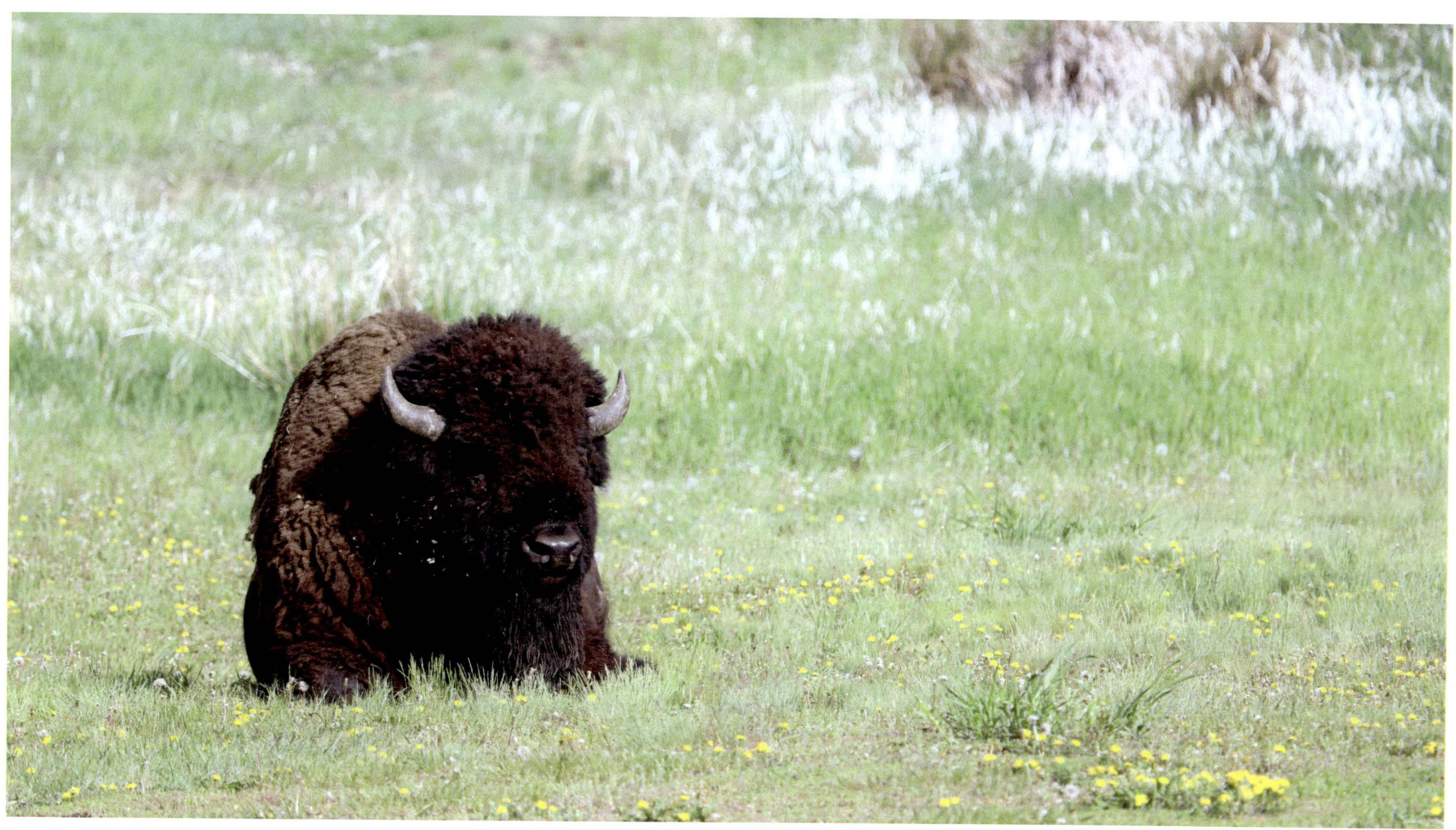

Above: Image 7X8A0047. Photograph copyright © Lochlainn Seabrook.

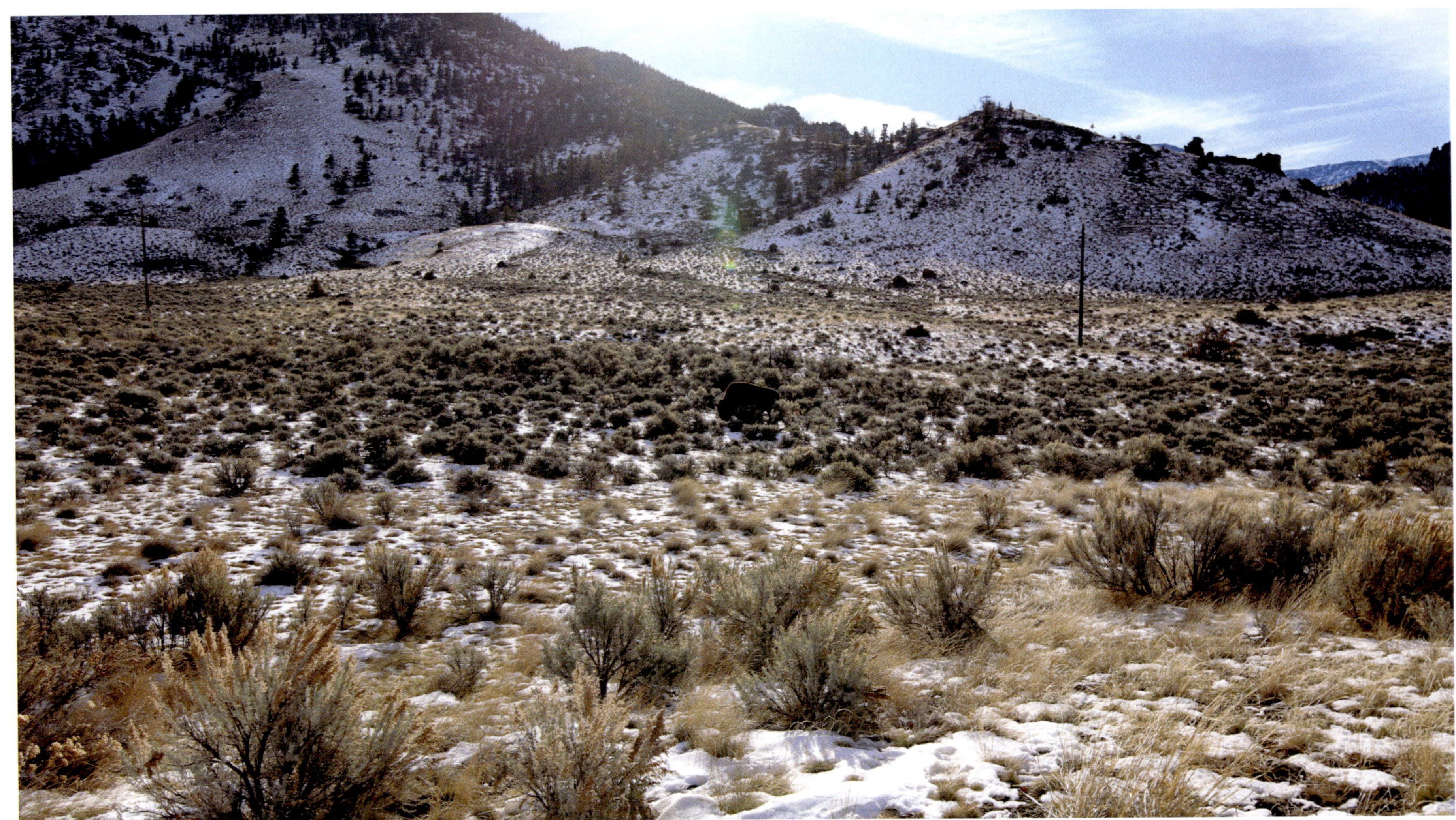

Above: Image 7X8A3378. Photograph copyright © Lochlainn Seabrook.

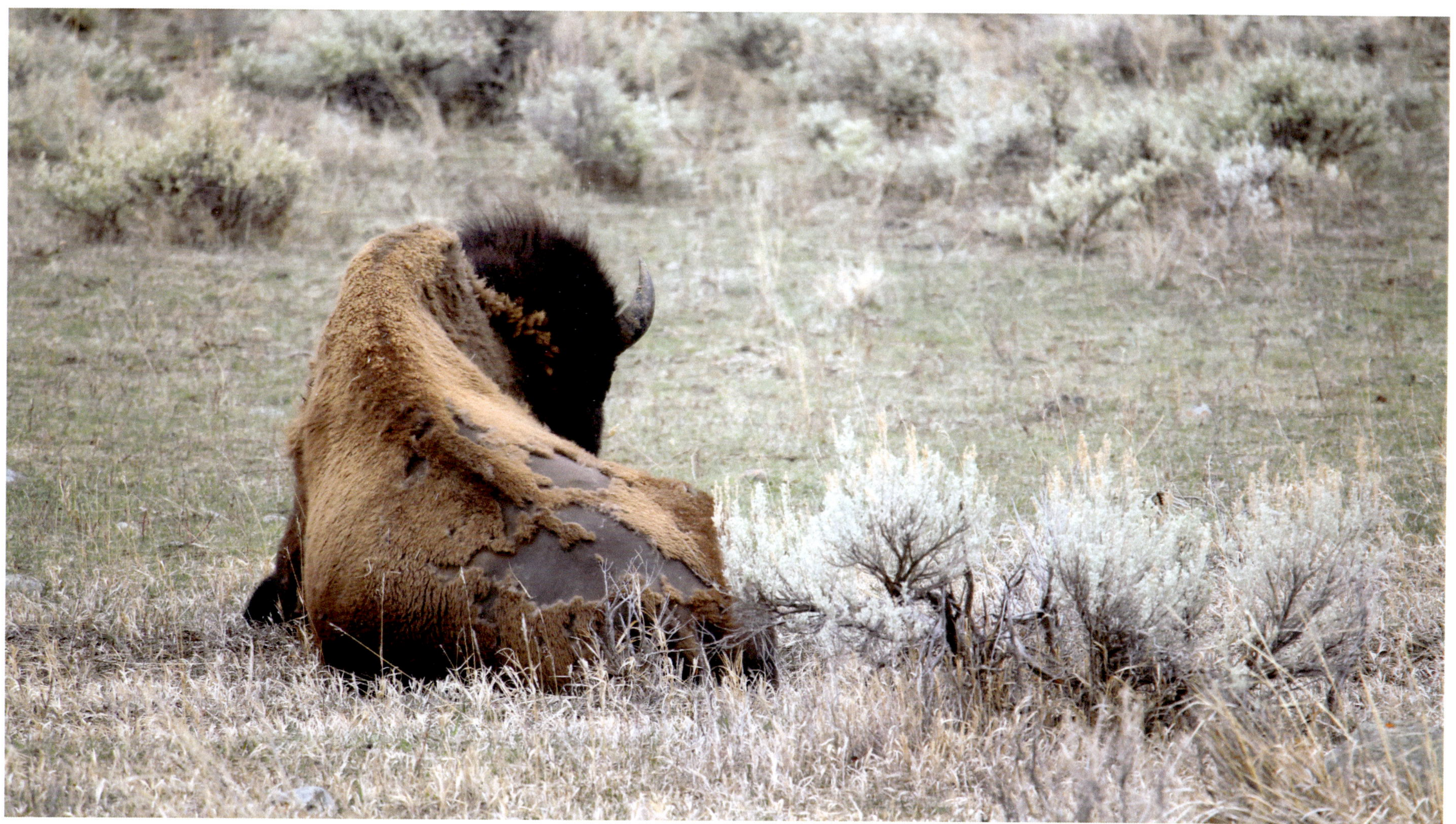

Above: Image 7X8A6505. Photograph copyright © Lochlainn Seabrook.

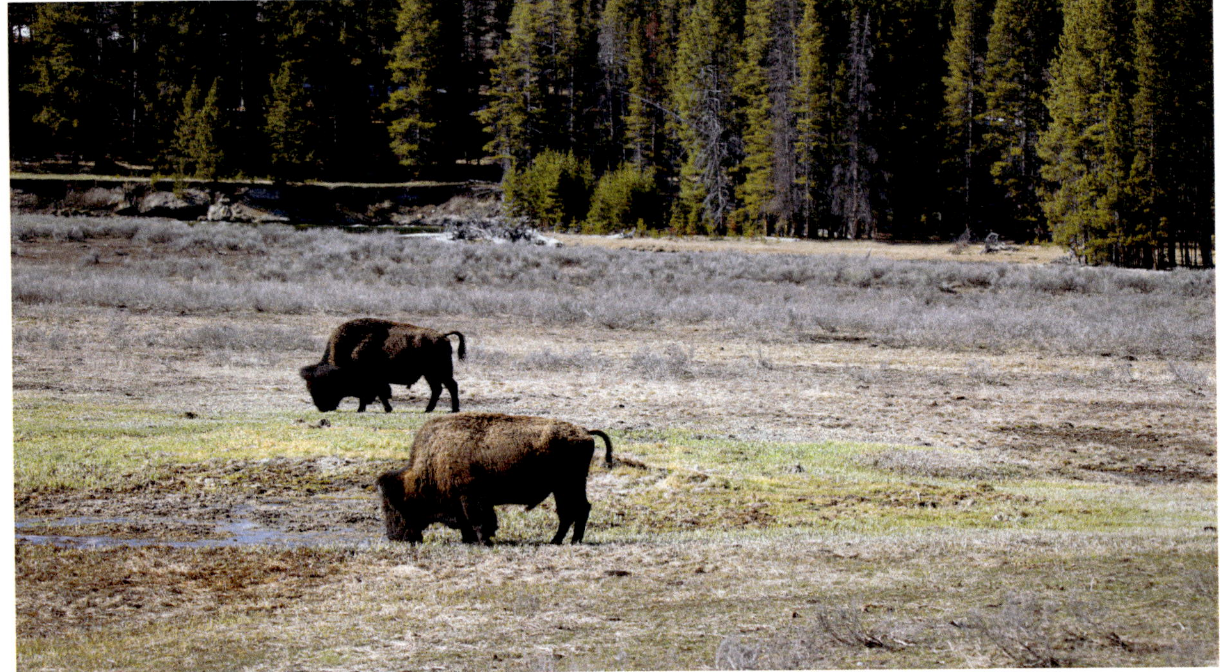

Left: Image 7X8A8962. Photograph copyright © Lochlainn Seabrook.

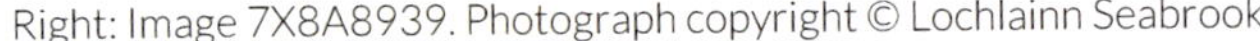

Right: Image 7X8A8939. Photograph copyright © Lochlainn Seabrook.

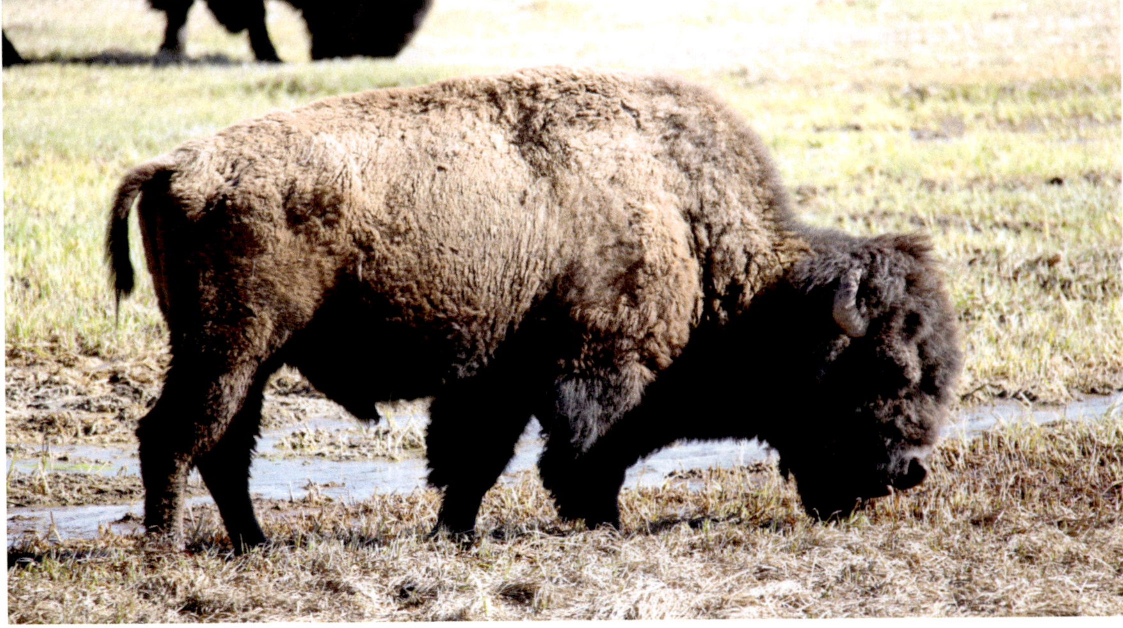

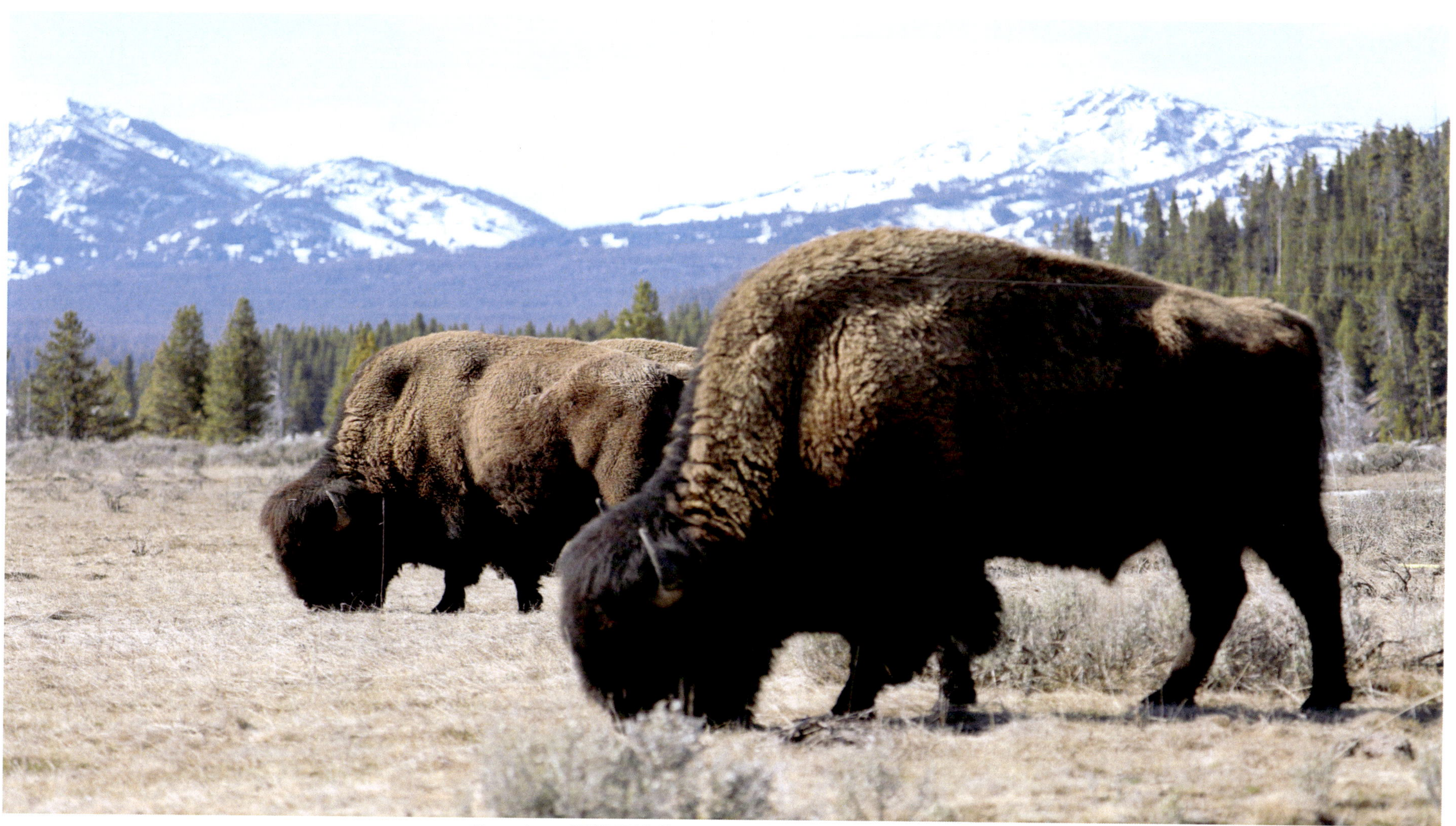

Above: Image 7X8A8939. Photograph copyright © Lochlainn Seabrook.

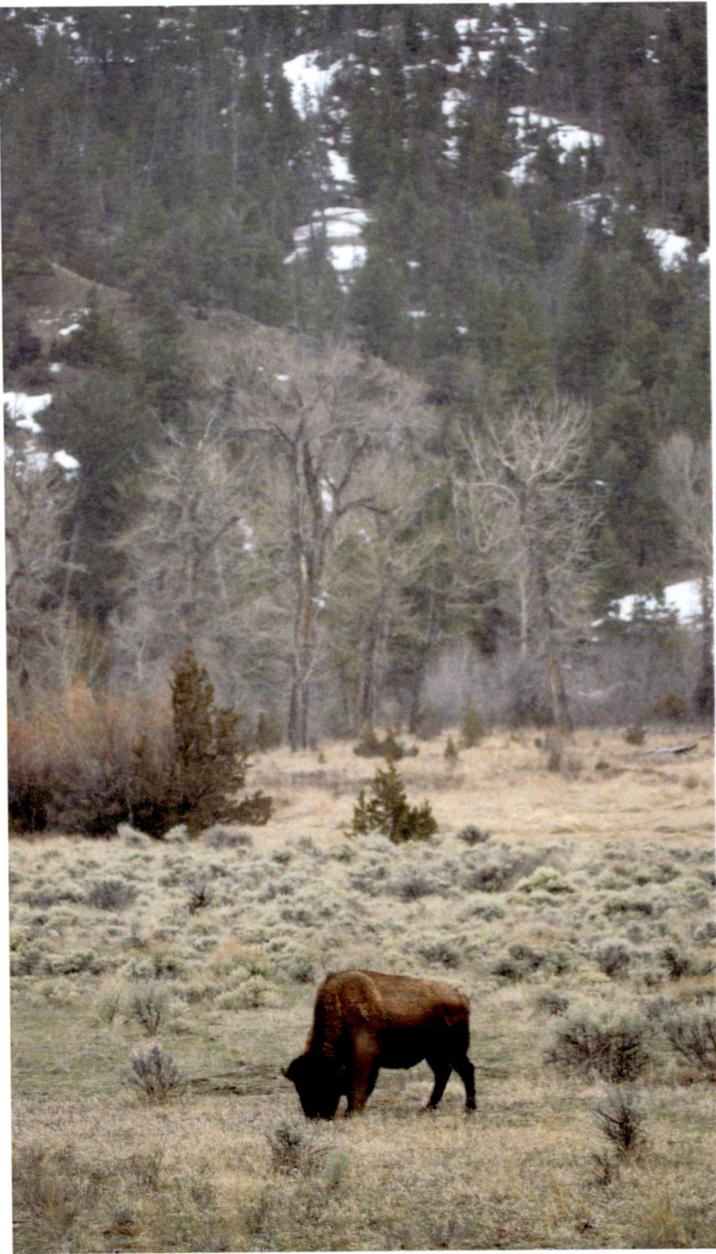

Above: Image 7X8A6490. Photograph copyright © Lochlainn Seabrook.

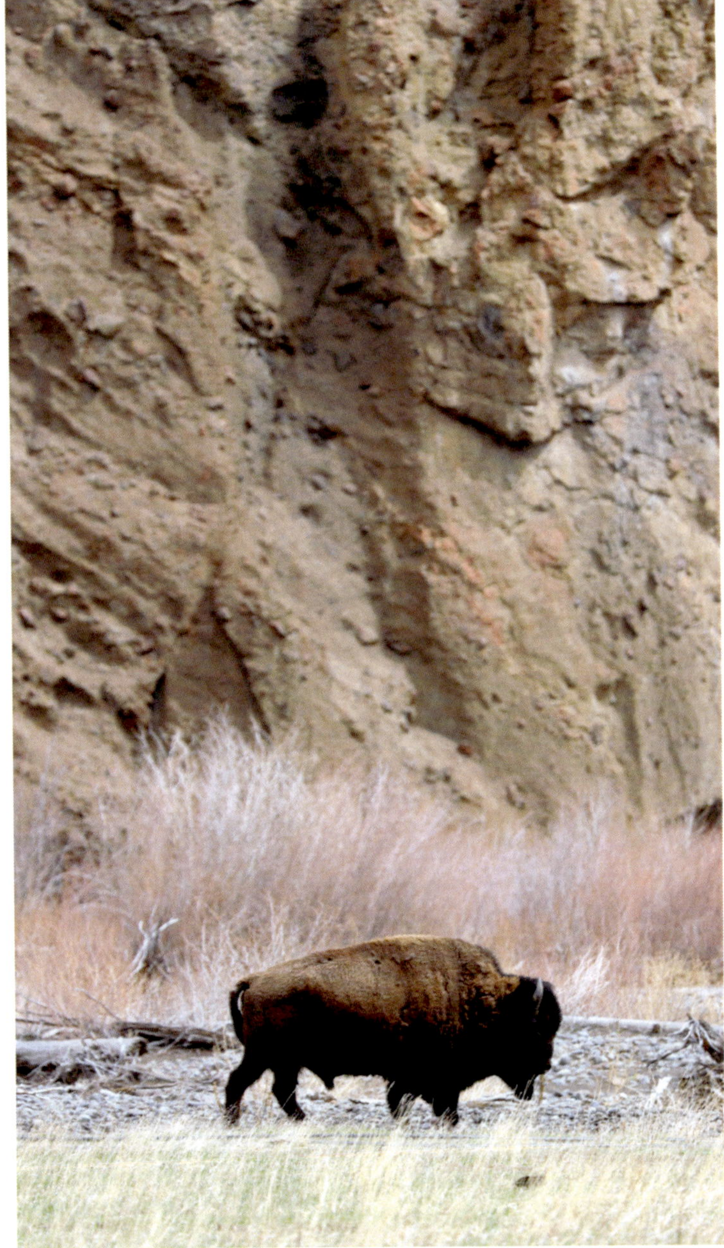

Above: Image 7X8A8099. Photograph copyright © Lochlainn Seabrook.

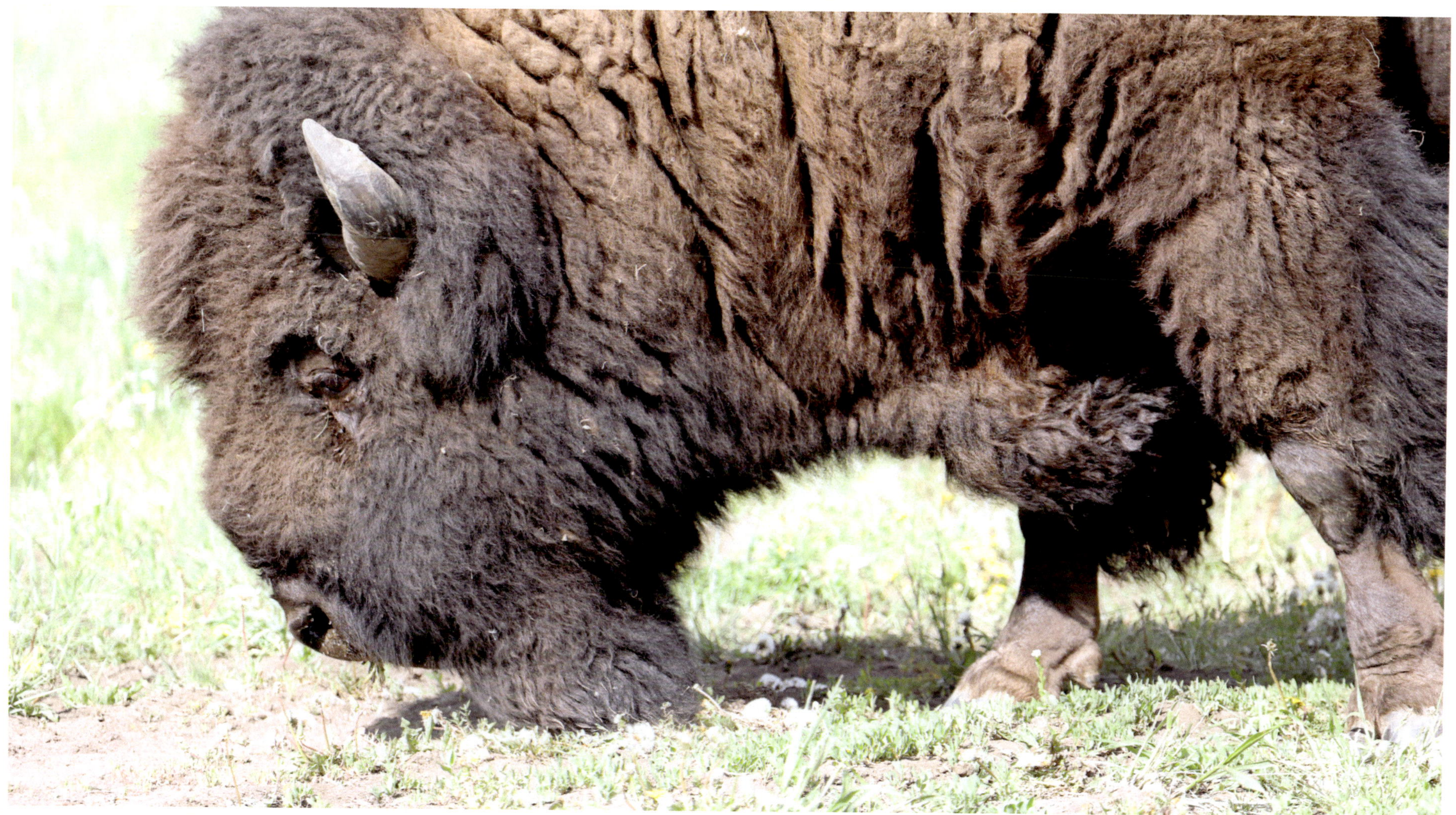

Above: Image 7X8A0531. Photograph copyright © Lochlainn Seabrook.

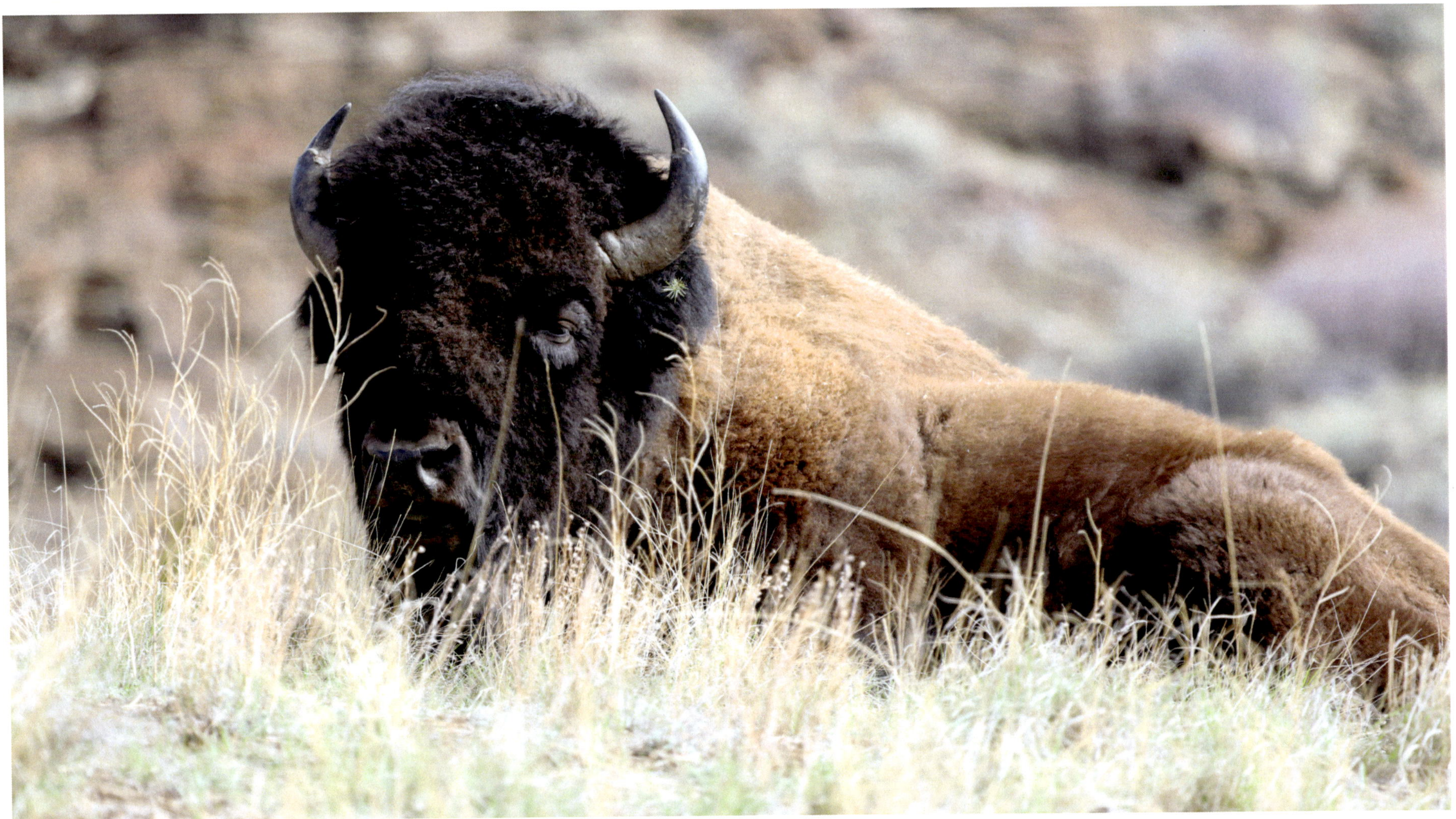

Above: Image 7X8A7145. Photograph copyright © Lochlainn Seabrook.

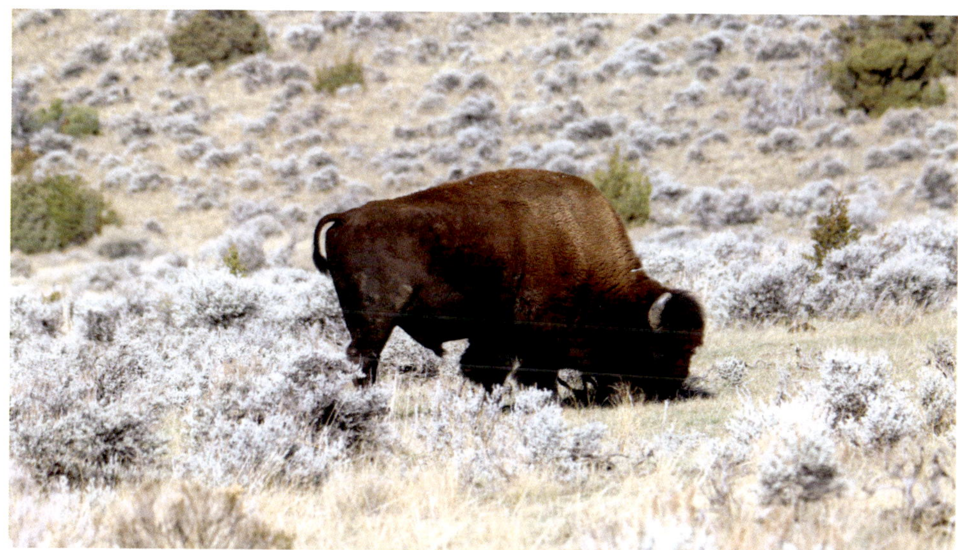

Above: Image 7X8A2239. Photograph copyright © Lochlainn Seabrook.

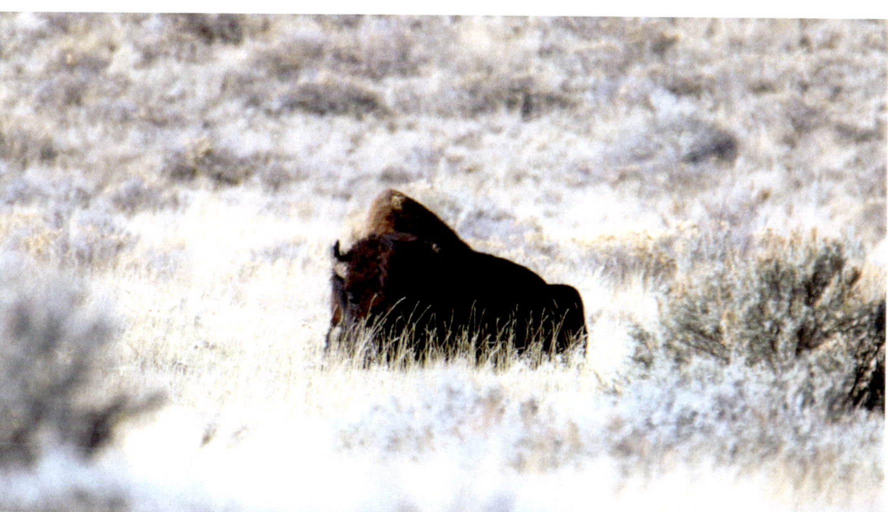

Above: Image 7X8A2552. Photograph copyright © Lochlainn Seabrook.

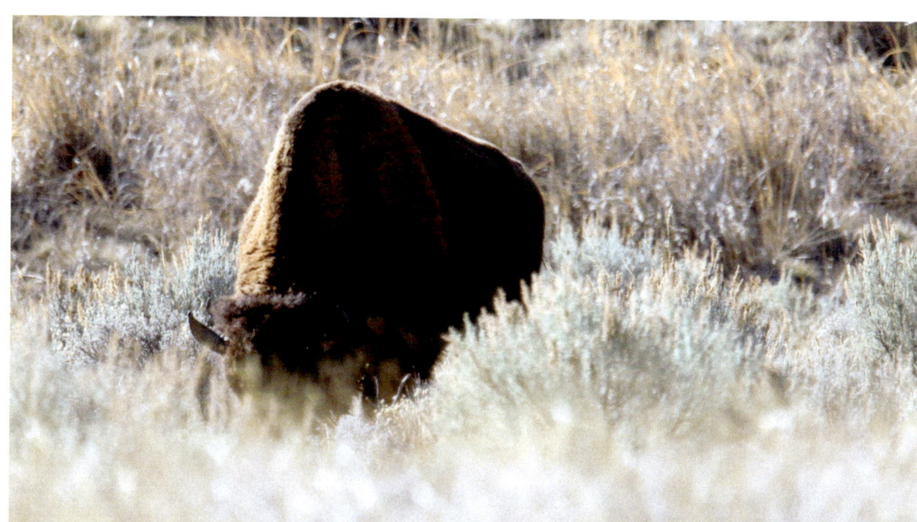

Above: Image 7X8A2555. Photograph copyright © Lochlainn Seabrook.

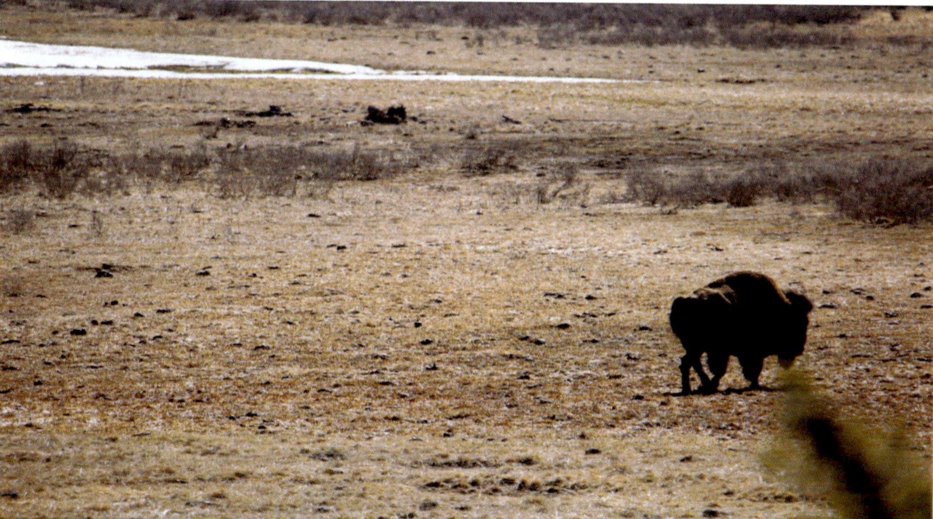

Above: Image 7X8A8961. Photograph copyright © Lochlainn Seabrook.

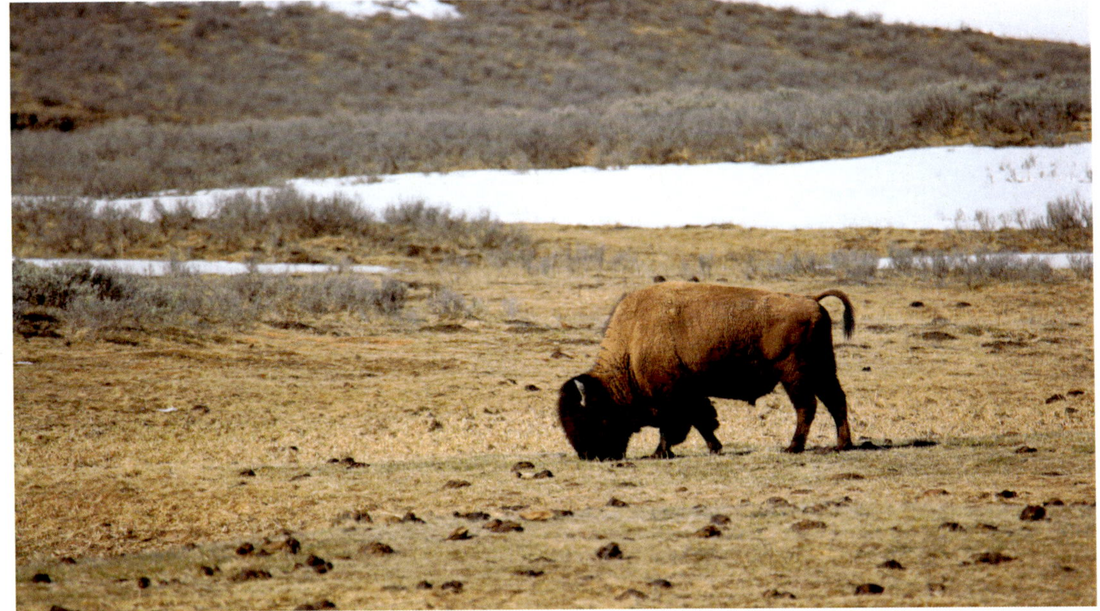

Left: Image 7X8A8953. Photograph copyright © Lochlainn Seabrook.

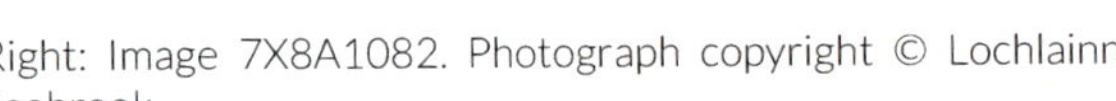

Right: Image 7X8A1082. Photograph copyright © Lochlainn Seabrook.

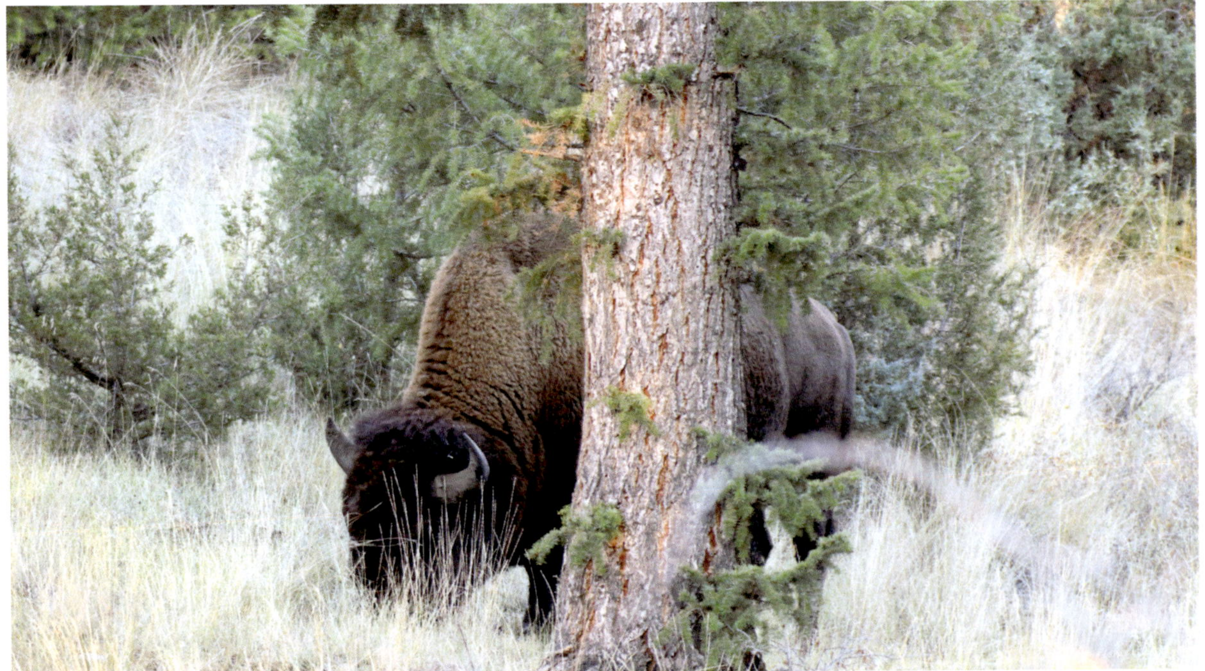

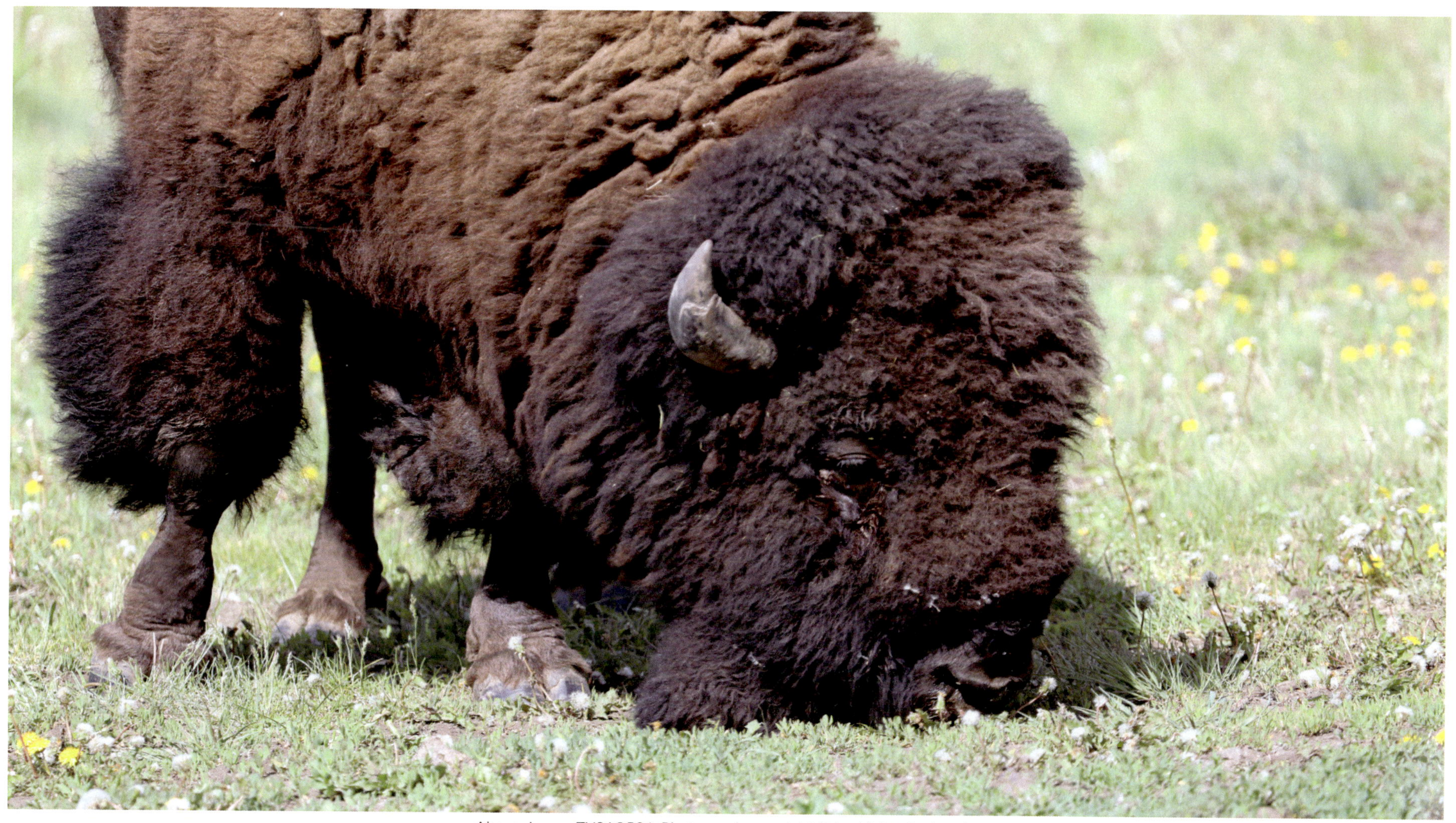

Above: Image 7X8A0521. Photograph copyright © Lochlainn Seabrook.

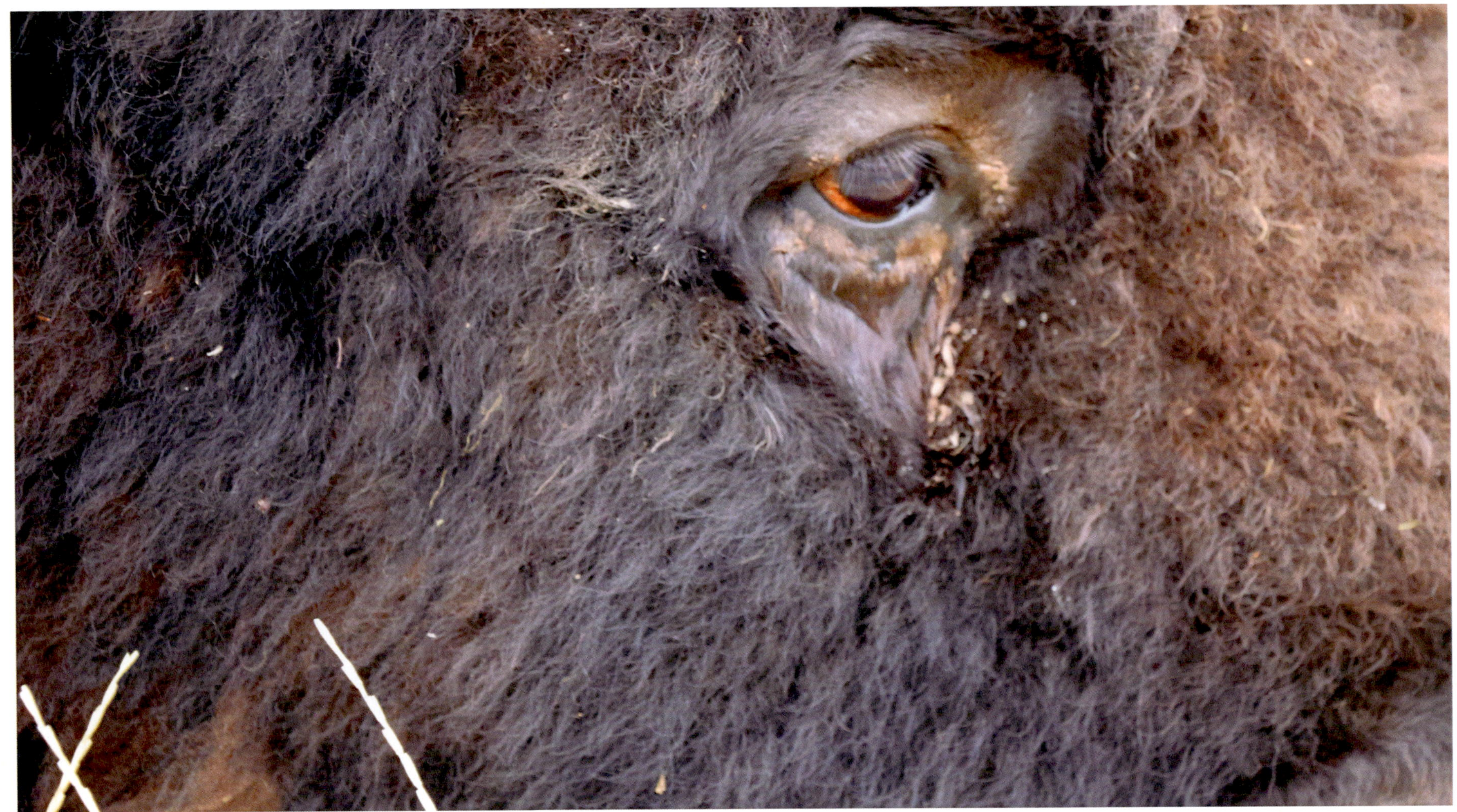

Above: Image 7X8A8667. Photograph copyright © Lochlainn Seabrook.

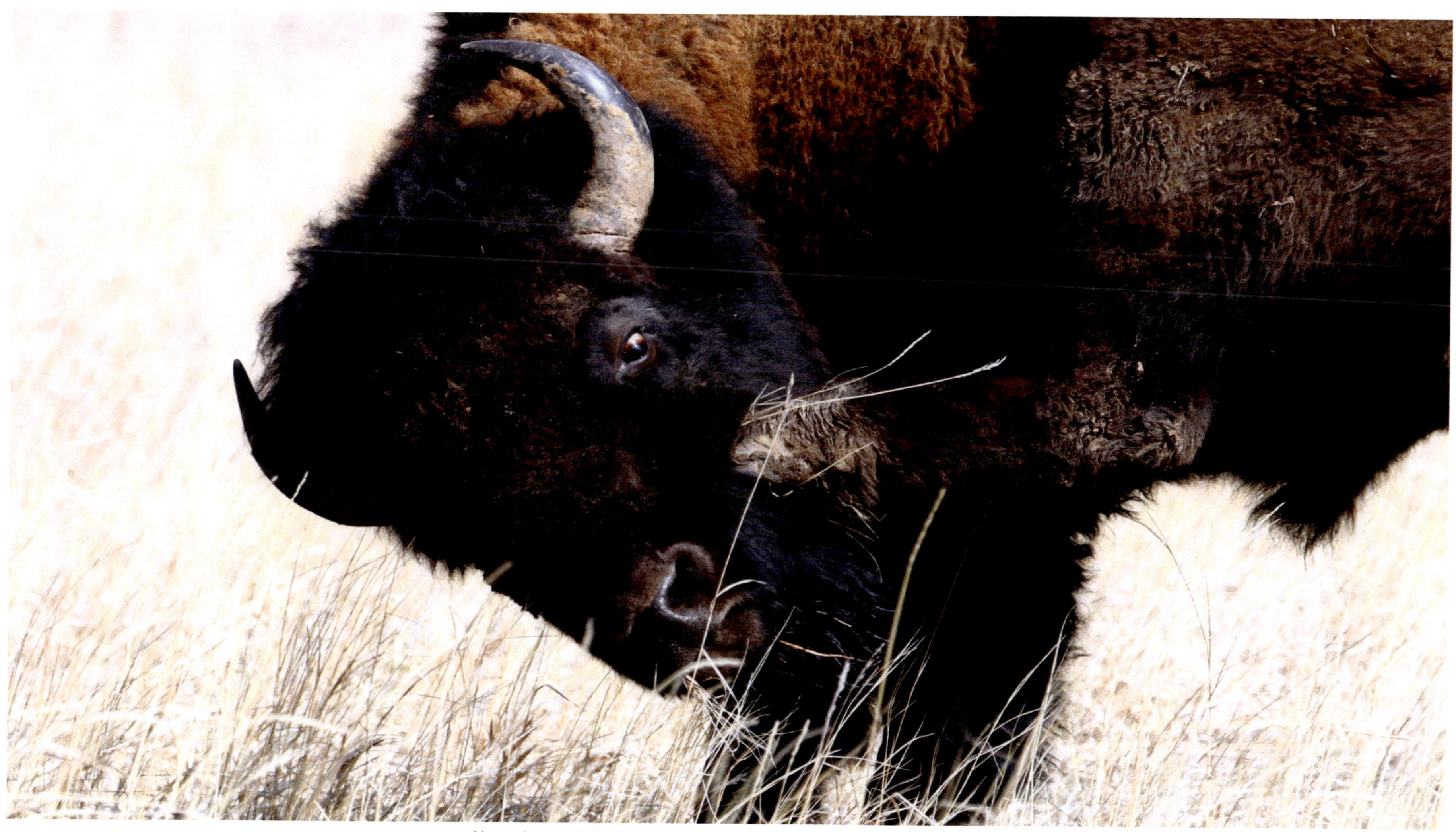

Above: Image IMG_4971. Photograph copyright © Lochlainn Seabrook.

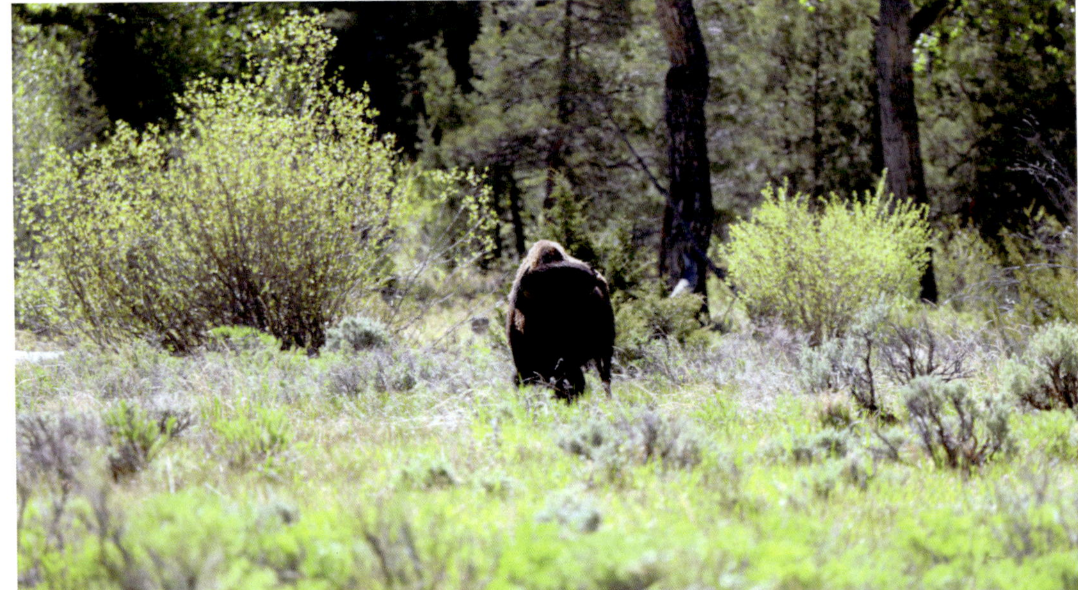

Left: Image 7X8A0259. Photograph copyright © Lochlainn Seabrook.

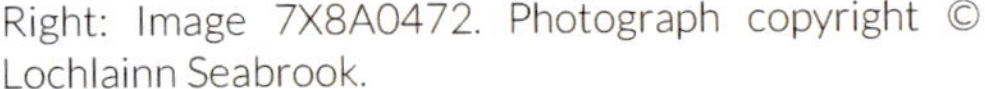

Right: Image 7X8A0472. Photograph copyright © Lochlainn Seabrook.

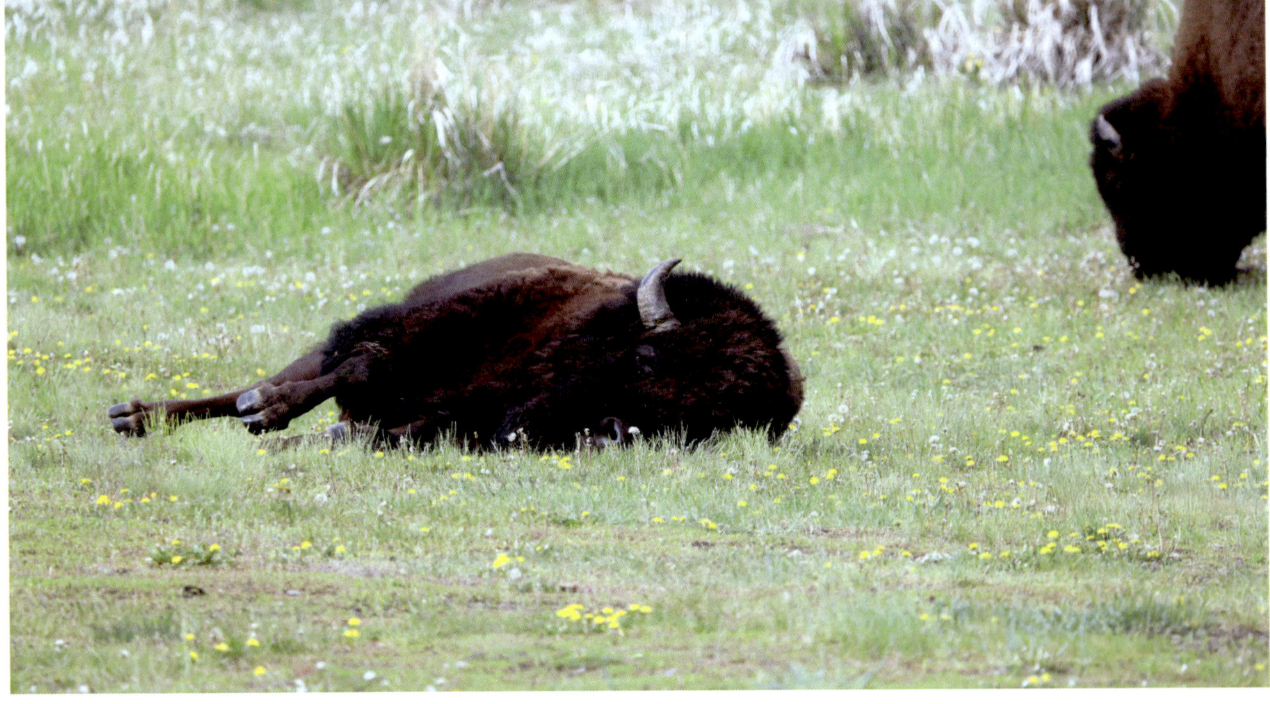

Right: Image 7X8A0886. Photograph copyright © Lochlainn Seabrook.

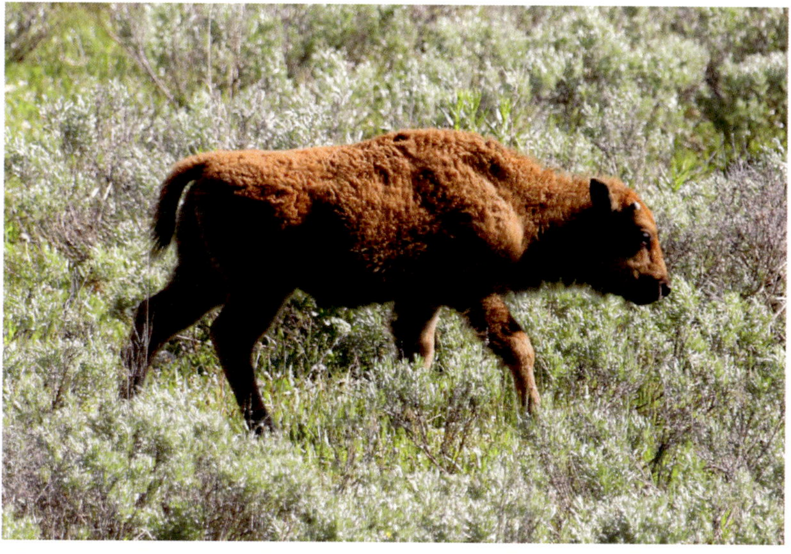

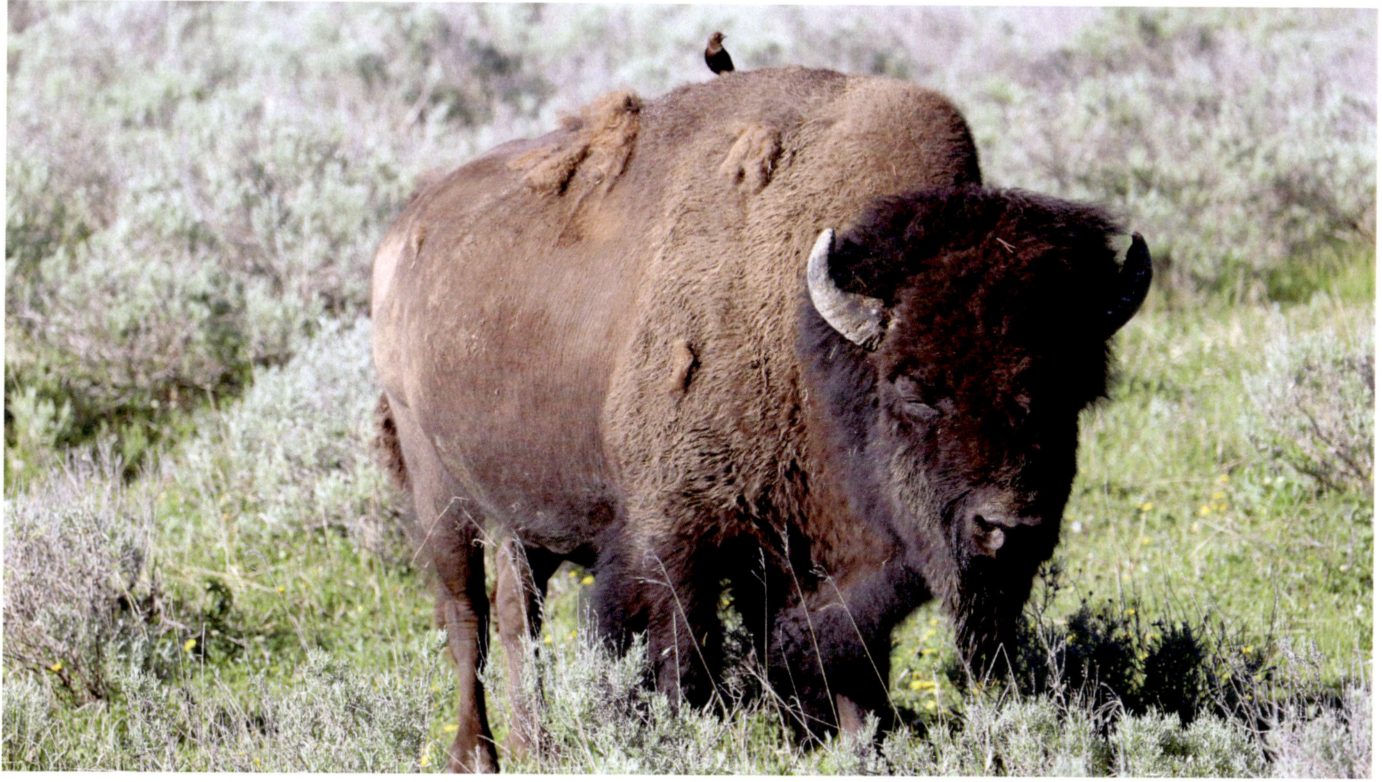

Left: Image 7X8A0726. Photograph copyright © Lochlainn Seabrook.

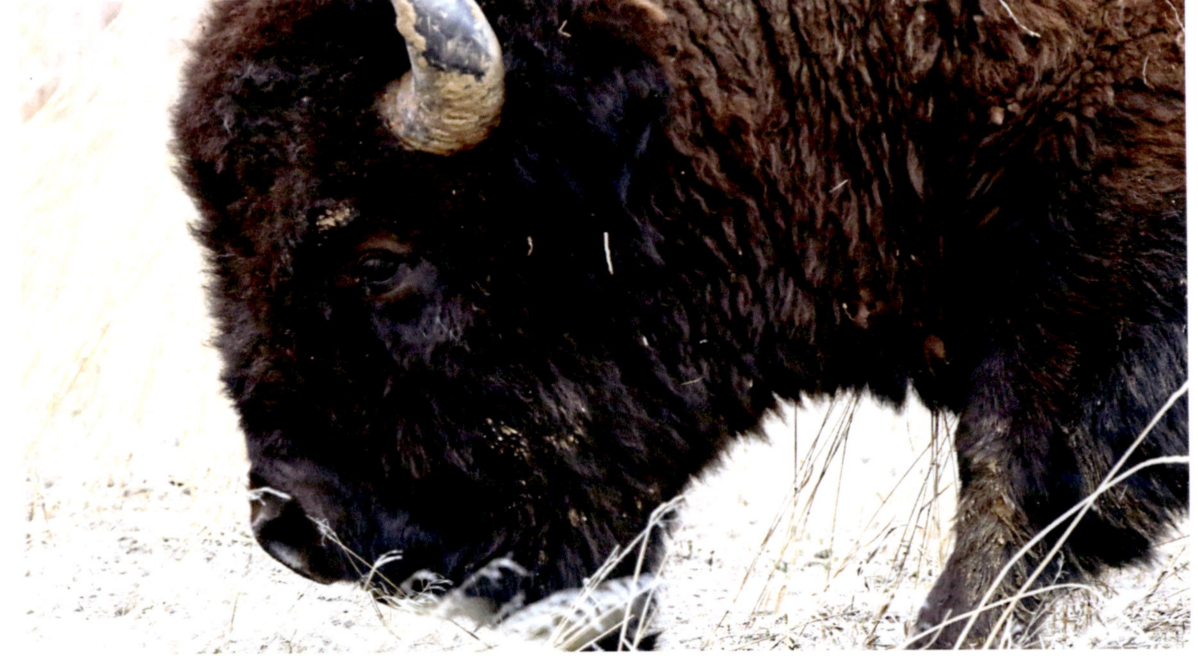

Left: Image IMG_4991. Photograph copyright © Lochlainn Seabrook.

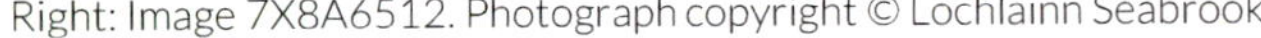

Right: Image 7X8A6512. Photograph copyright © Lochlainn Seabrook

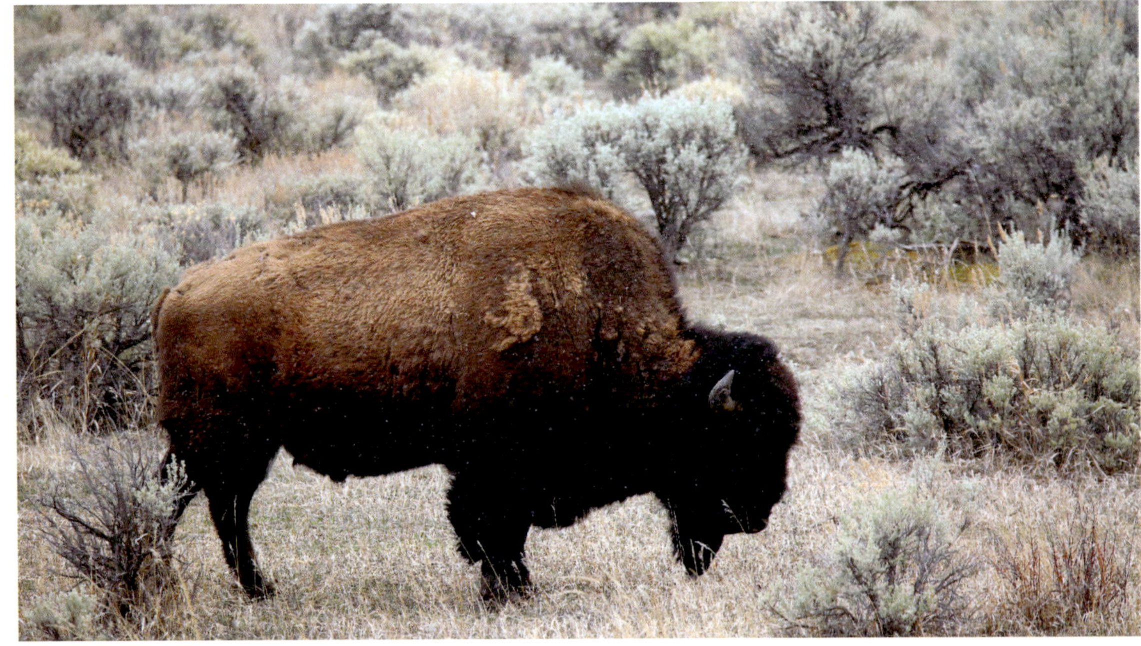

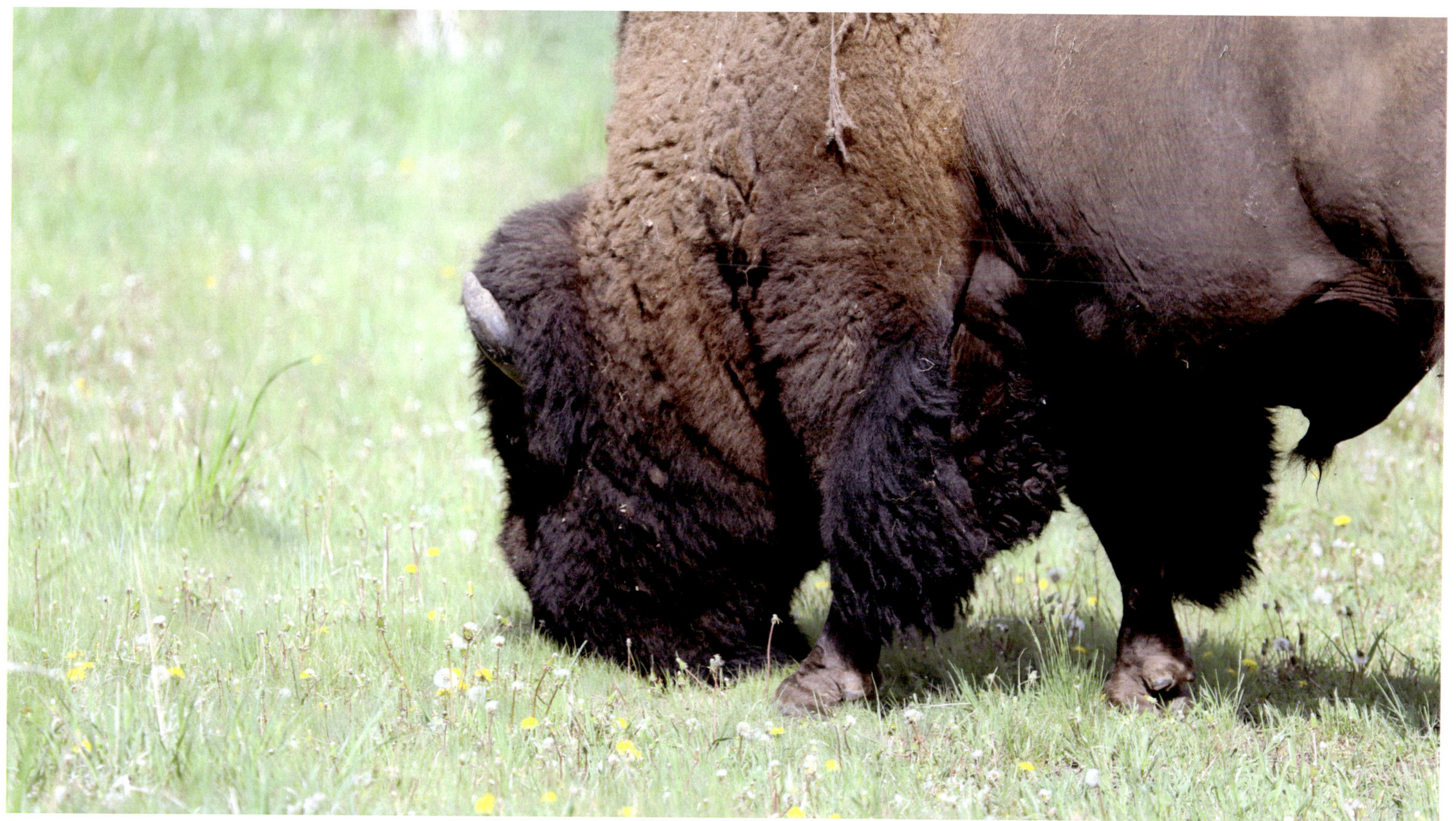

Above: Image 7X8A0537. Photograph copyright © Lochlainn Seabrook.

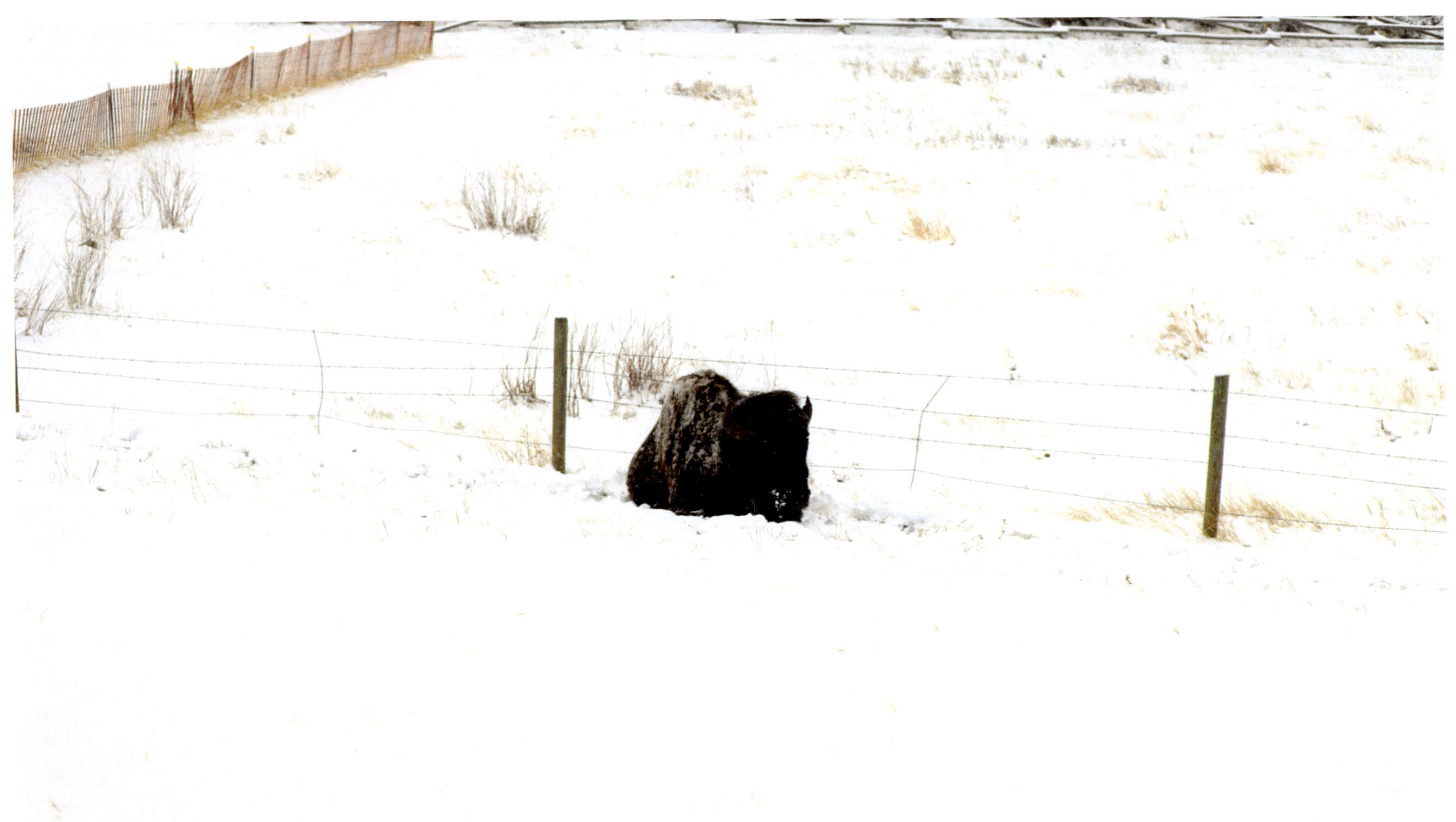

Above: Image 7X8A6008. Photograph copyright © Lochlainn Seabrook.

Right: Image 7X8A0989. Photograph copyright © Lochlainn Seabrook.

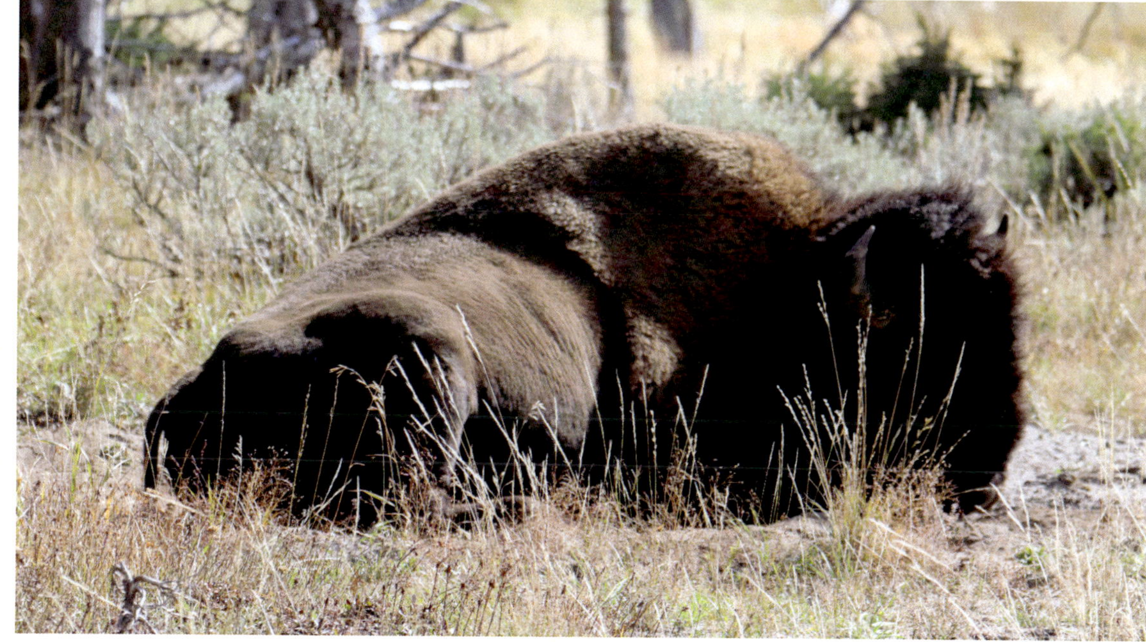

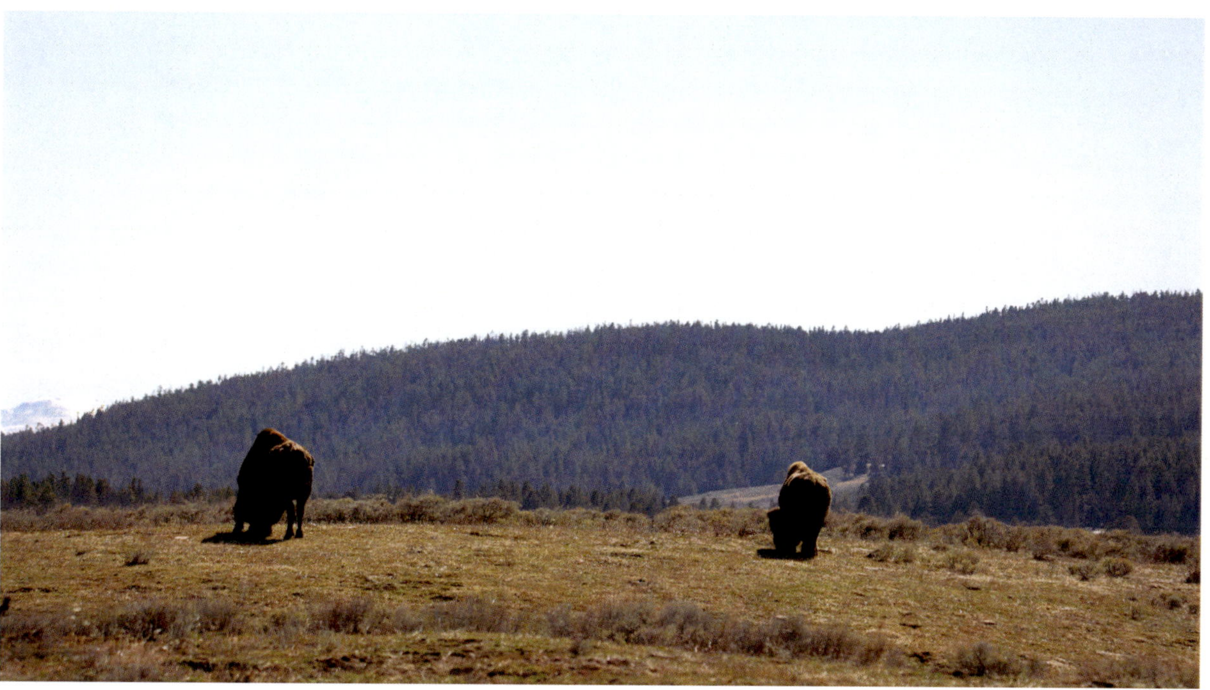

Left: Image 7X8A8960. Photograph copyright © Lochlainn Seabrook.

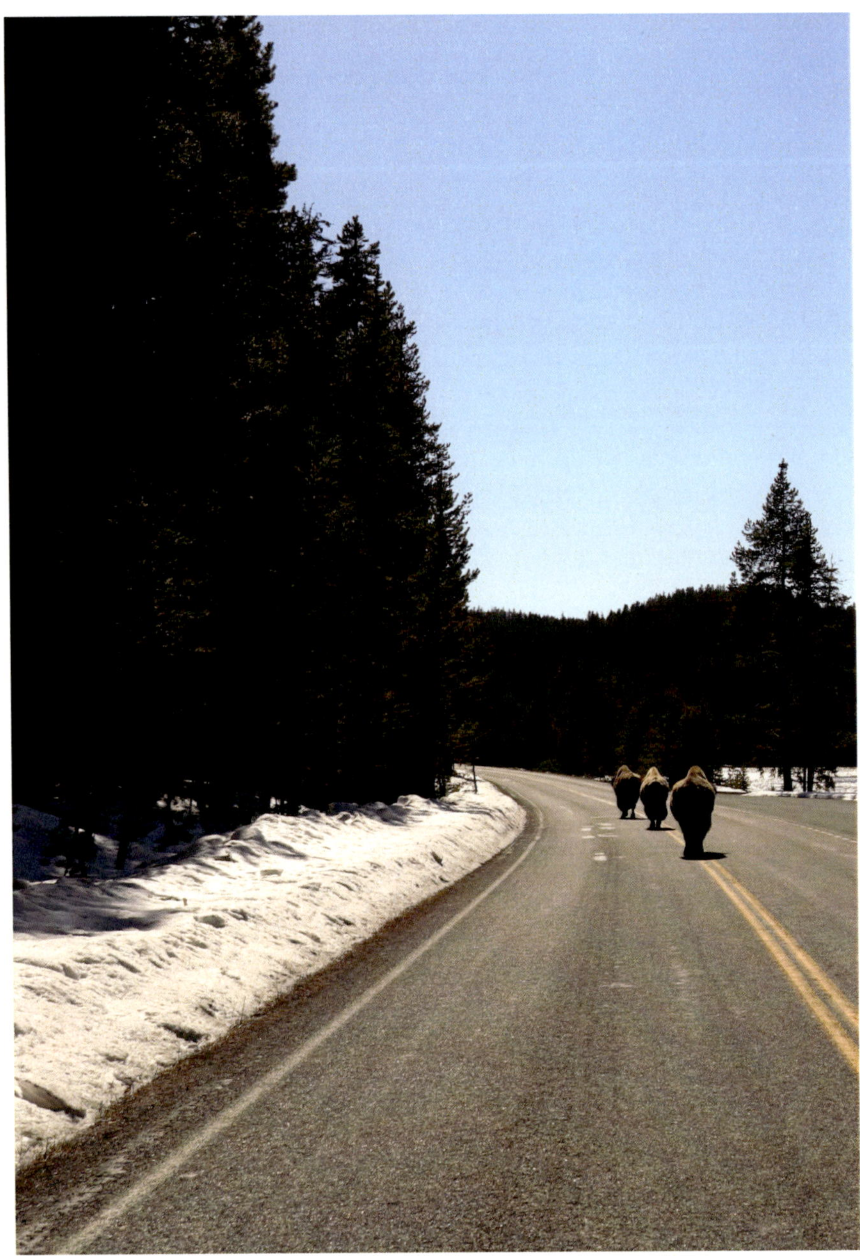

Above: Image IMG_5457. Photograph copyright © Lochlainn Seabrook.

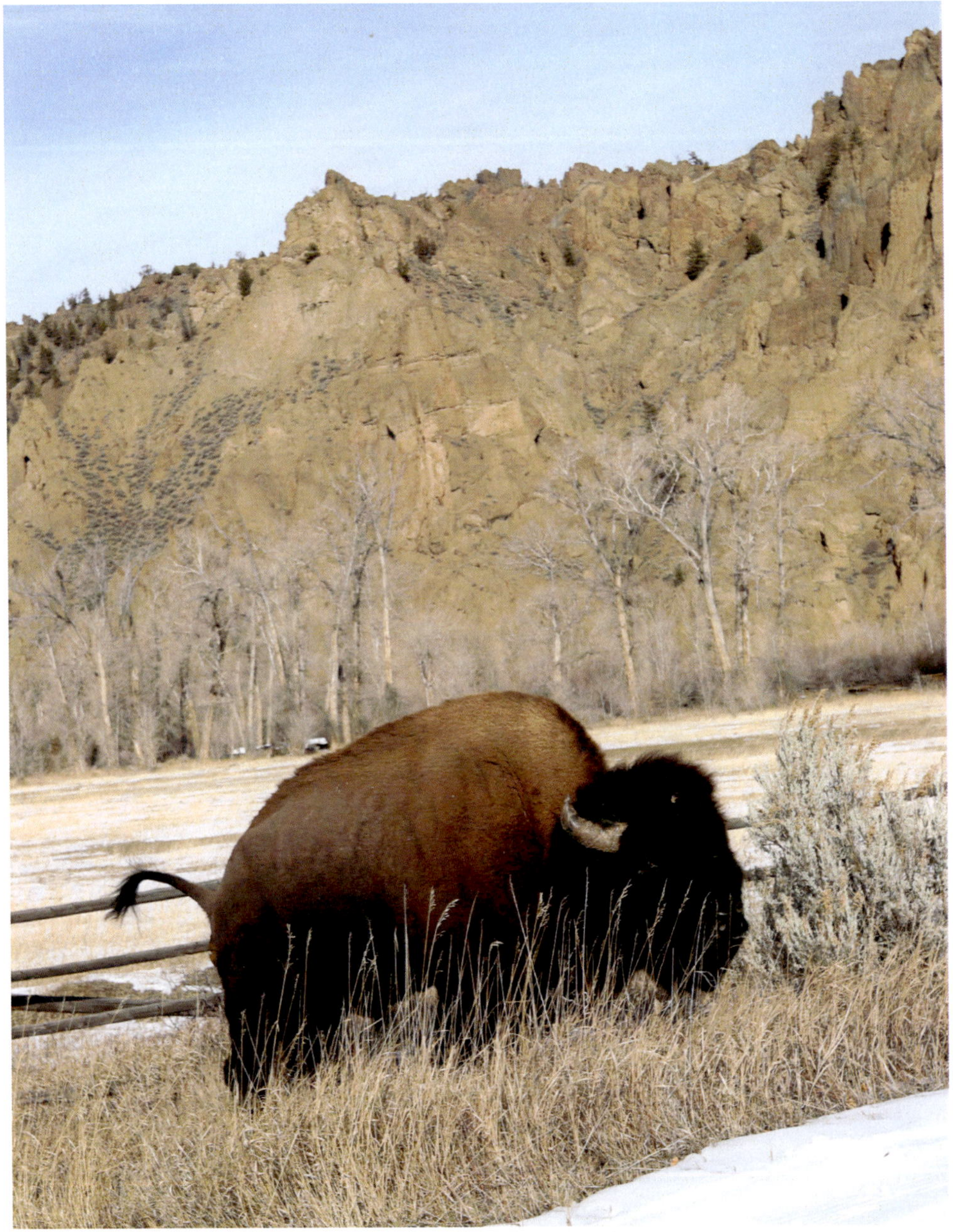

Above: Image 7X8A3324. Photograph copyright © Lochlainn Seabrook.

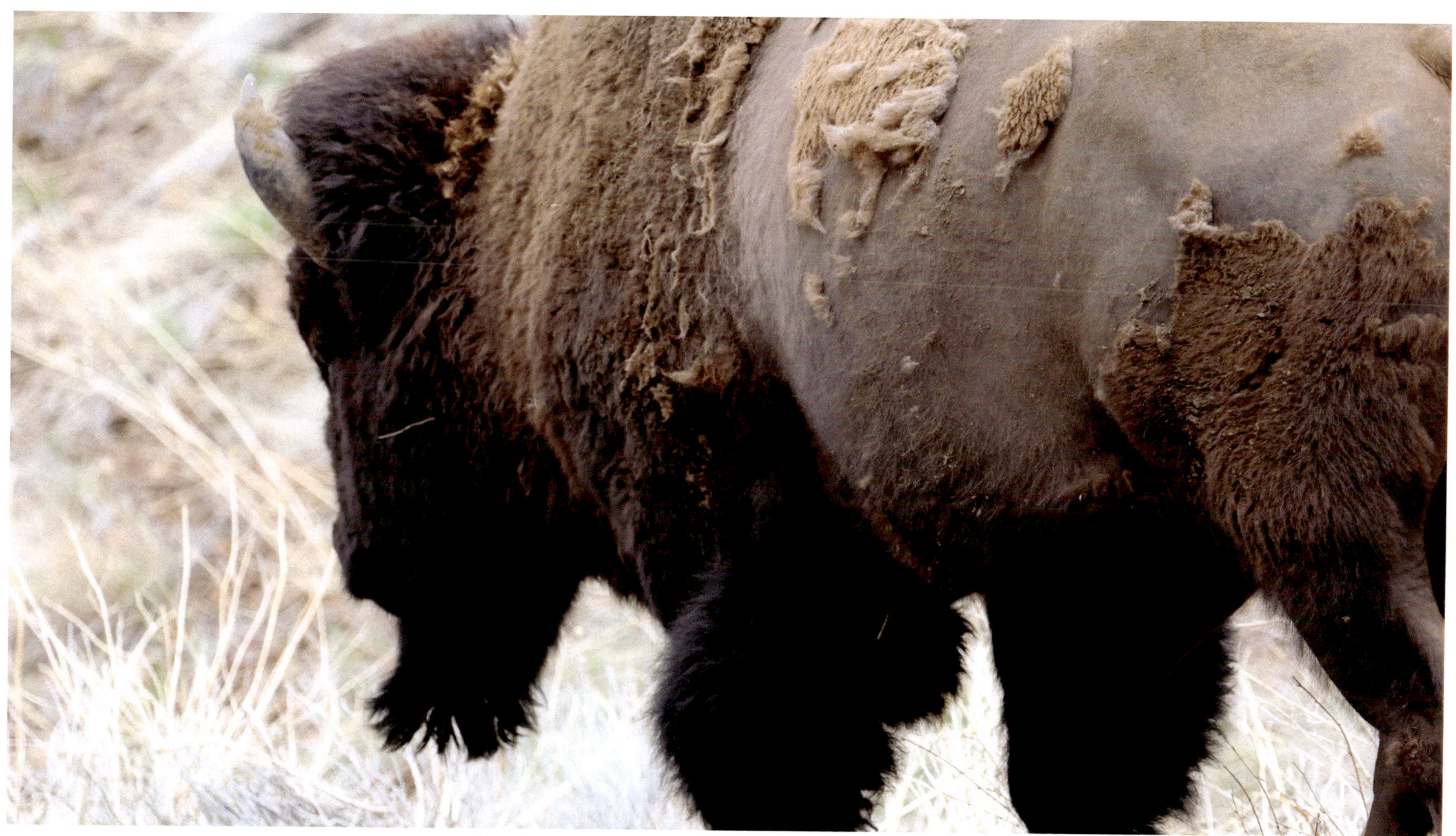

Above: Image 7X8A7923. Photograph copyright © Lochlainn Seabrook.

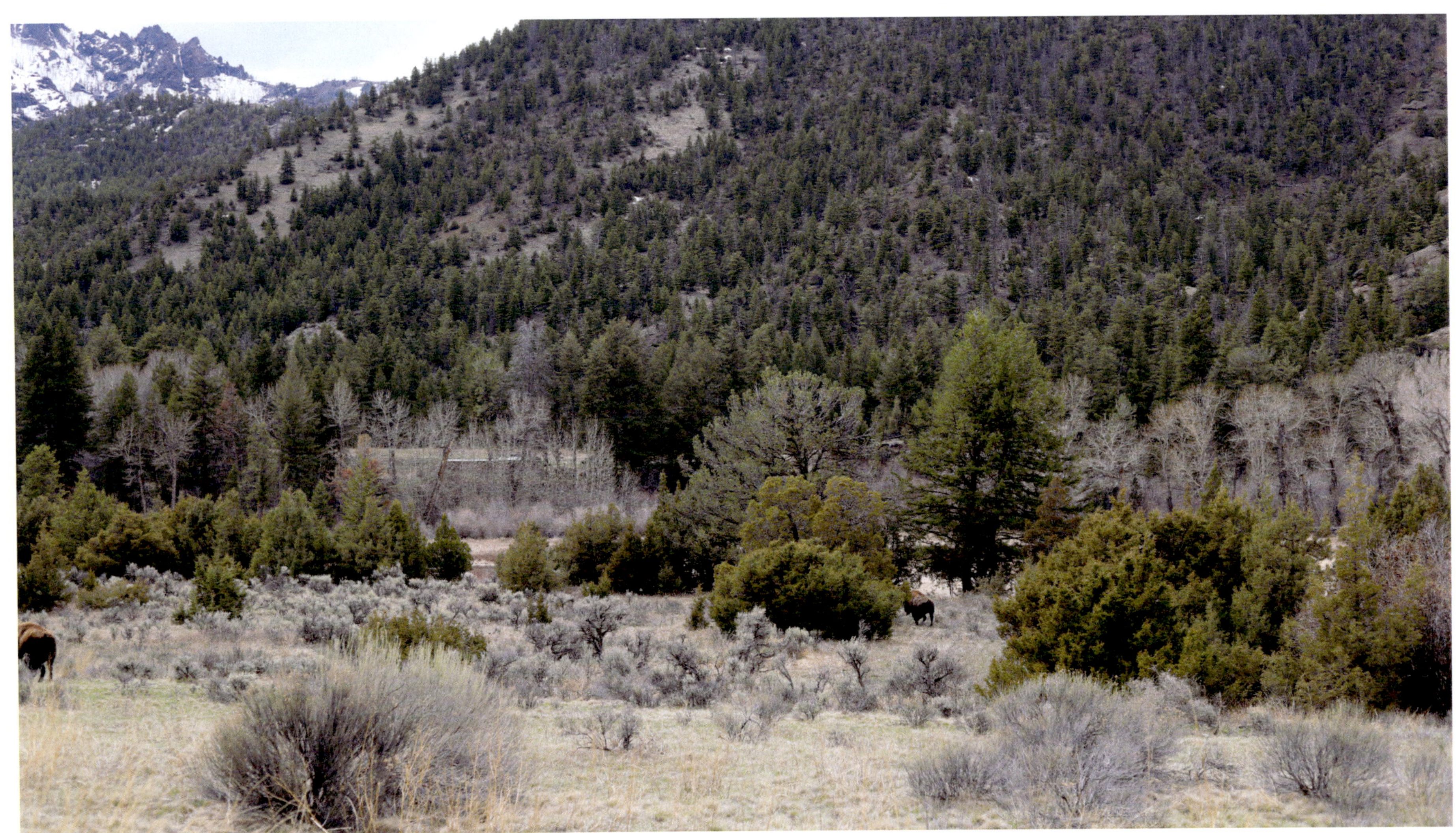

Above: Image 7X8A7717. Photograph copyright © Lochlainn Seabrook.

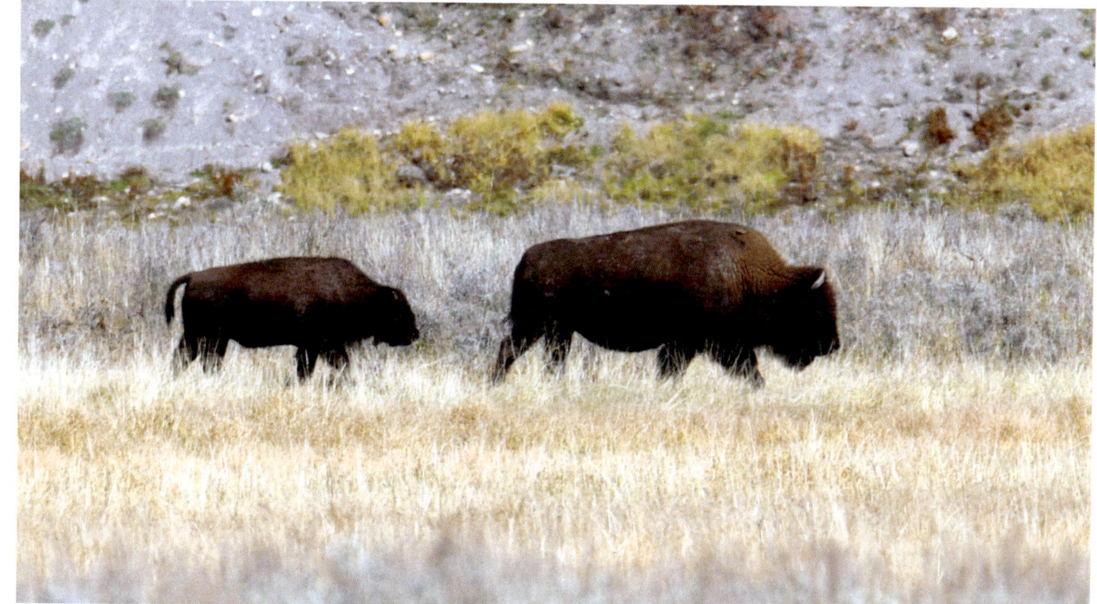

Left: Image IMG_Still1. Photograph copyright © Lochlainn Seabrook.

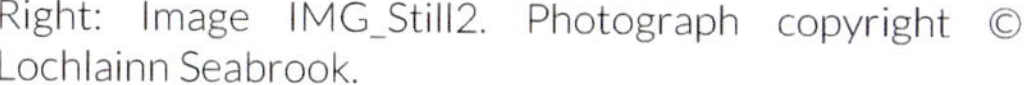

Right: Image IMG_Still2. Photograph copyright © Lochlainn Seabrook.

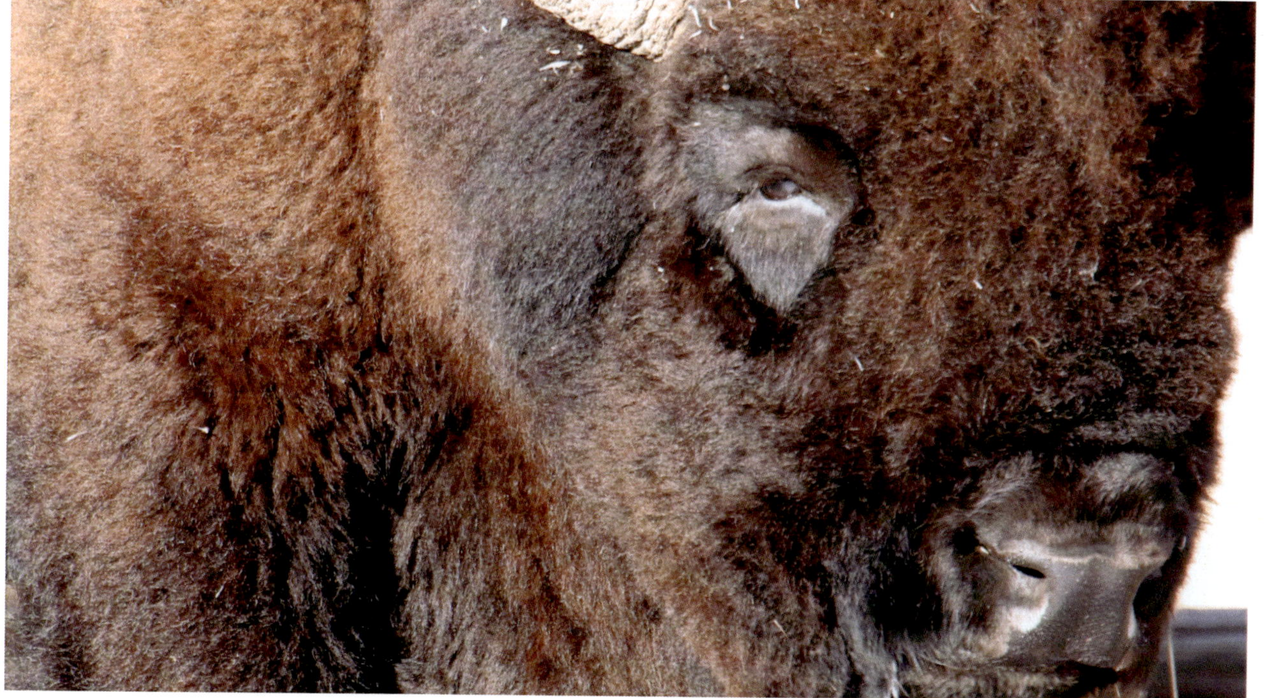

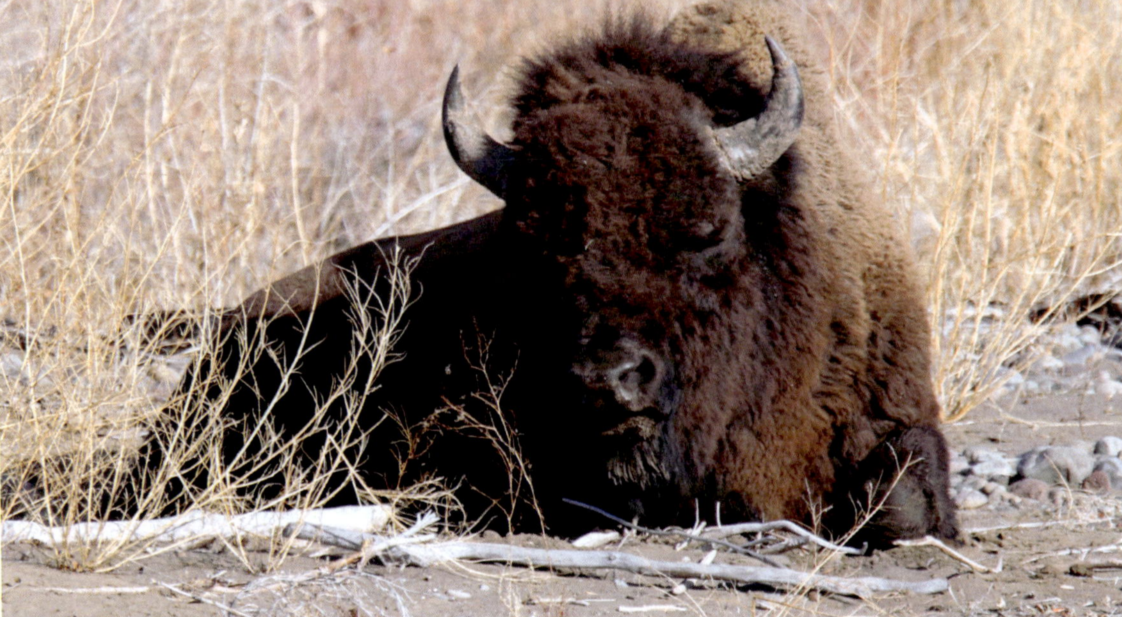

Right: Image IMG_Still3. Photograph copyright © Lochlainn Seabrook.

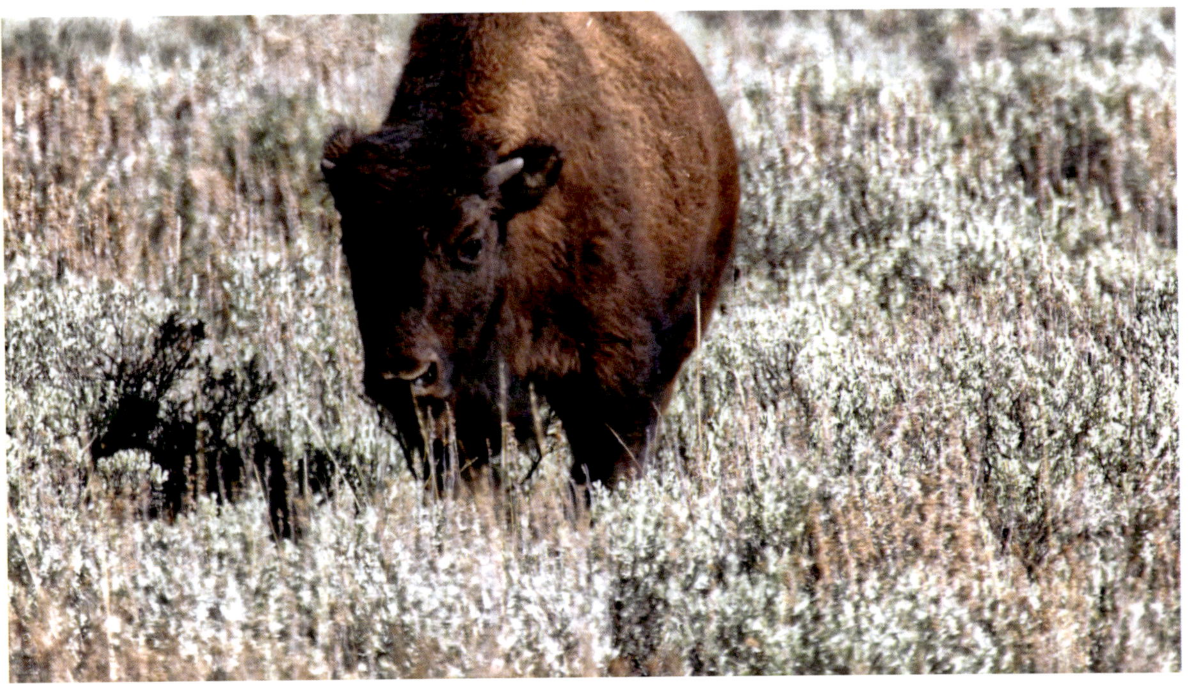

Left: Image IMG_Still4. Photograph copyright © Lochlainn Seabrook.

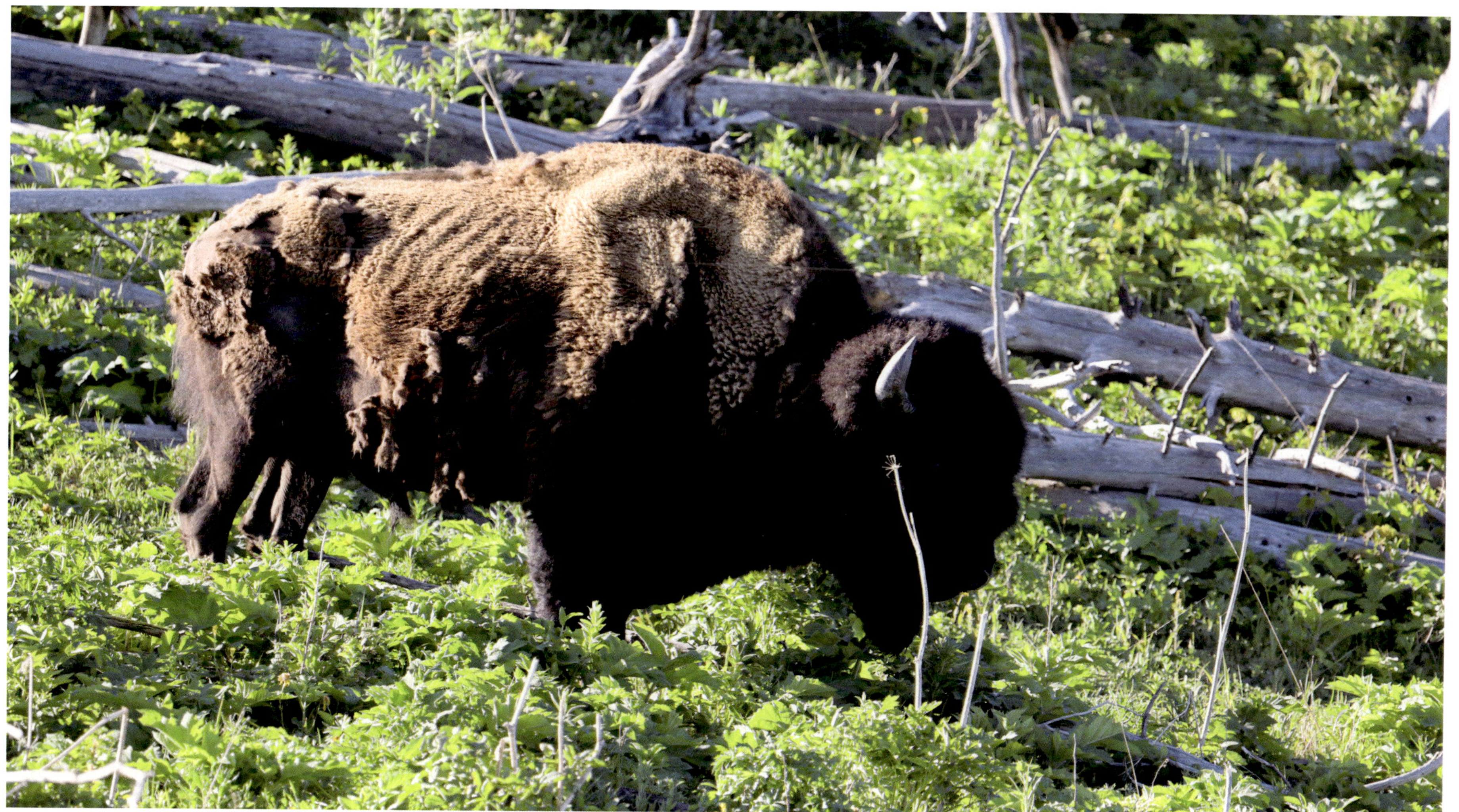

Above: Image 7X8A0673. Photograph copyright © Lochlainn Seabrook.

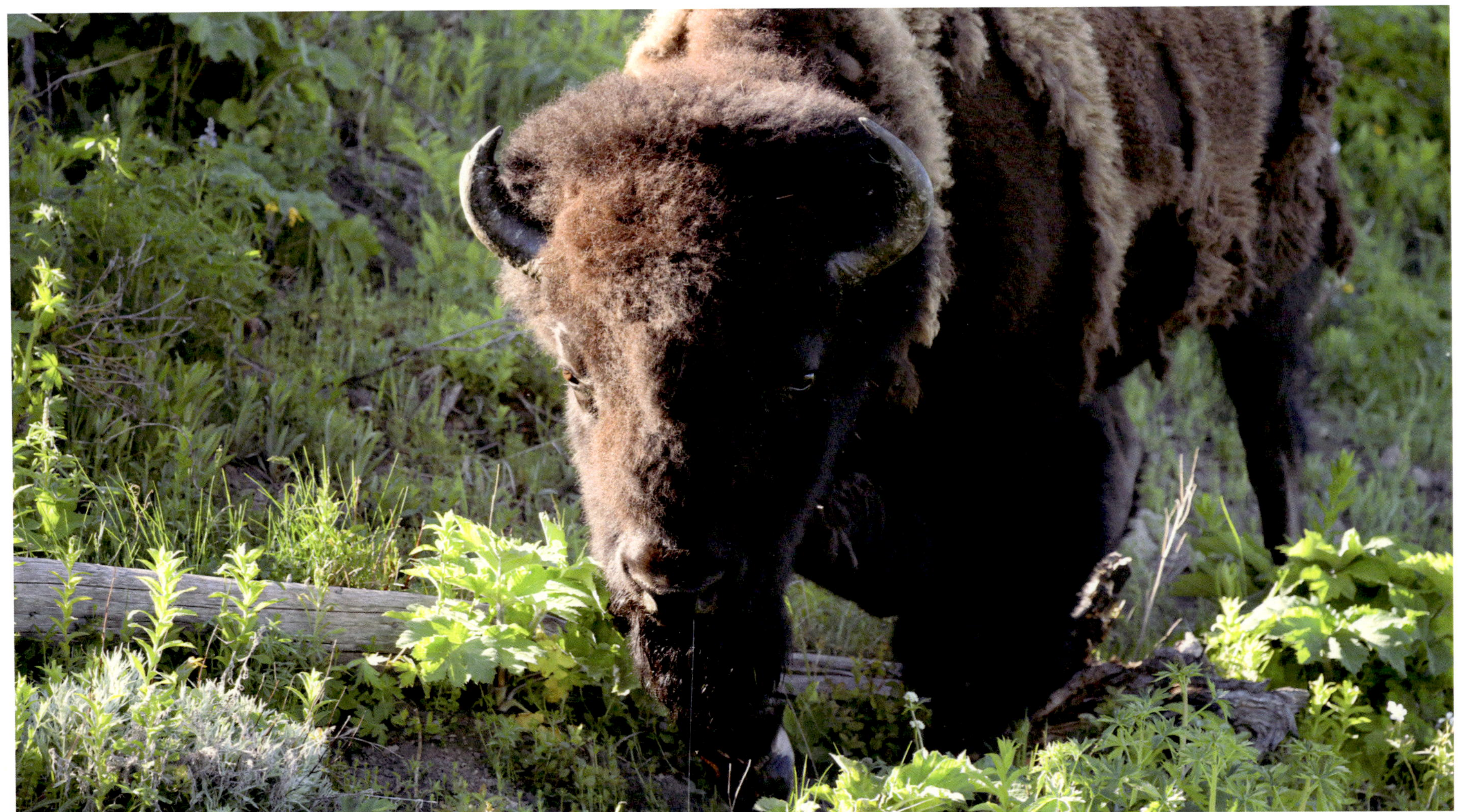

Above: Image 7X8A0682. Photograph copyright © Lochlainn Seabrook.

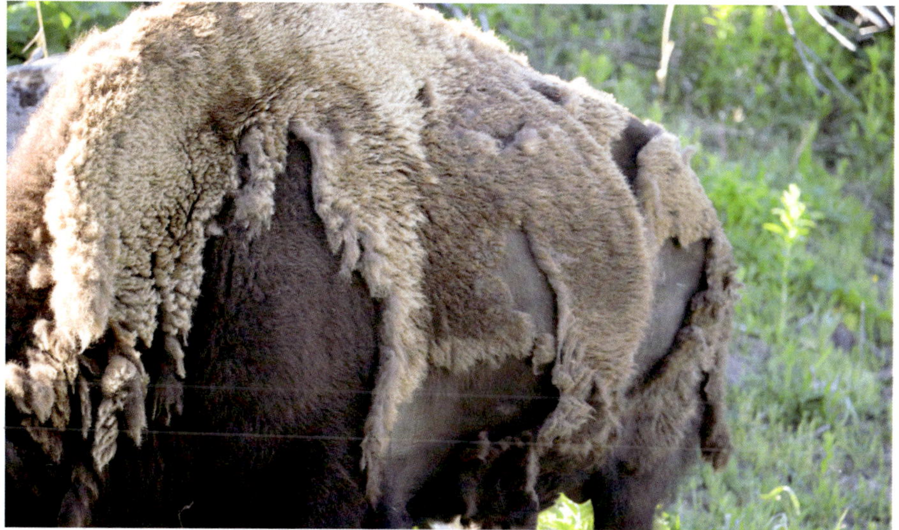

Above: Image 7X8A0686. Photograph copyright © Lochlainn Seabrook.

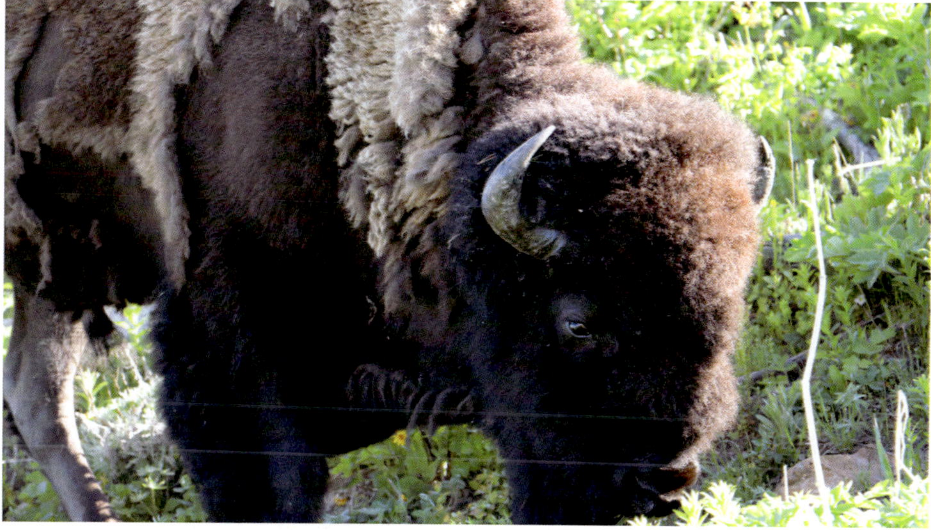

Above: Image 7X8A0687. Photograph copyright © Lochlainn Seabrook.

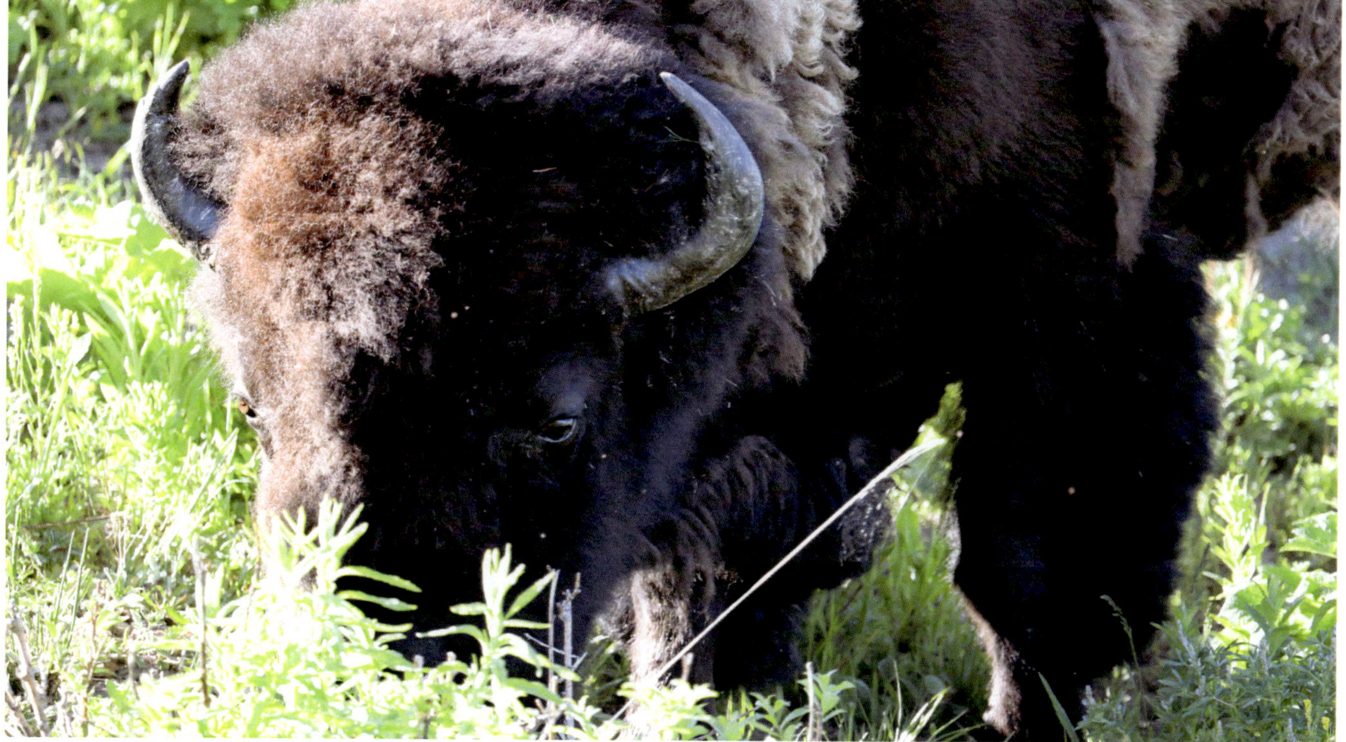

Left: Image 7X8A0695. Photograph copyright © Lochlainn Seabrook.

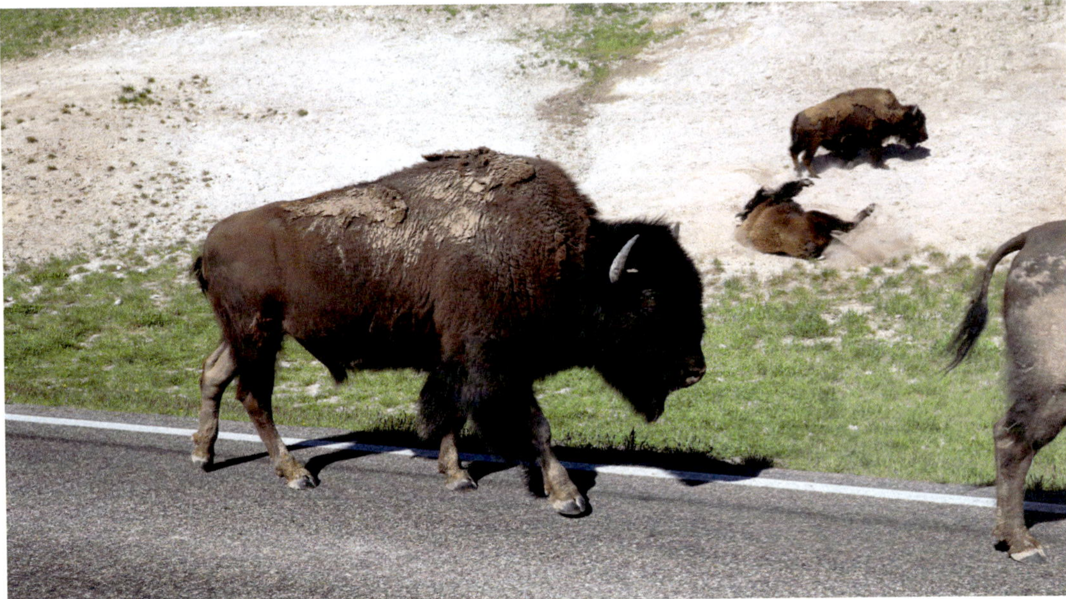

Above: Image IMG_6740. Photograph copyright © Lochlainn Seabrook.

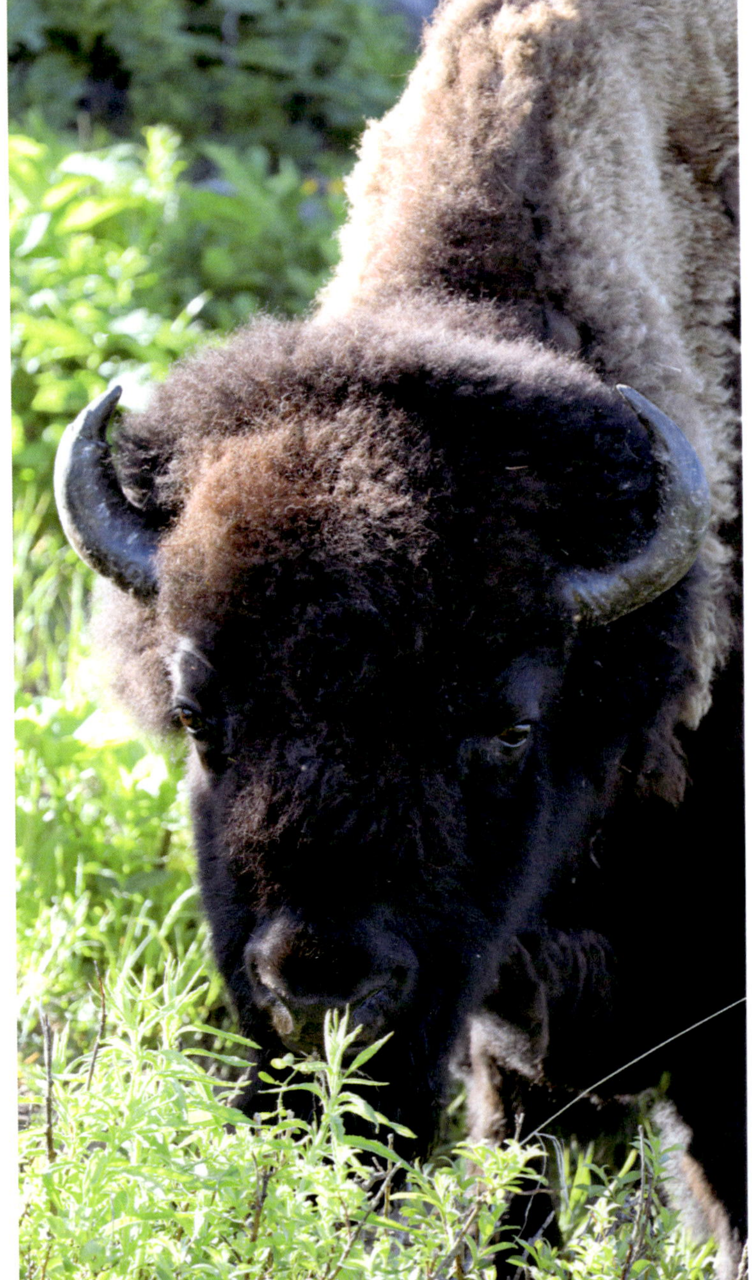

Above: Image 7X8A0701. Photograph copyright © Lochlainn Seabrook.

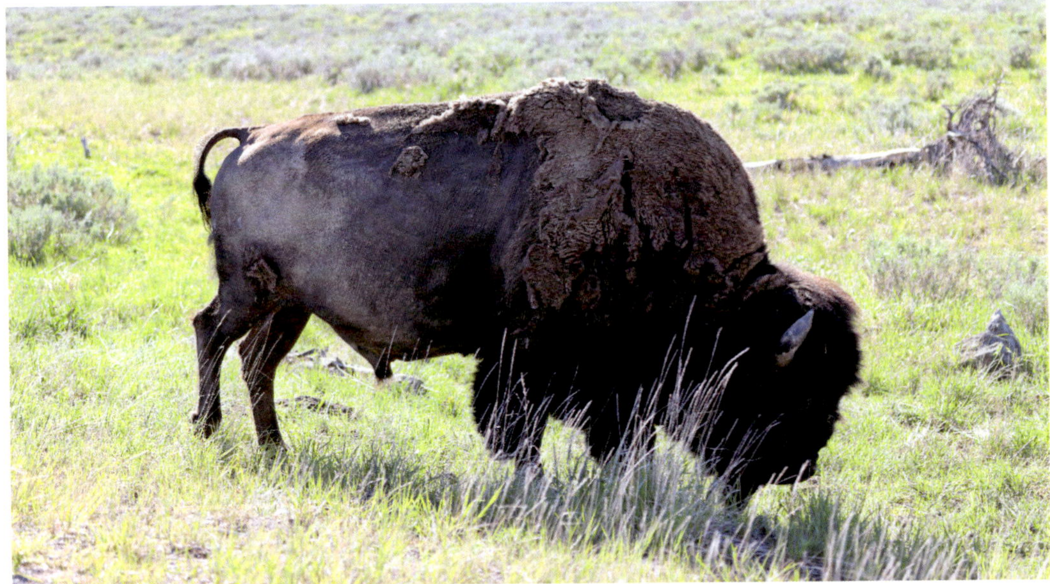

Above: Image 7X8A0704. Photograph copyright © Lochlainn Seabrook.

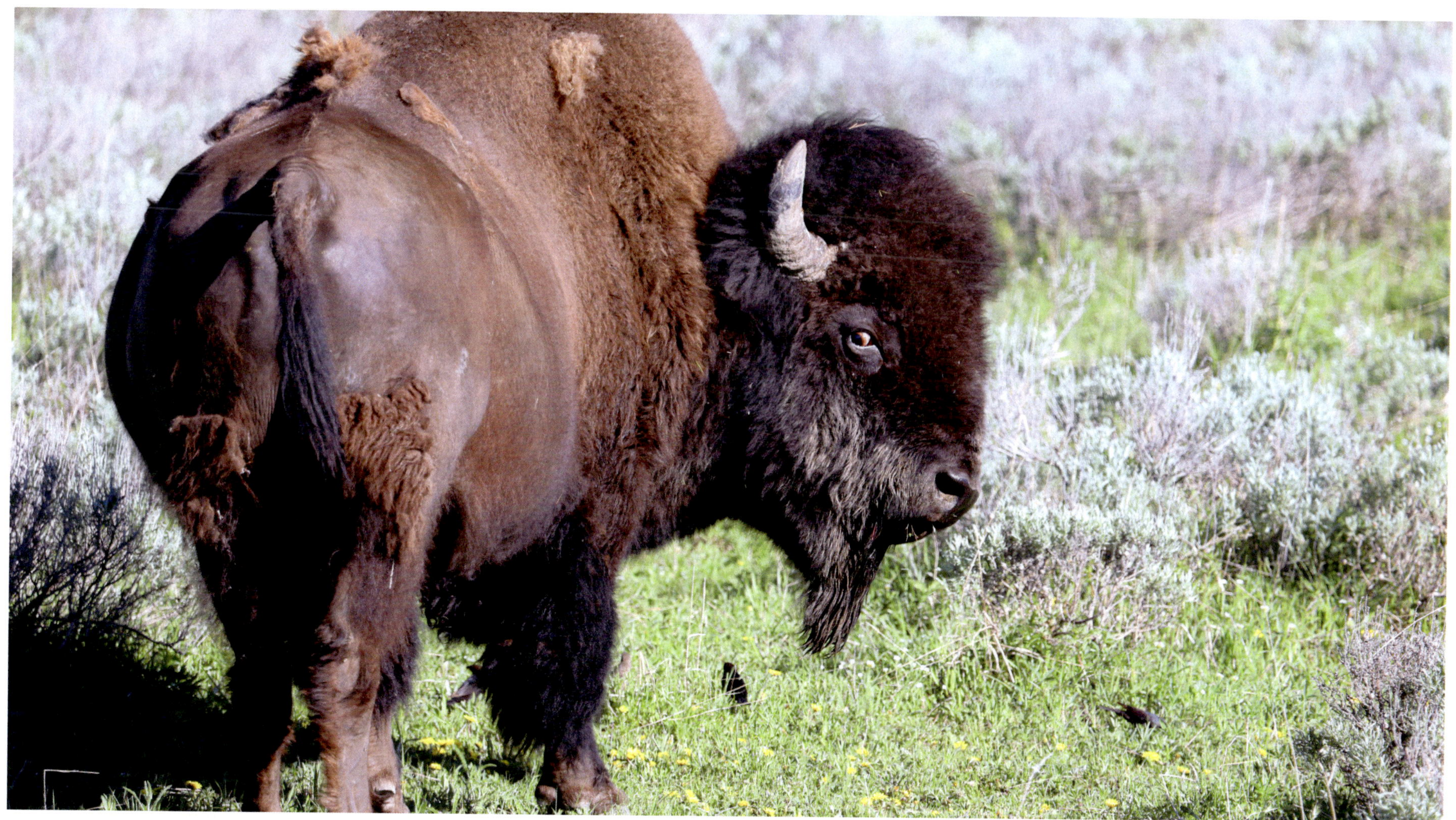

Above: Image 7X8A0704. Photograph copyright © Lochlainn Seabrook.

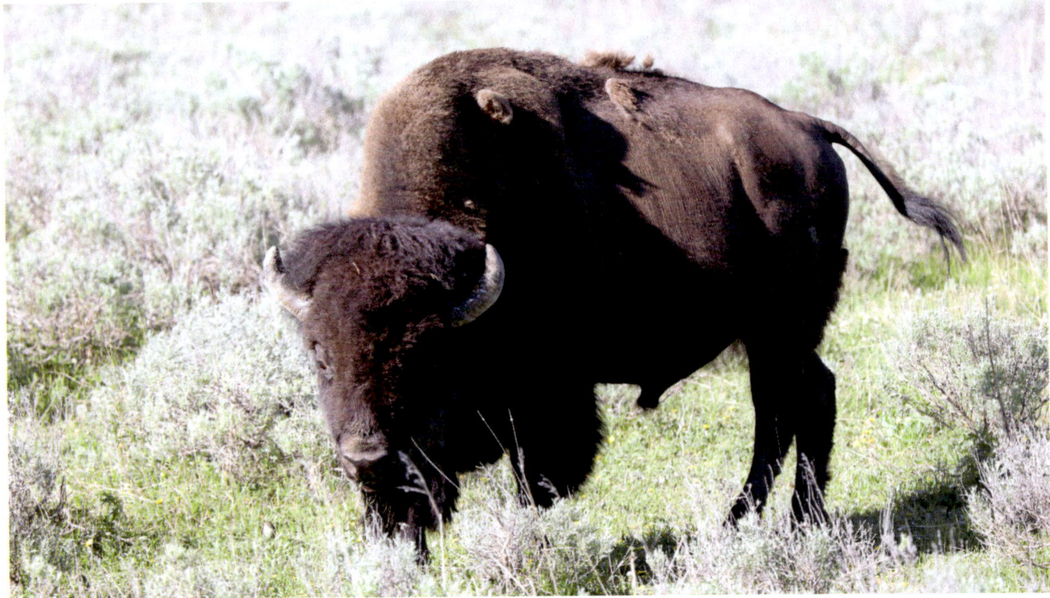

Above: Image 7X8A0717. Photograph copyright © Lochlainn Seabrook.

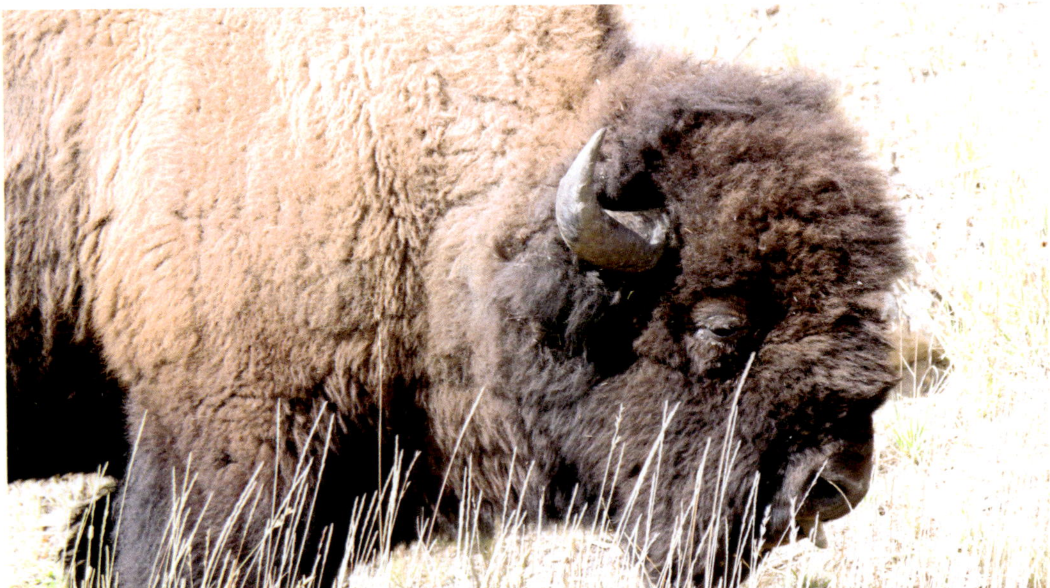

Above: Image 7X8A0259. Photograph copyright © Lochlainn Seabrook.

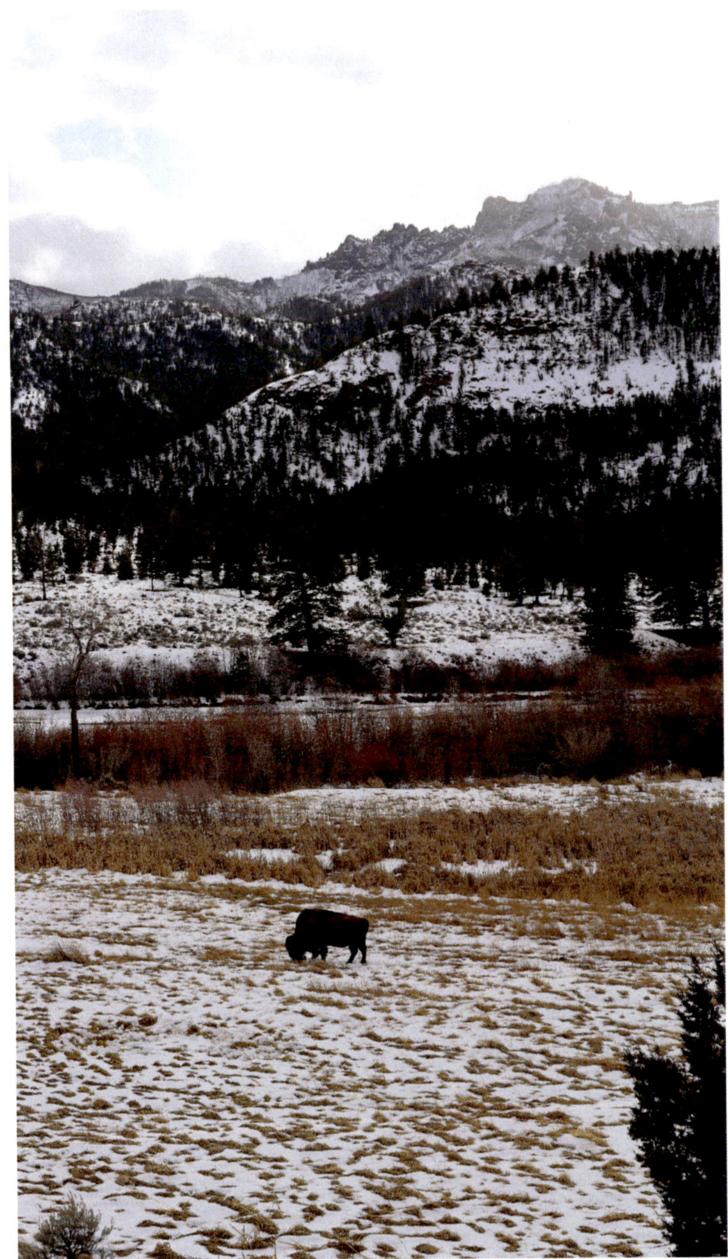

Above: Image 7X8A5140. Photograph copyright © Lochlainn Seabrook.

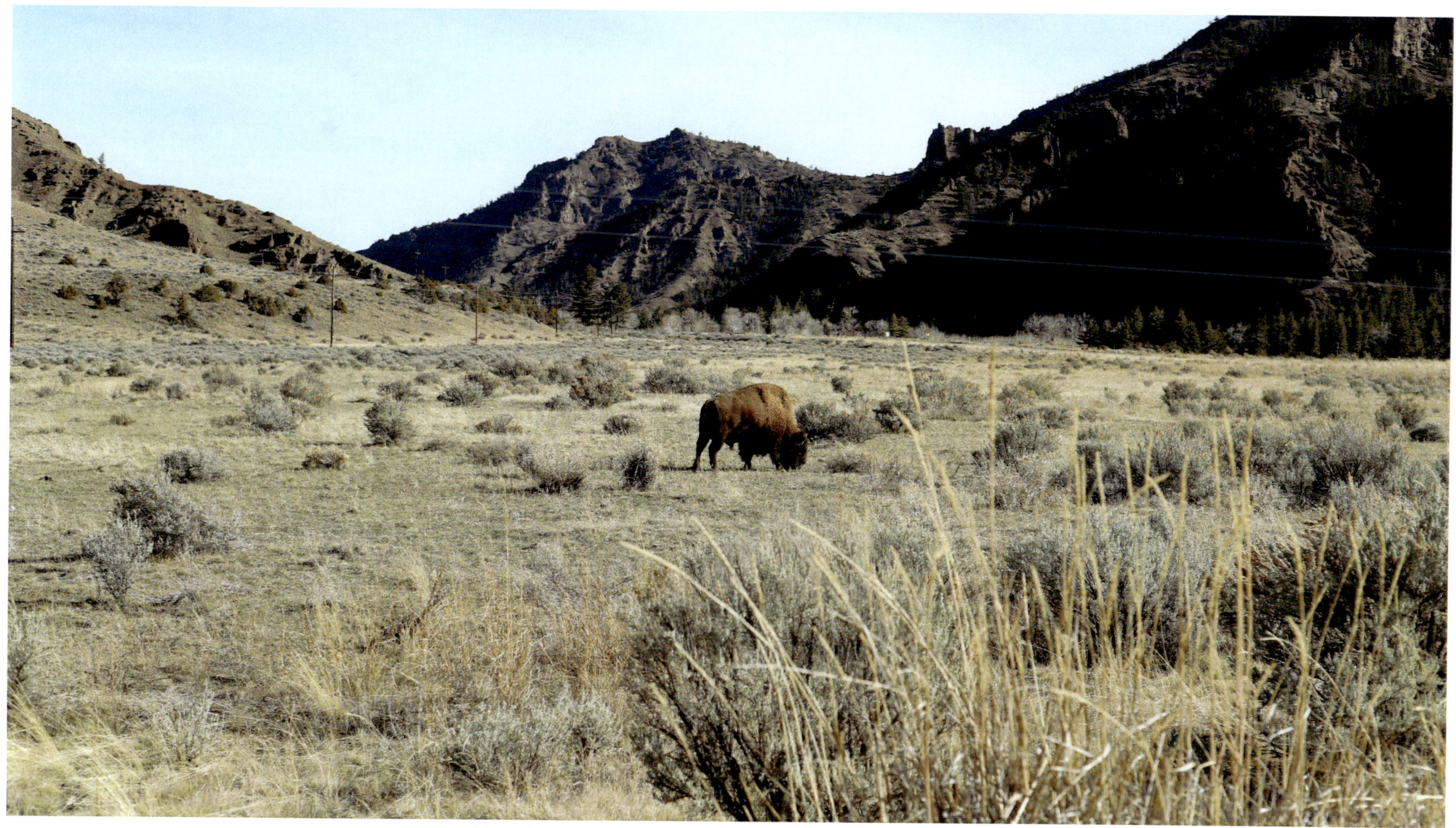

Above: Image 7X8A2578. Photograph copyright © Lochlainn Seabrook.

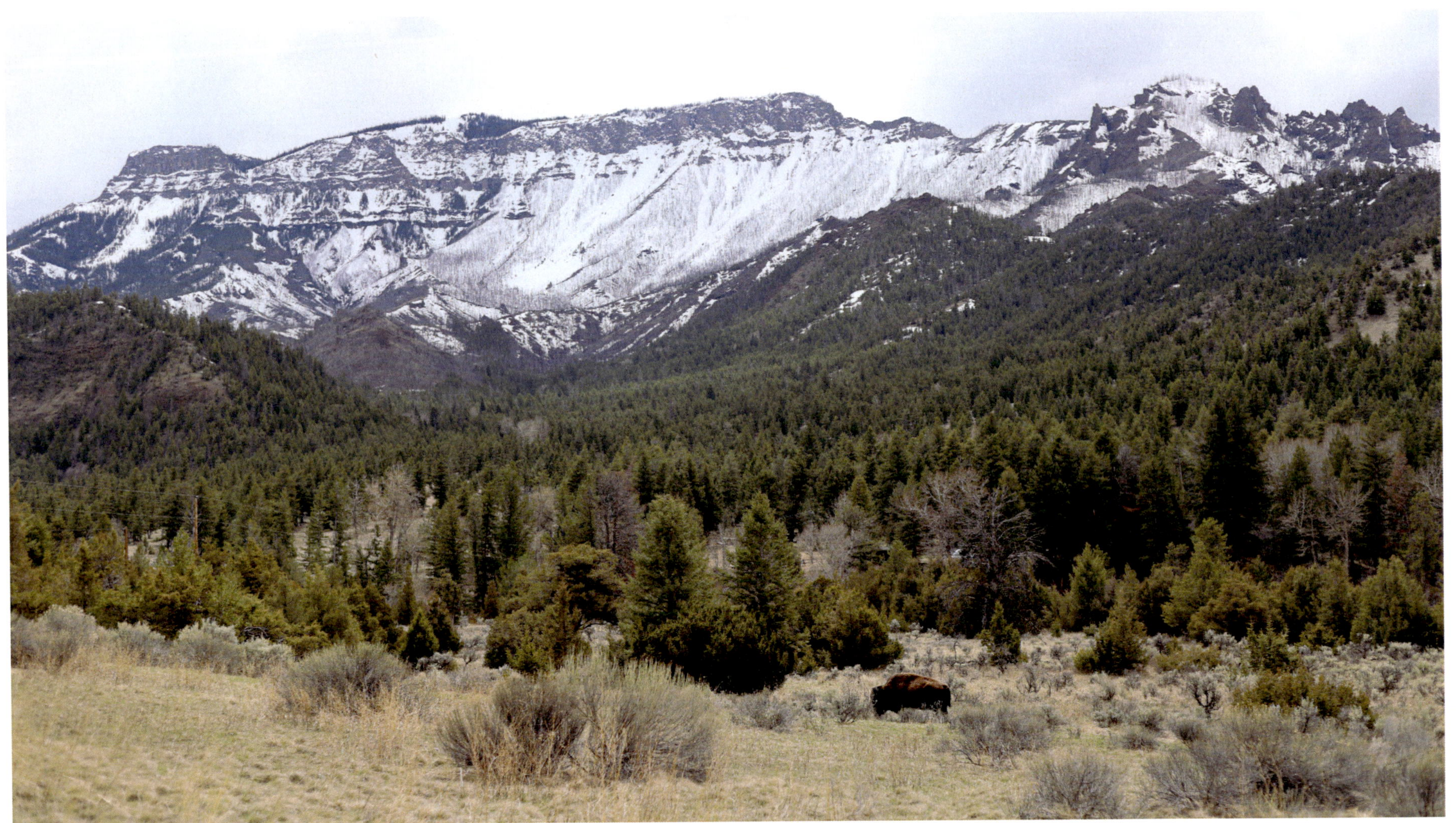

Above: Image 7X8A7718. Photograph copyright © Lochlainn Seabrook.

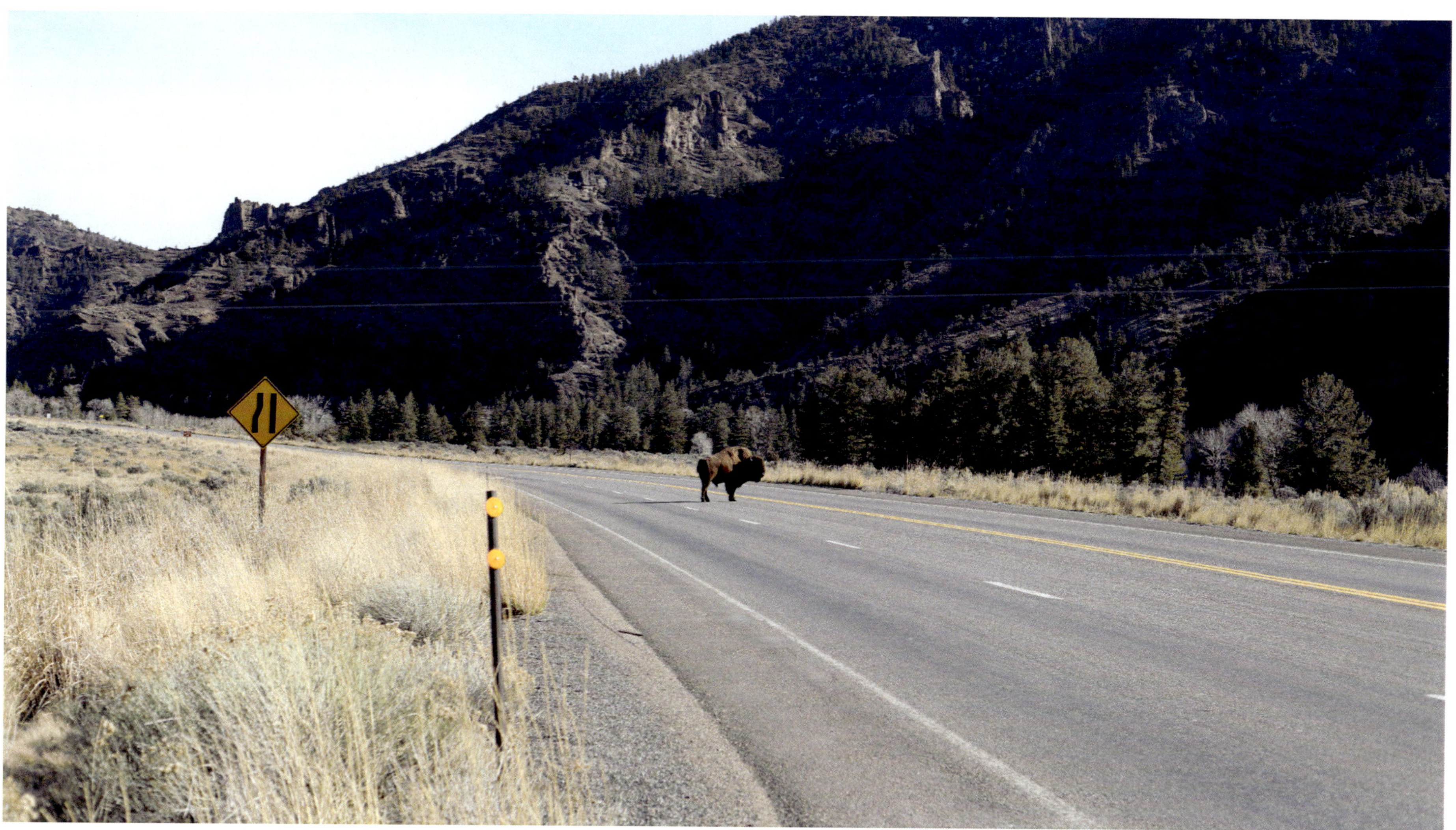

Above: Image 7X8A2595. Photograph copyright © Lochlainn Seabrook.

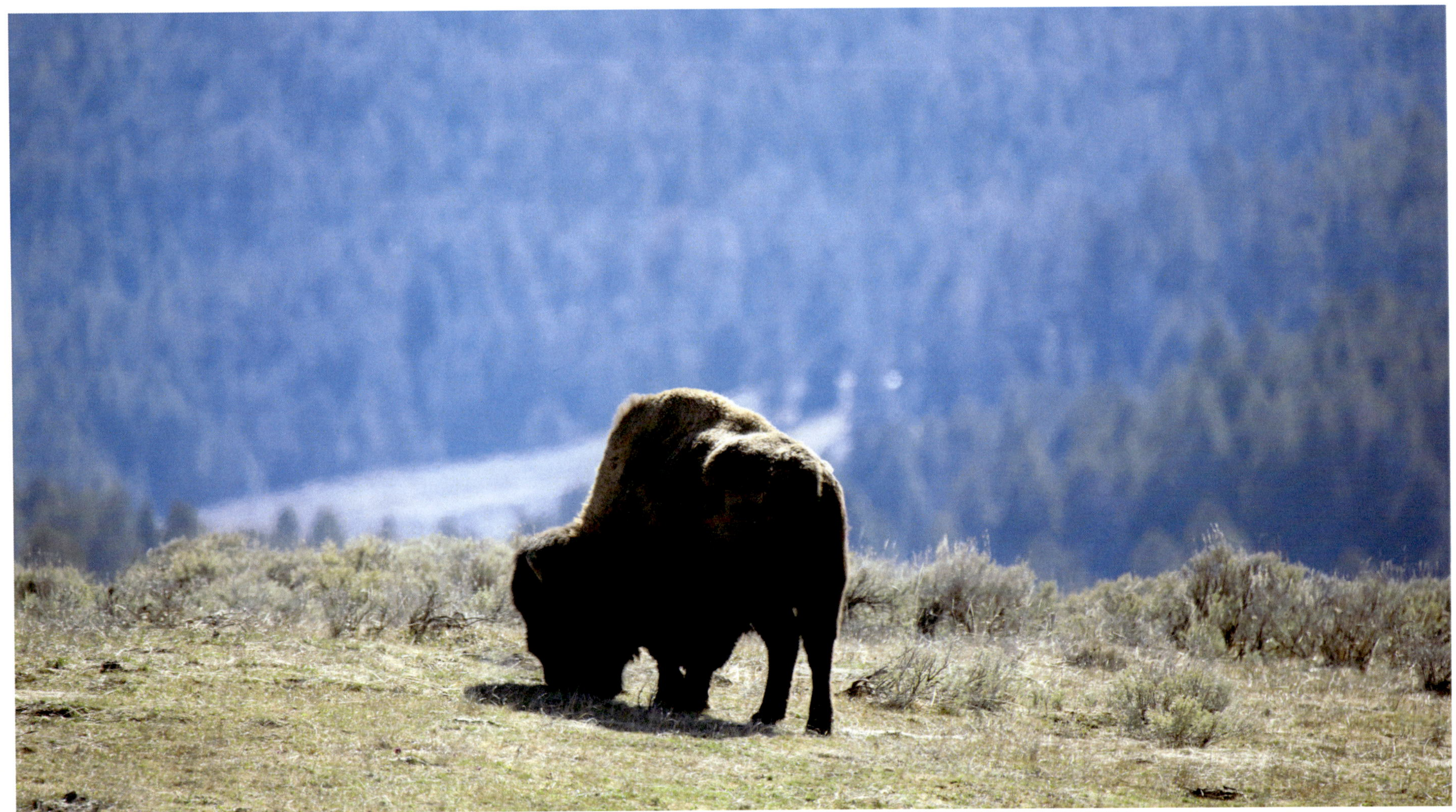

Above: Image 7X8A8958. Photograph copyright © Lochlainn Seabrook.

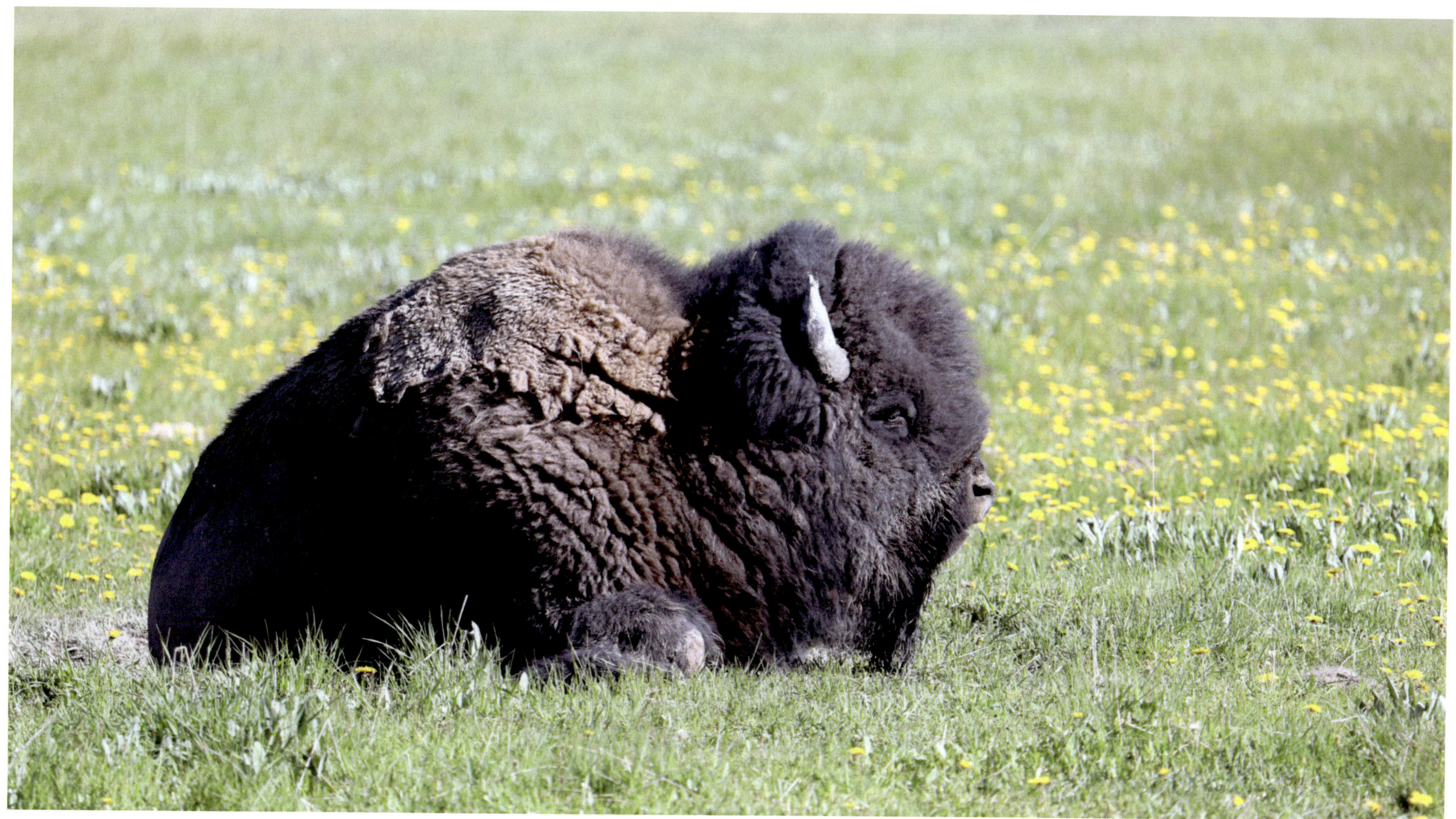

Above: Image 7X8A0781. Photograph copyright © Lochlainn Seabrook.

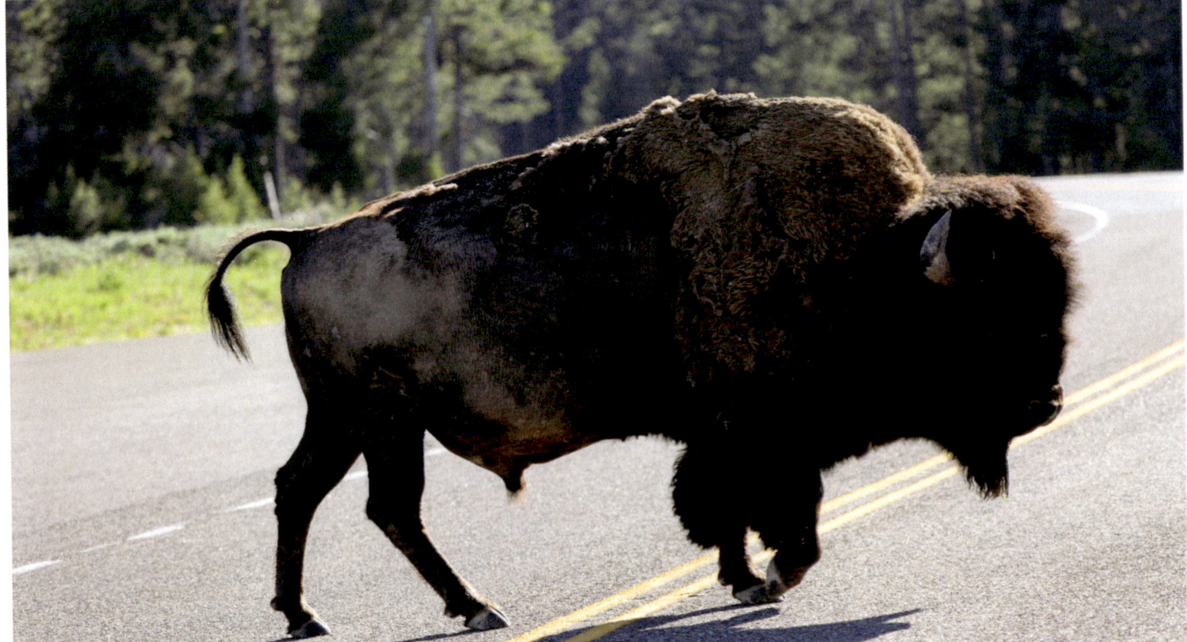

Right: Image 7X8A0740. Photograph copyright © Lochlainn Seabrook.

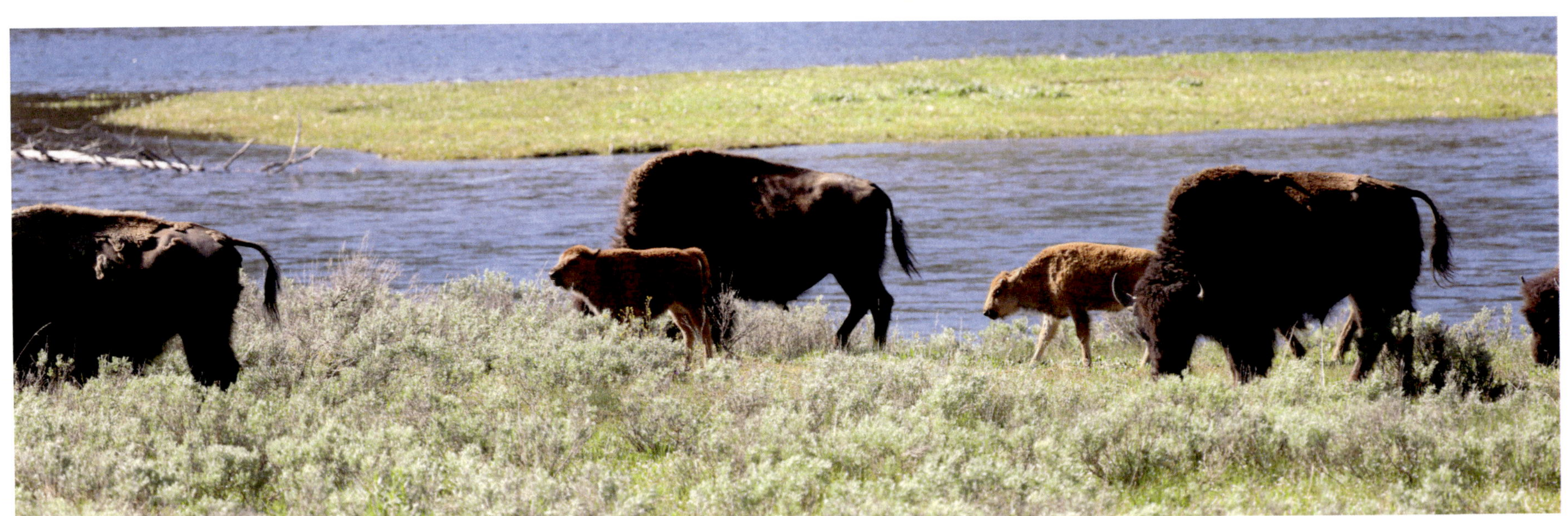

Above: Image 7X8A0827. Photograph copyright © Lochlainn Seabrook.

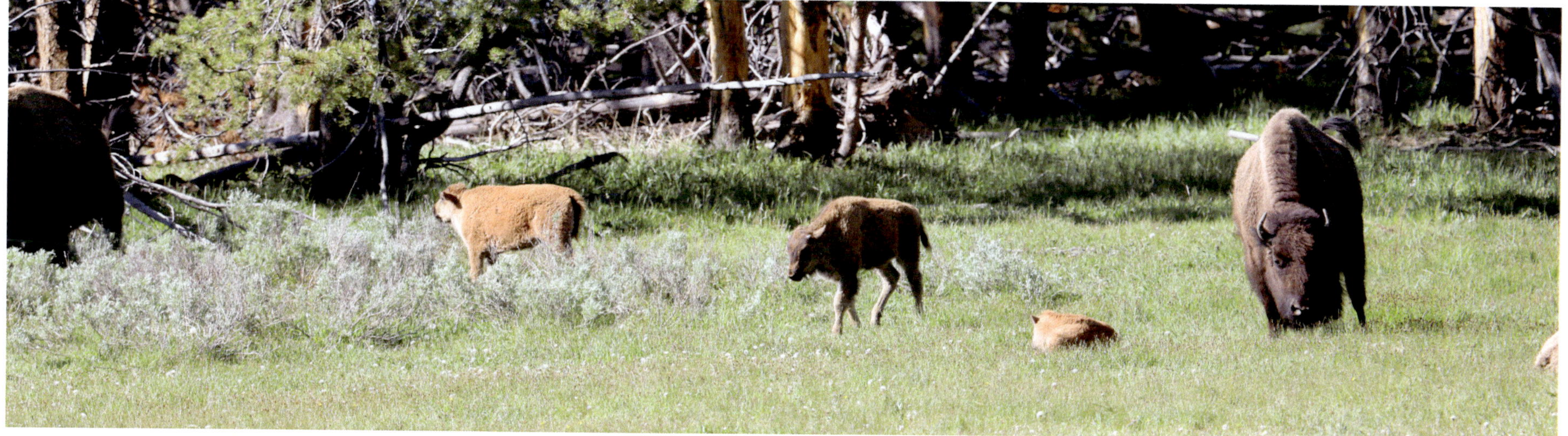

Above: Image 7X8A0837. Photograph copyright © Lochlainn Seabrook.

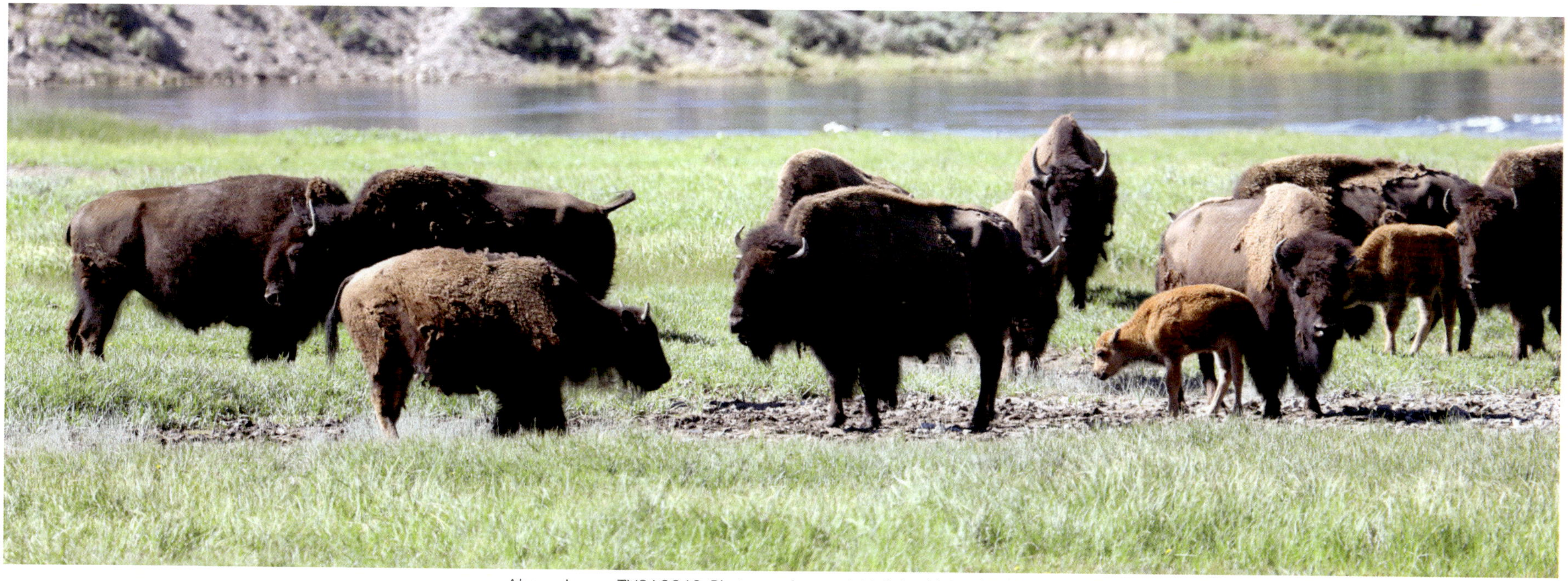

Above: Image 7X8A0960. Photograph copyright © Lochlainn Seabrook.

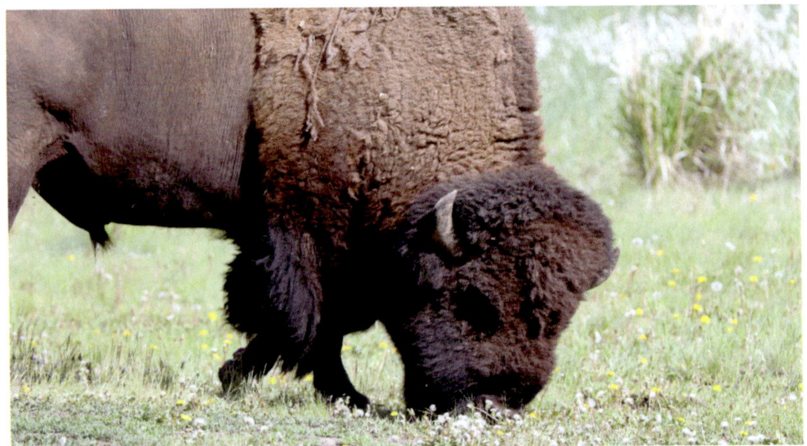

Above: Image 7X8A0511. Photograph copyright © Lochlainn Seabrook.

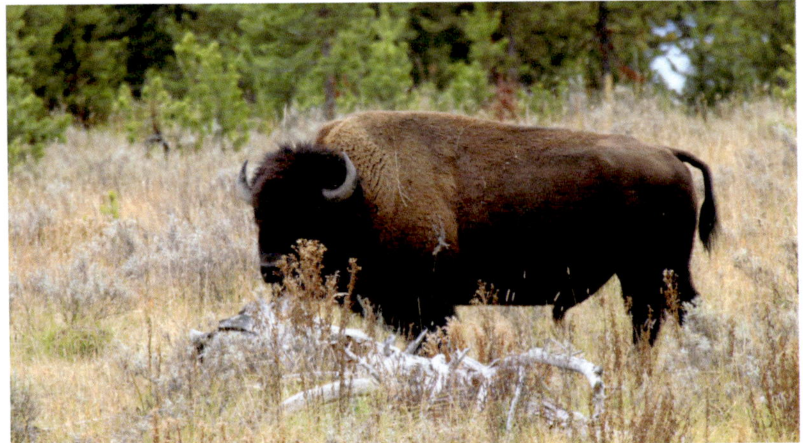

Above: Image 7X8A1481. Photograph copyright © Lochlainn Seabrook.

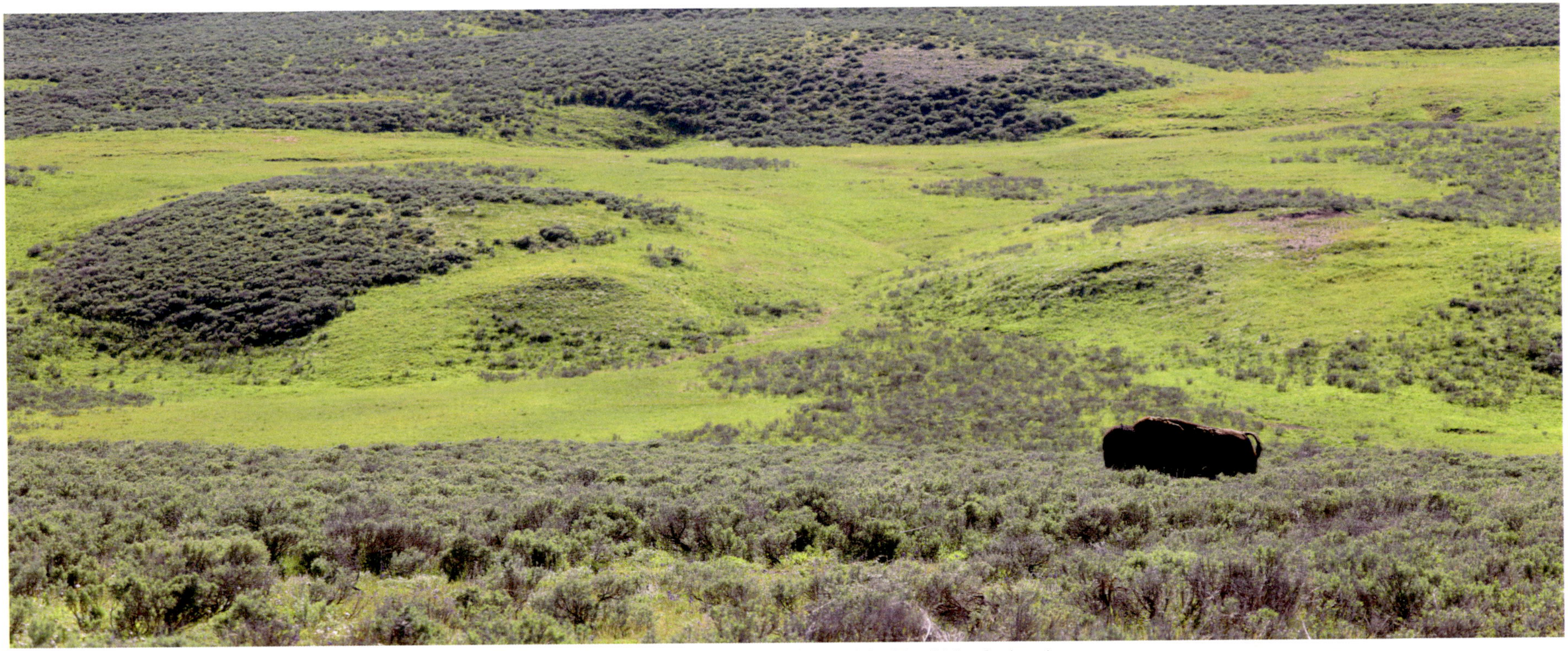

Above: Image 7X8A0933. Photograph copyright © Lochlainn Seabrook.

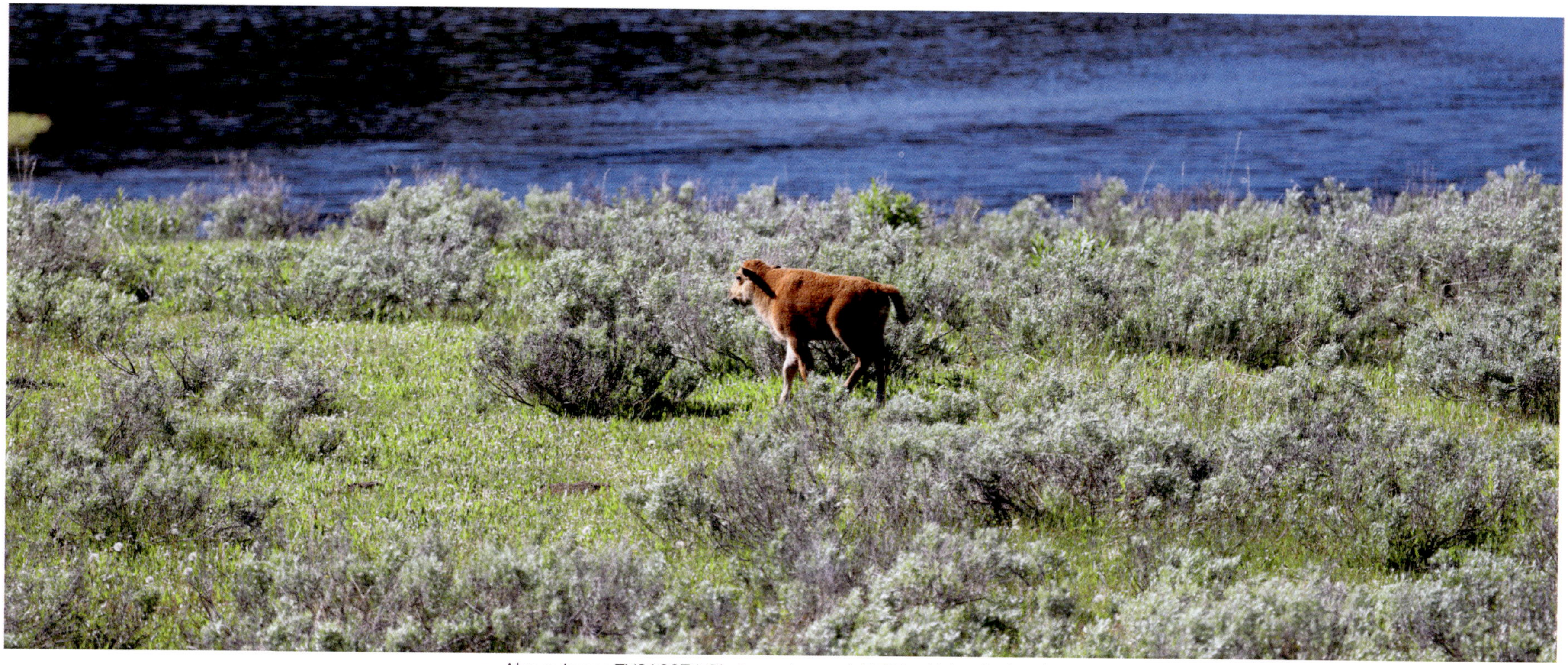

Above: Image 7X8A0876. Photograph copyright © Lochlainn Seabrook.

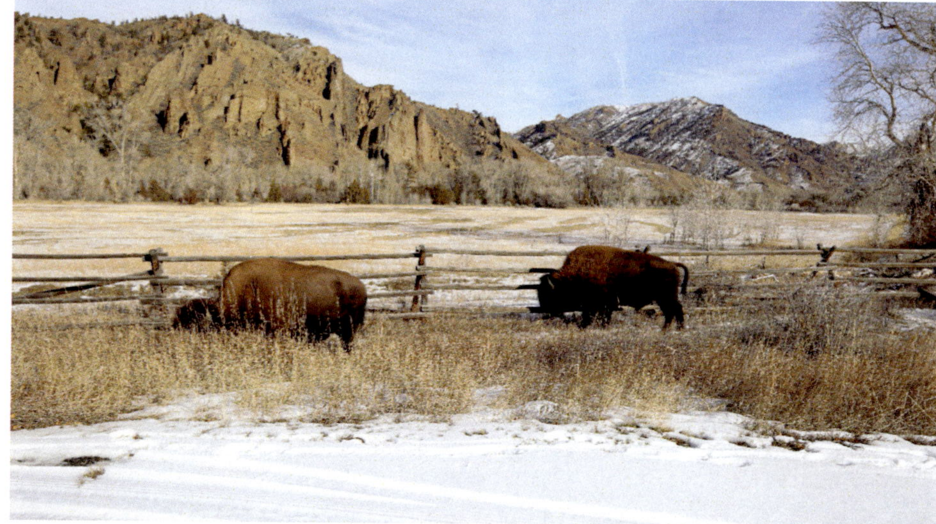

Right: Image 7X8A3322. Photograph copyright © Lochlainn Seabrook.

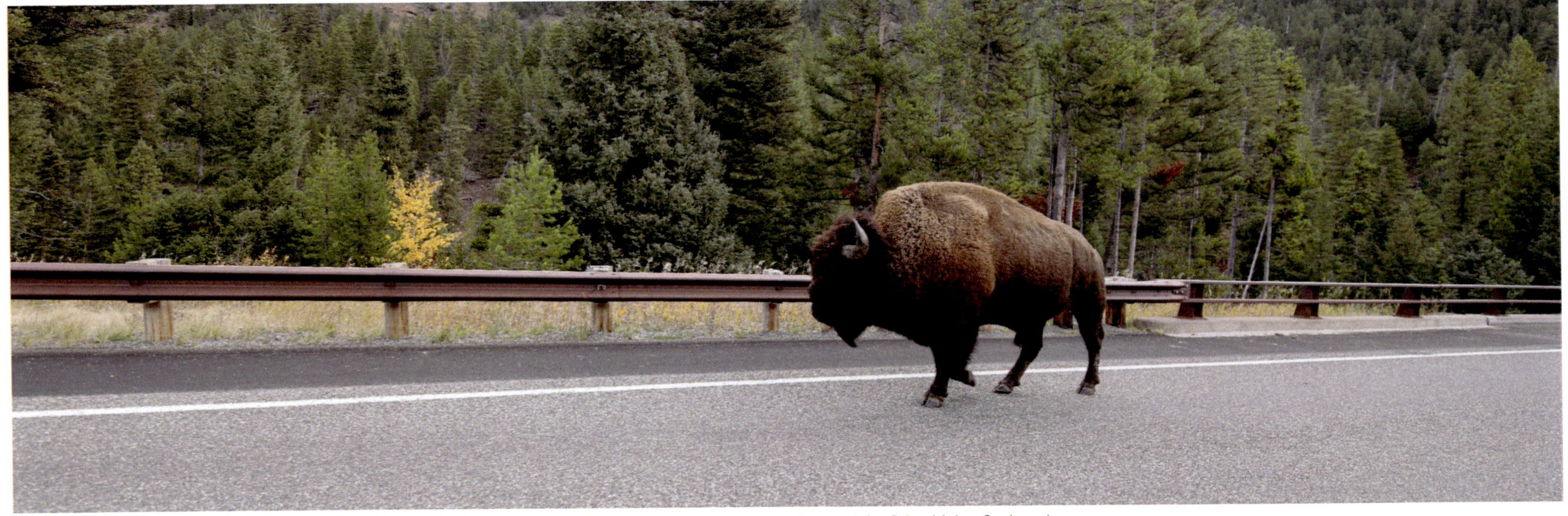

Above: Image 7X8A1506. Photograph copyright © Lochlainn Seabrook.

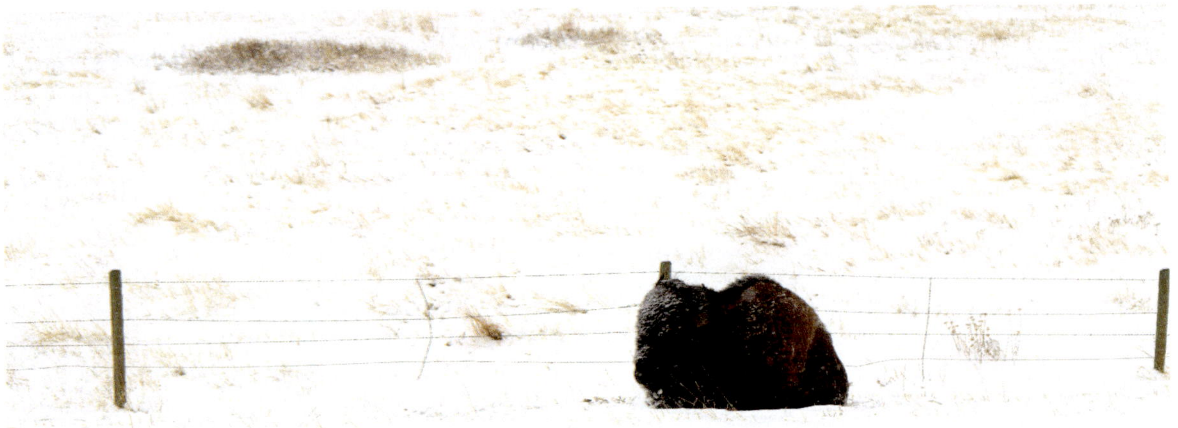

Left: Image 7X8A6011. Photograph copyright © Lochlainn Seabrook.

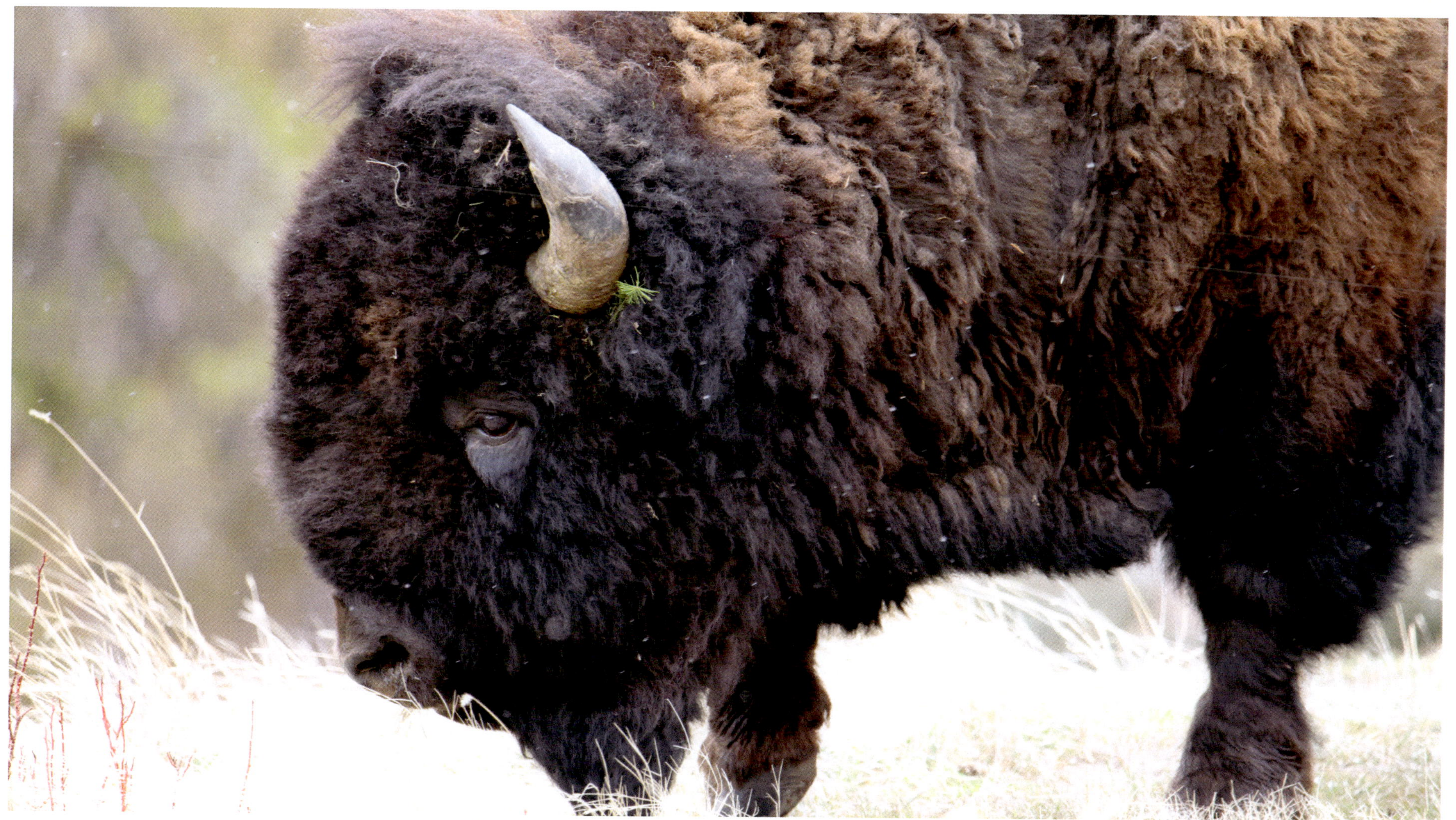

Above: Image 7X8A6609. Photograph copyright © Lochlainn Seabrook.

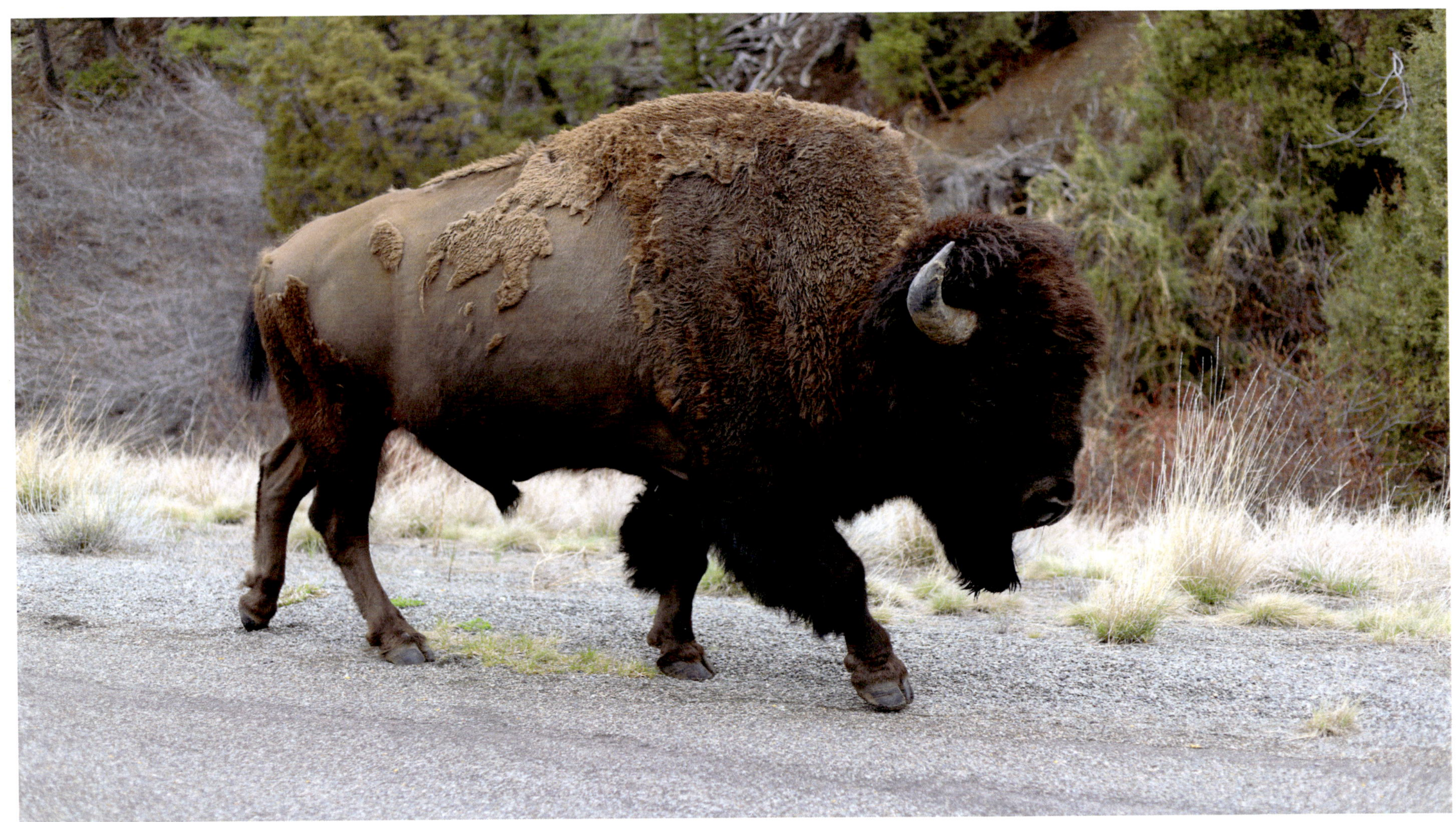

Above: Image 7X8A7854. Photograph copyright © Lochlainn Seabrook.

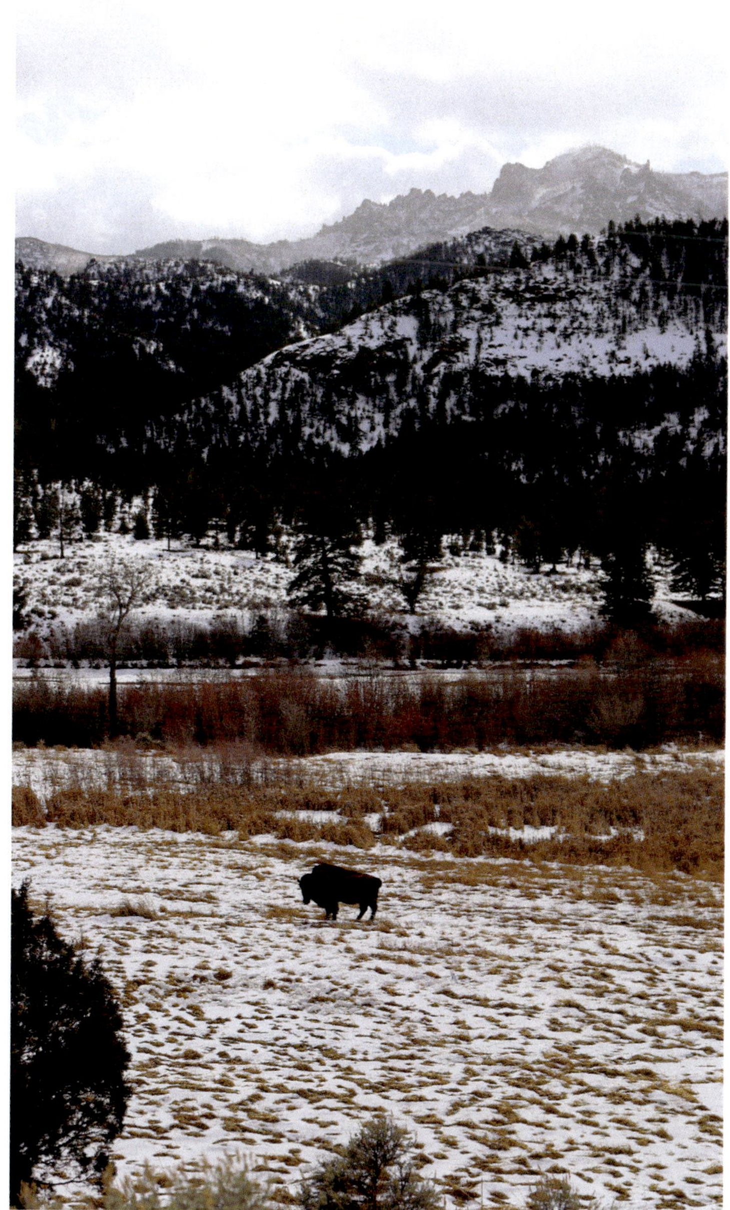

Above: Image 7X8A5145. Photograph copyright © Lochlainn Seabrook.

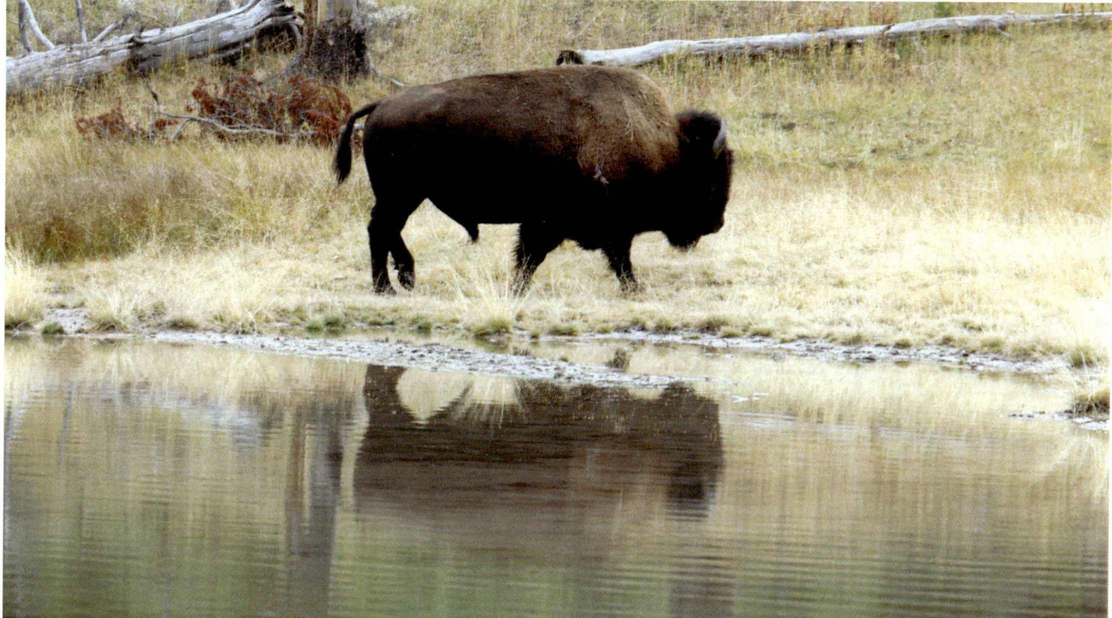

Above: Image 7X8A1477. Photograph copyright © Lochlainn Seabrook.

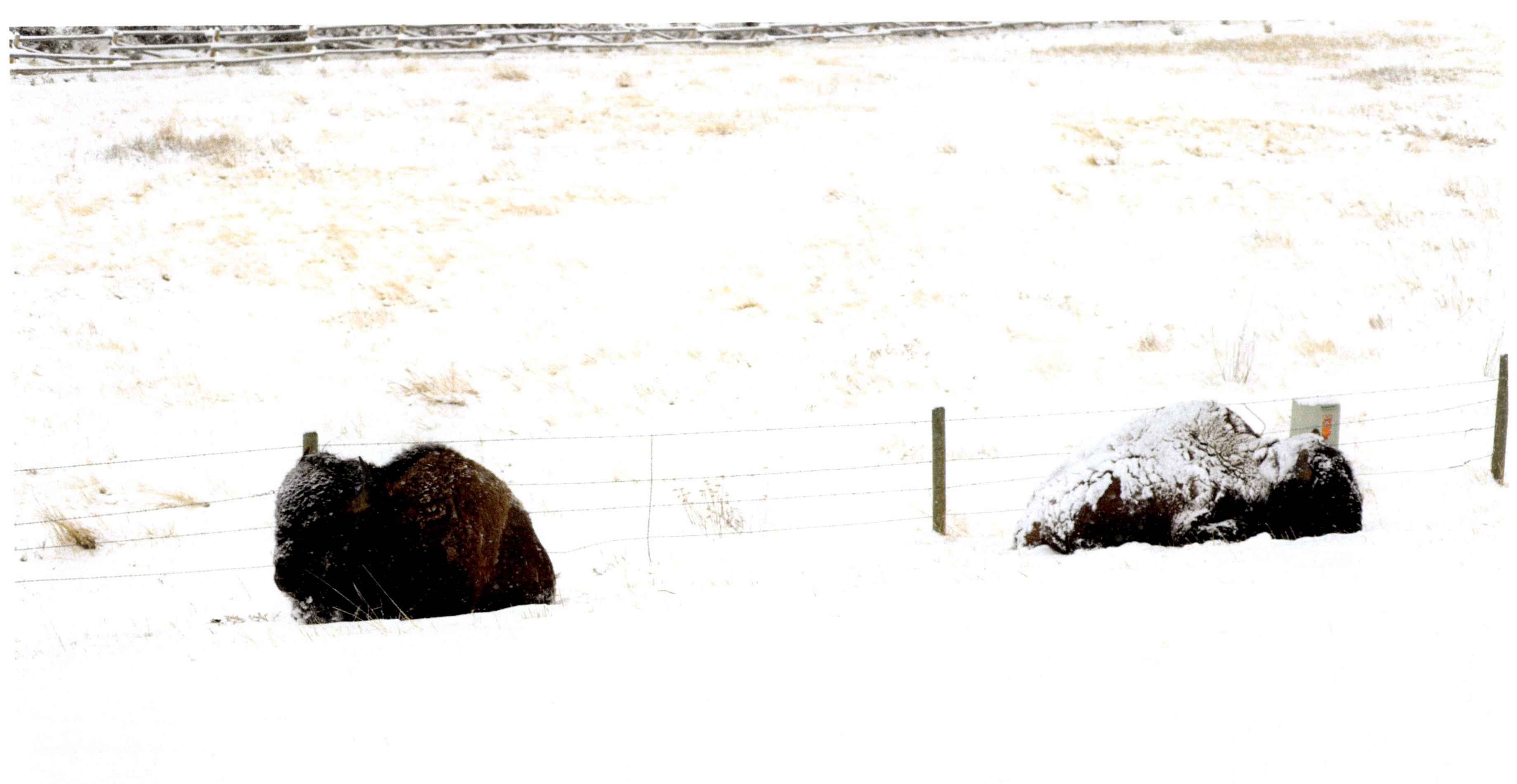

Above: Image 7X8A6010. Photograph copyright © Lochlainn Seabrook.

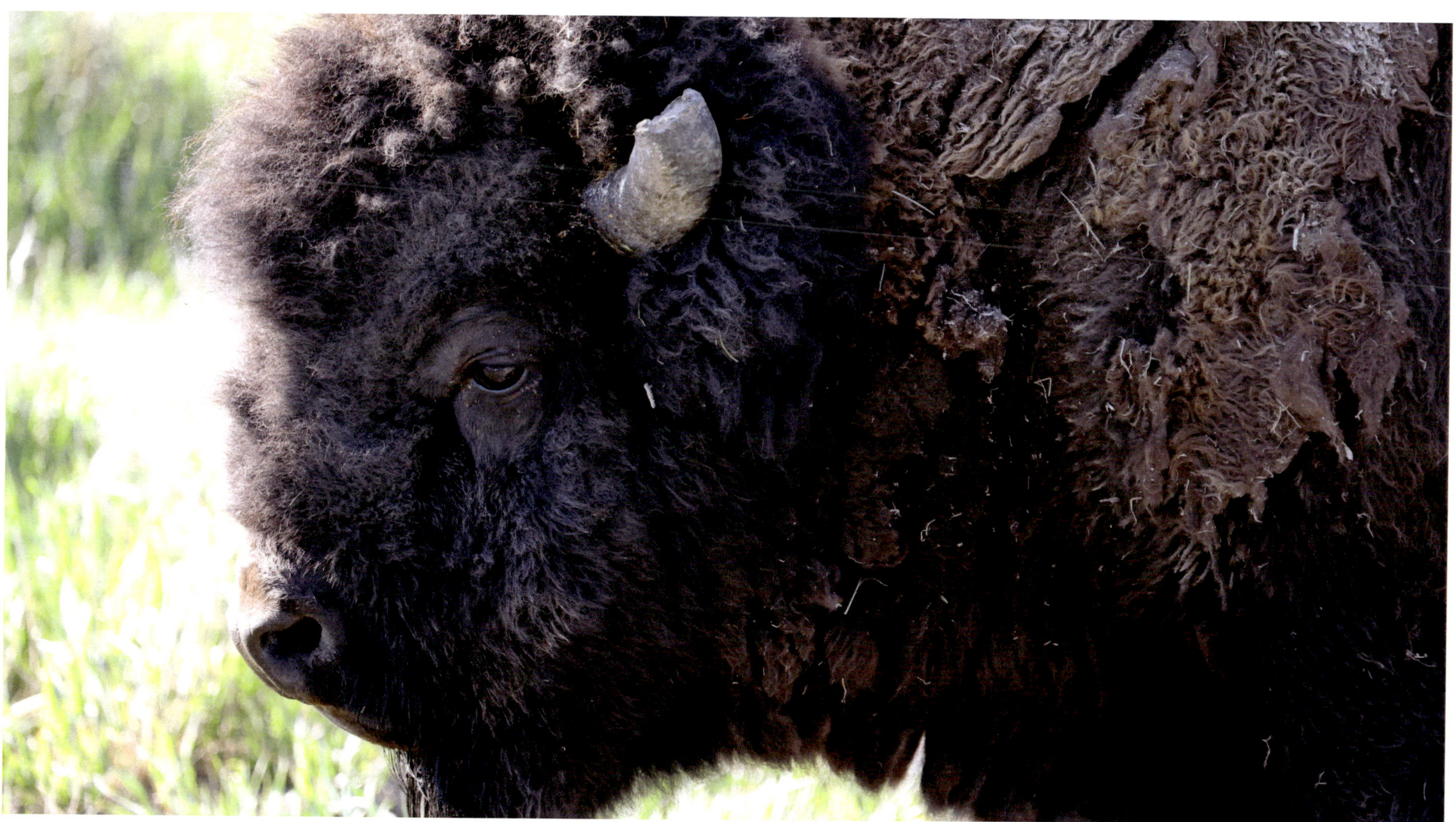

Above: Image 7X8A0771. Photograph copyright © Lochlainn Seabrook.

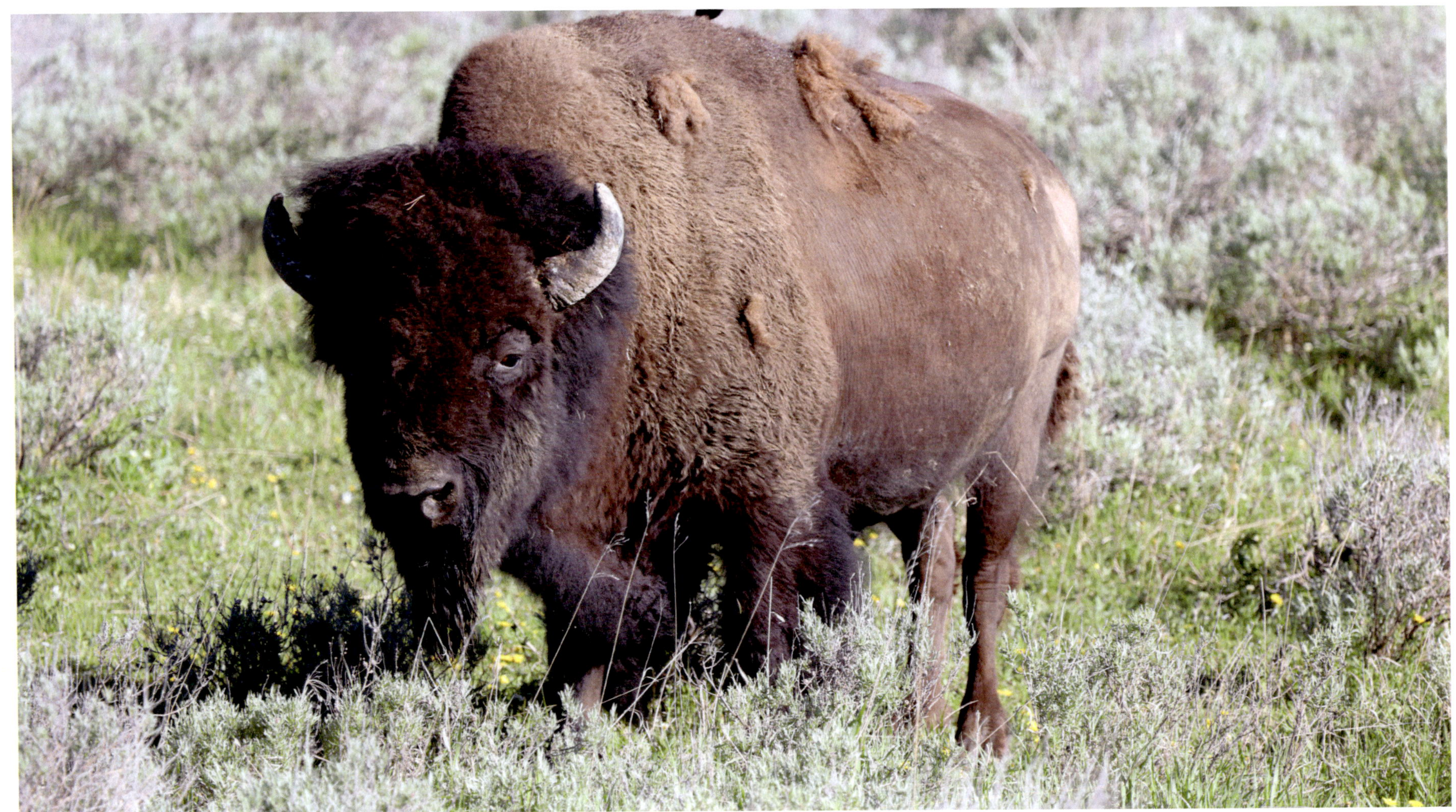

Above: Image 7X8A0724. Photograph copyright © Lochlainn Seabrook.

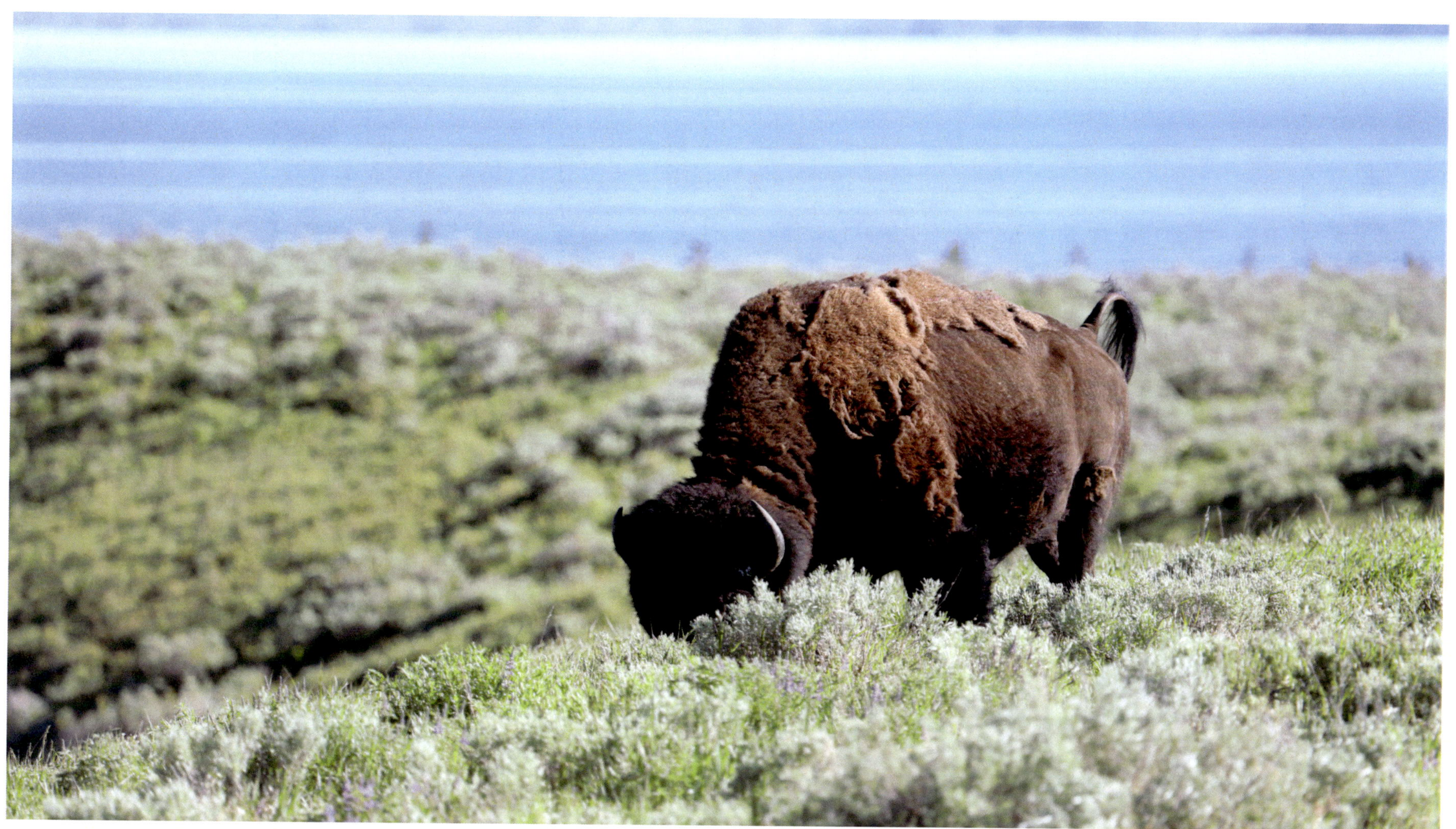

Above: Image 7X8A0763. Photograph copyright © Lochlainn Seabrook.

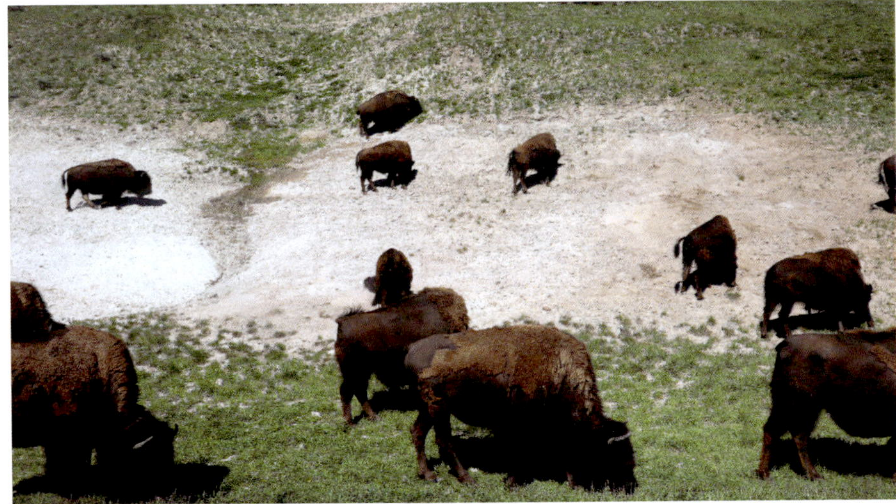

Right: Image IMG_6738. Photograph copyright © Lochlainn Seabrook.

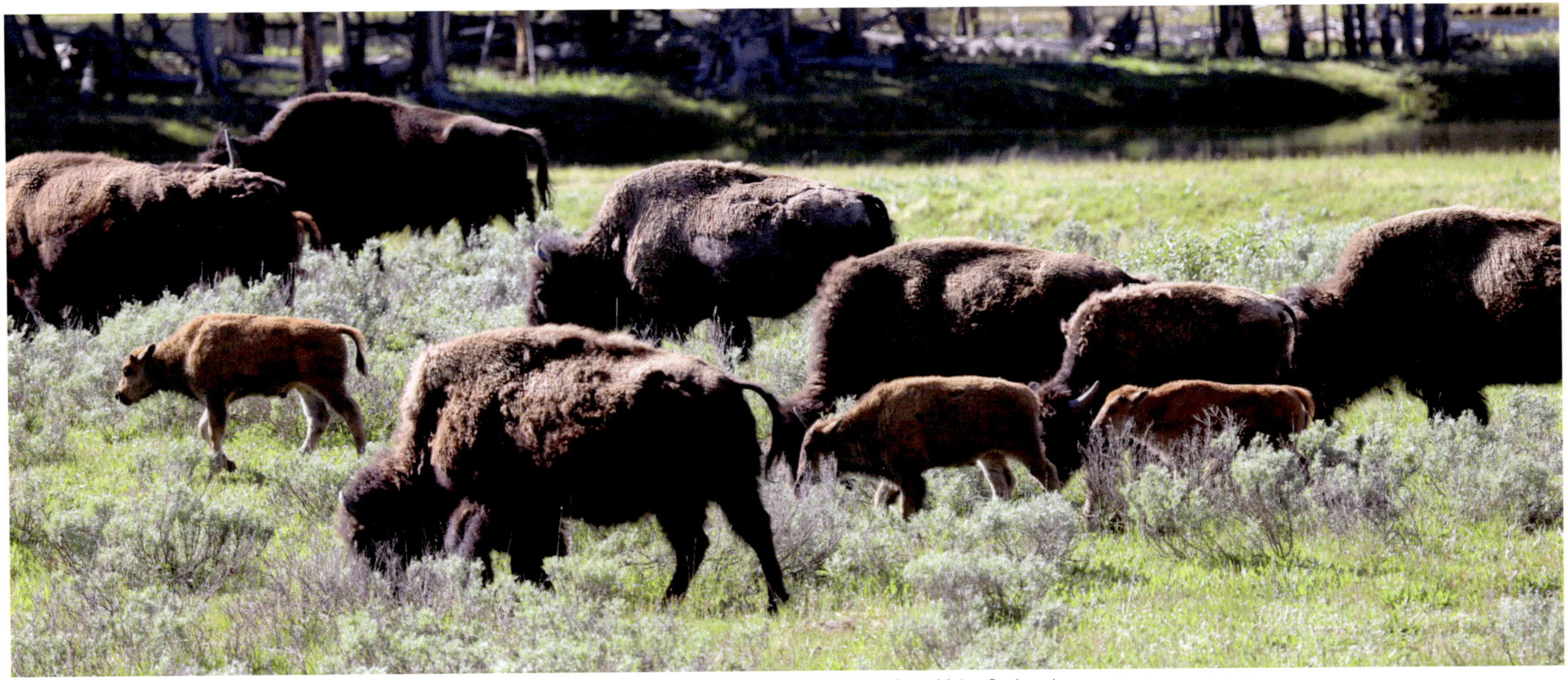

Above: Image 7X8A0857. Photograph copyright © Lochlainn Seabrook.

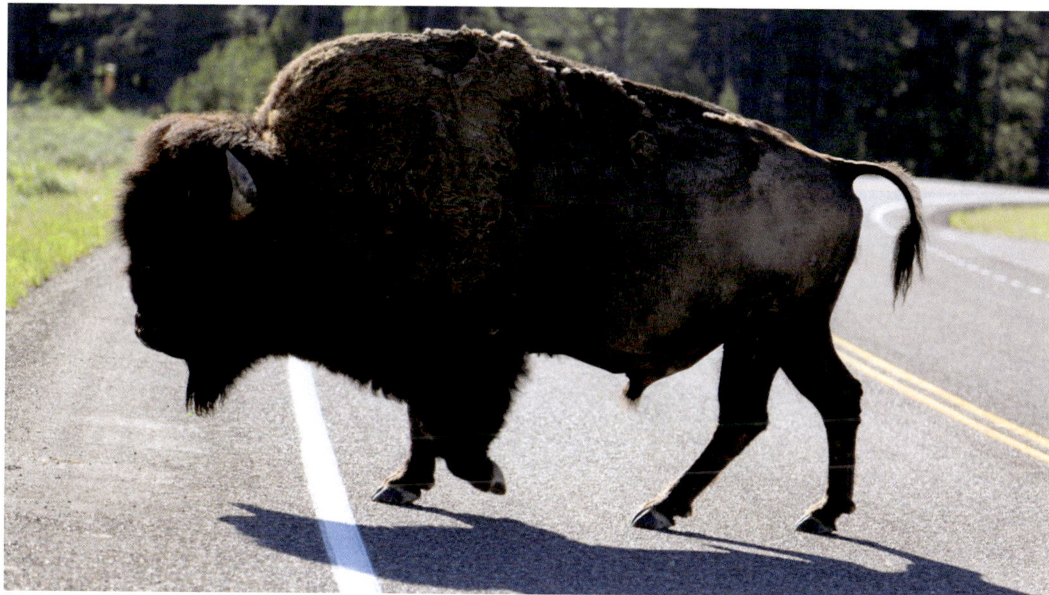

Above: Image 7X8A0741. Photograph copyright © Lochlainn Seabrook.

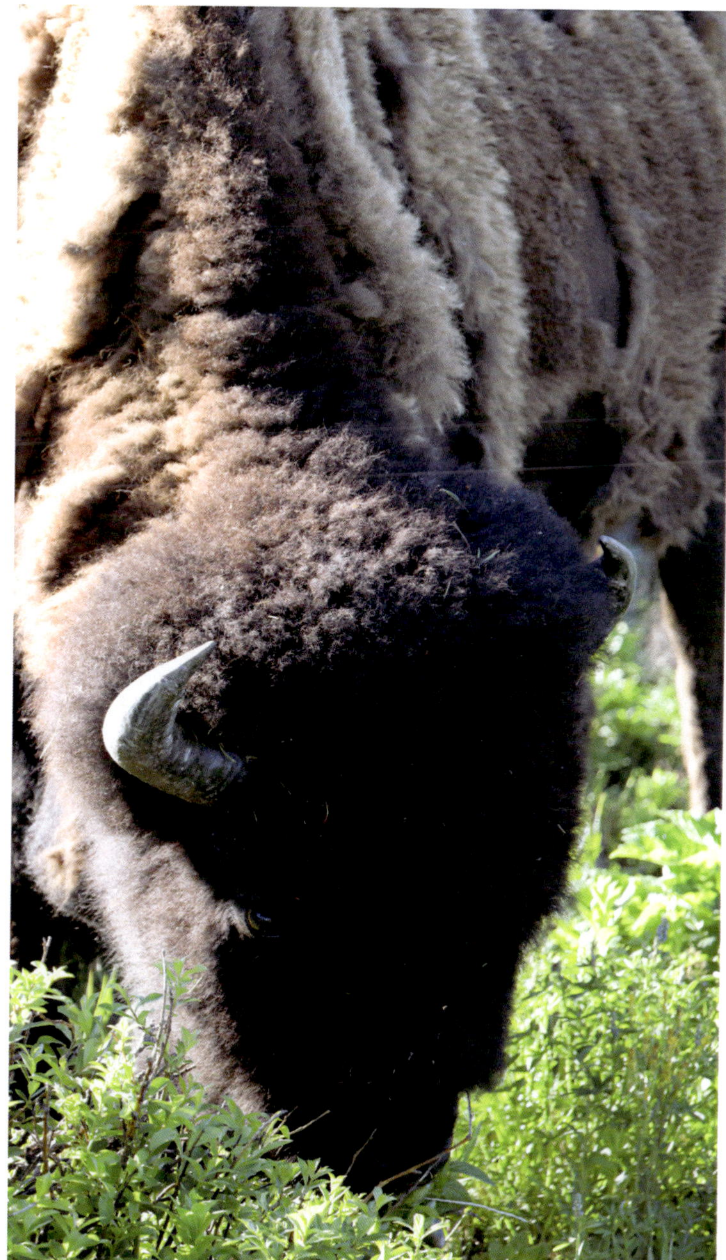

Above: Image 7X8A0702. Photograph copyright © Lochlainn Seabrook.

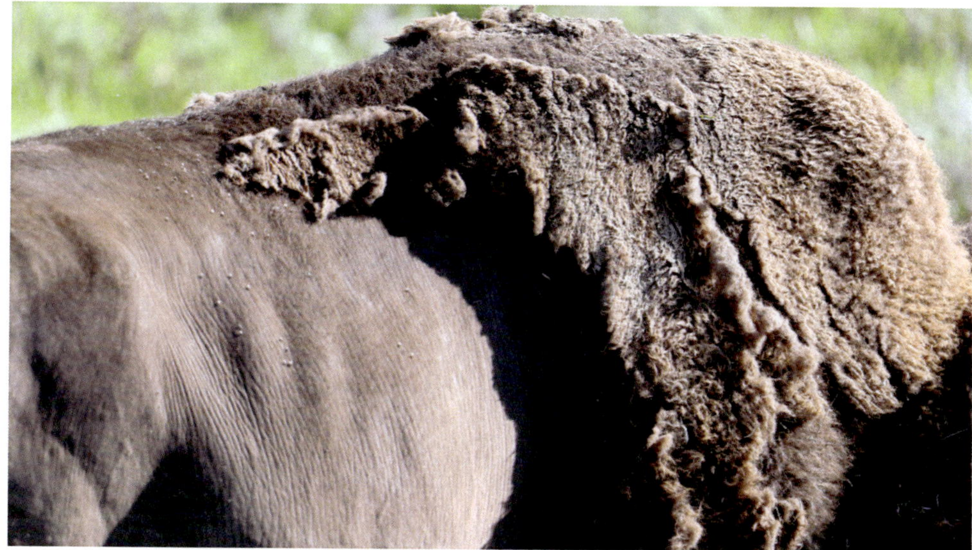

Above: Image 7X8A0777. Photograph copyright © Lochlainn Seabrook.

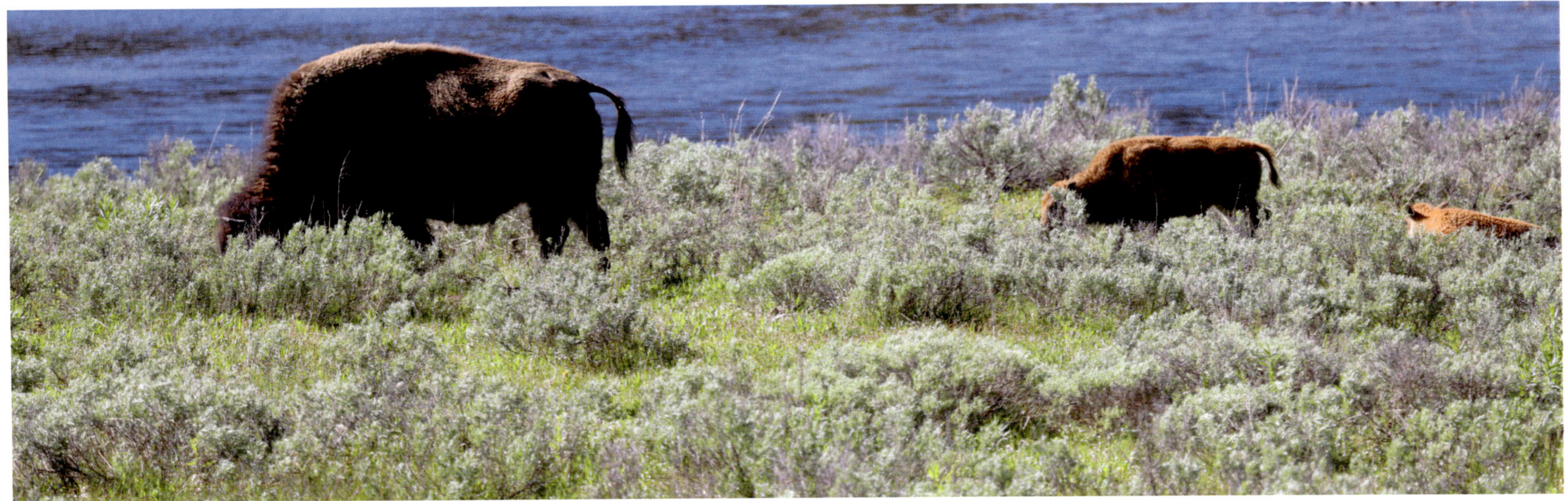

Above: Image 7X8A0842. Photograph copyright © Lochlainn Seabrook.

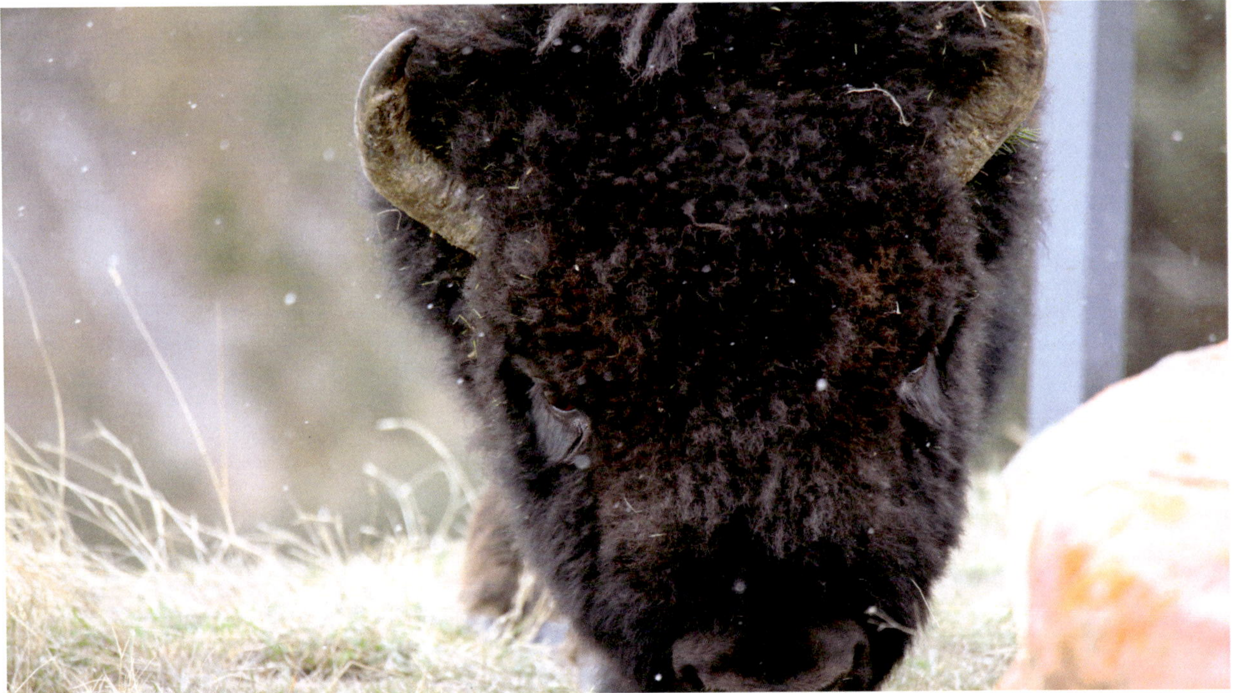

Left: Image 7X8A6603. Photograph copyright © Lochlainn Seabrook.

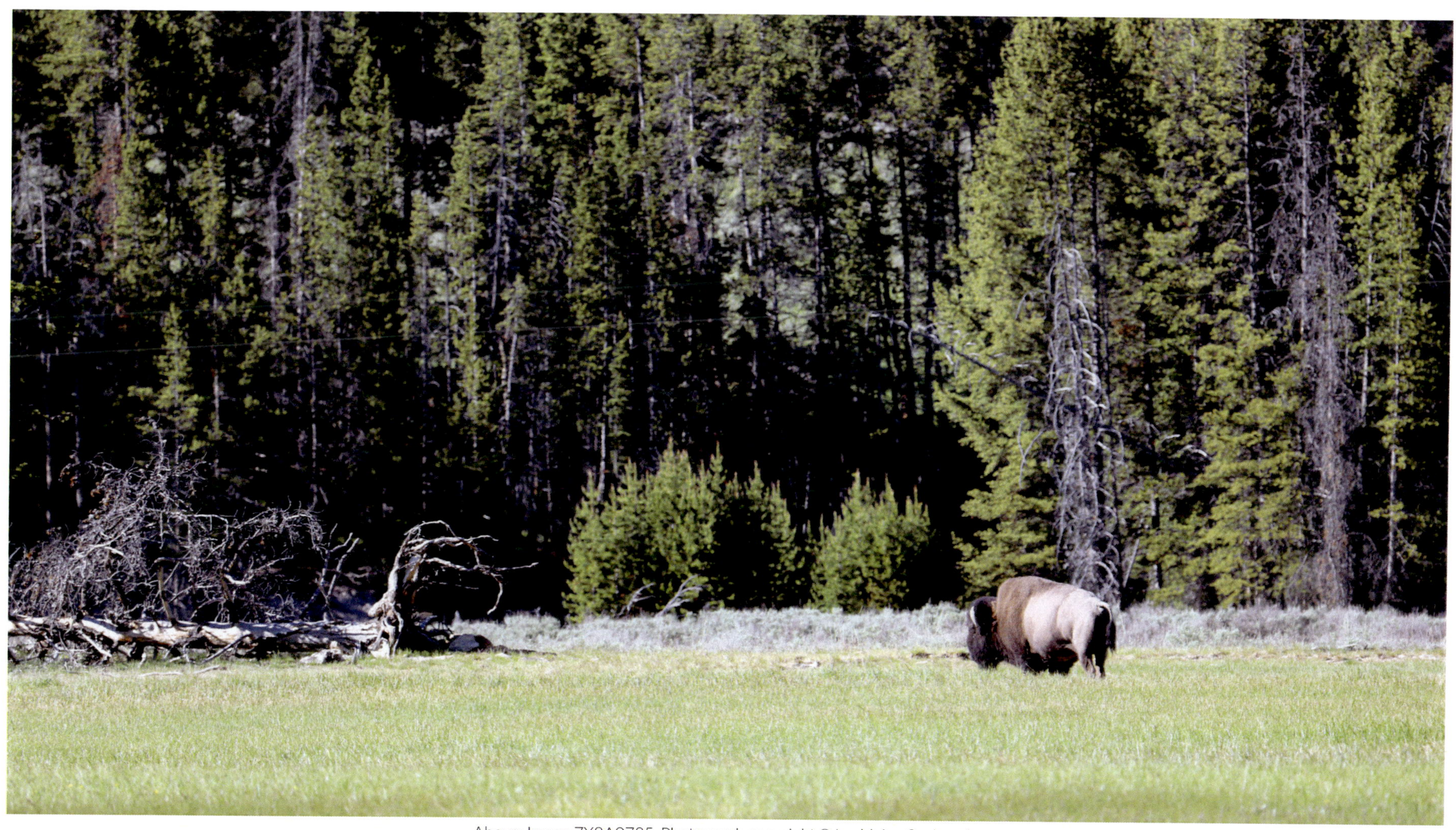

Above: Image 7X8A0785. Photograph copyright © Lochlainn Seabrook.

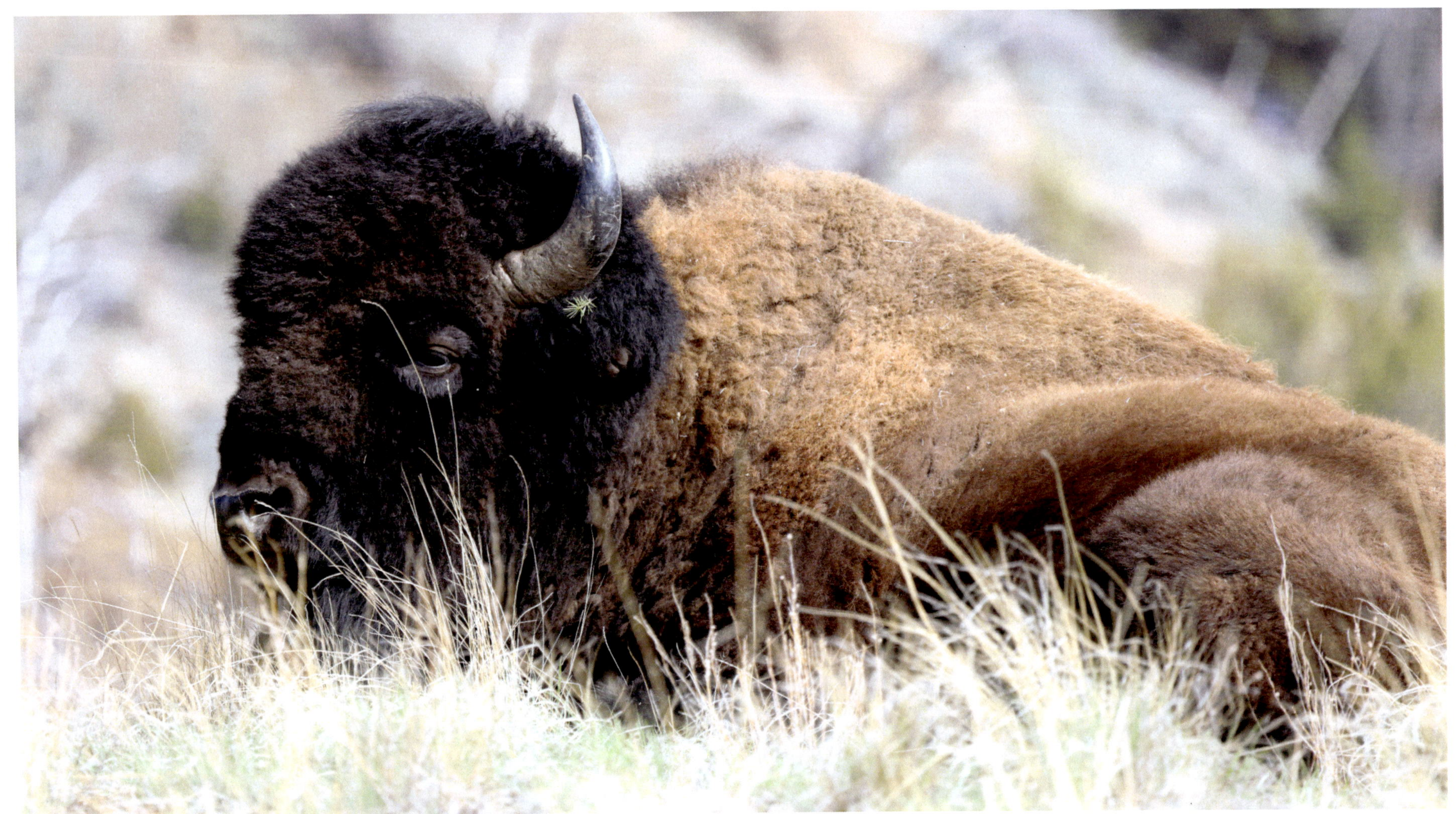

Above: Image 7X8A7149. Photograph copyright © Lochlainn Seabrook.

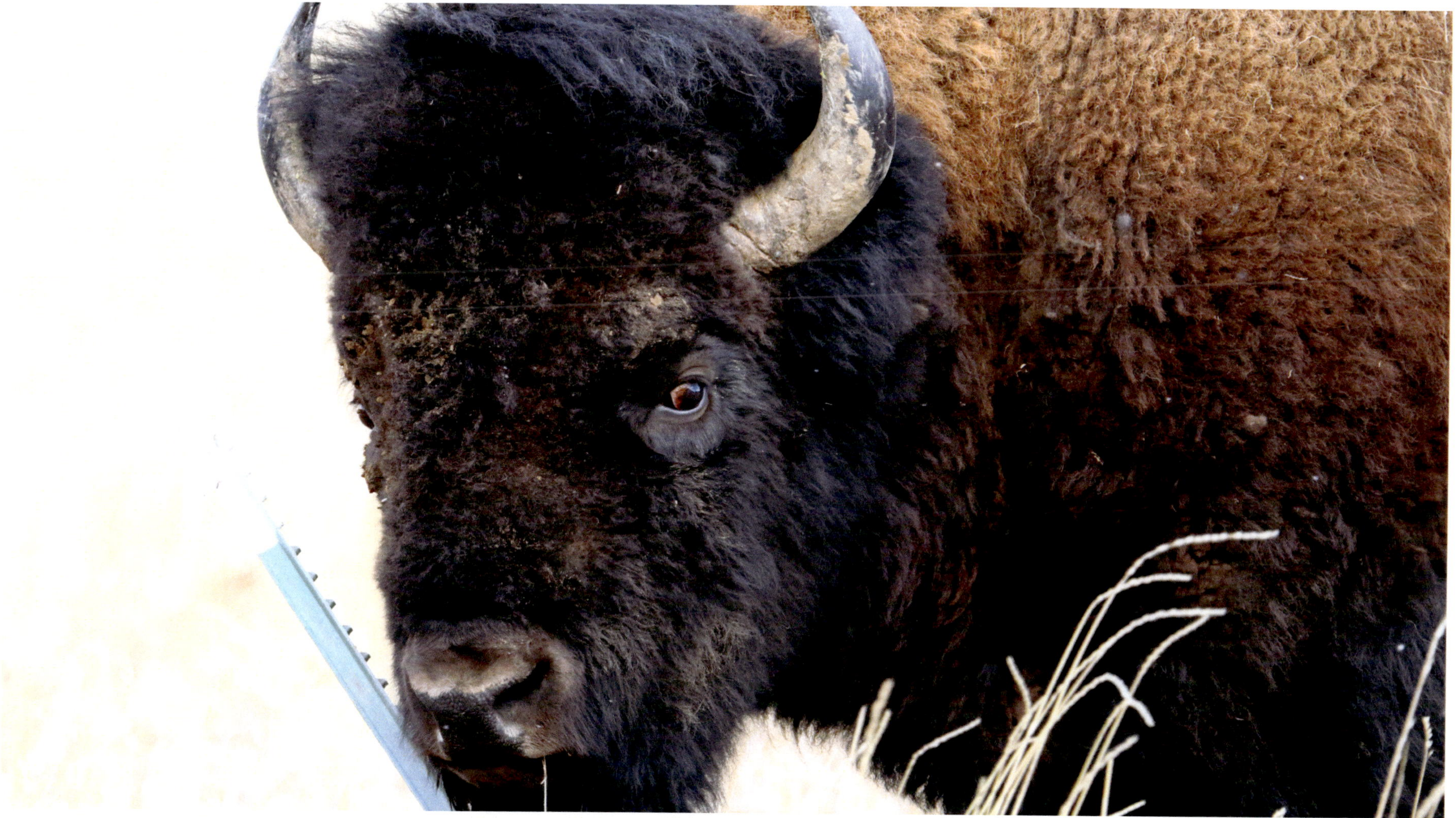

Above: Image IMG_5001. Photograph copyright © Lochlainn Seabrook.

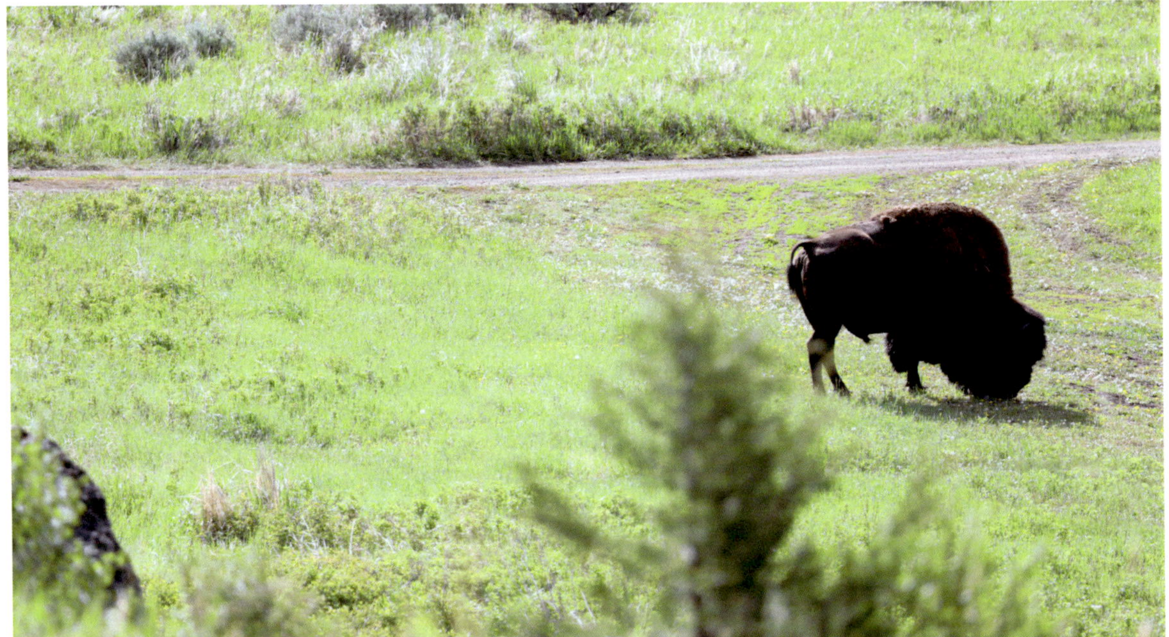

Left: Image 7X8A0491. Photograph copyright © Lochlainn Seabrook.

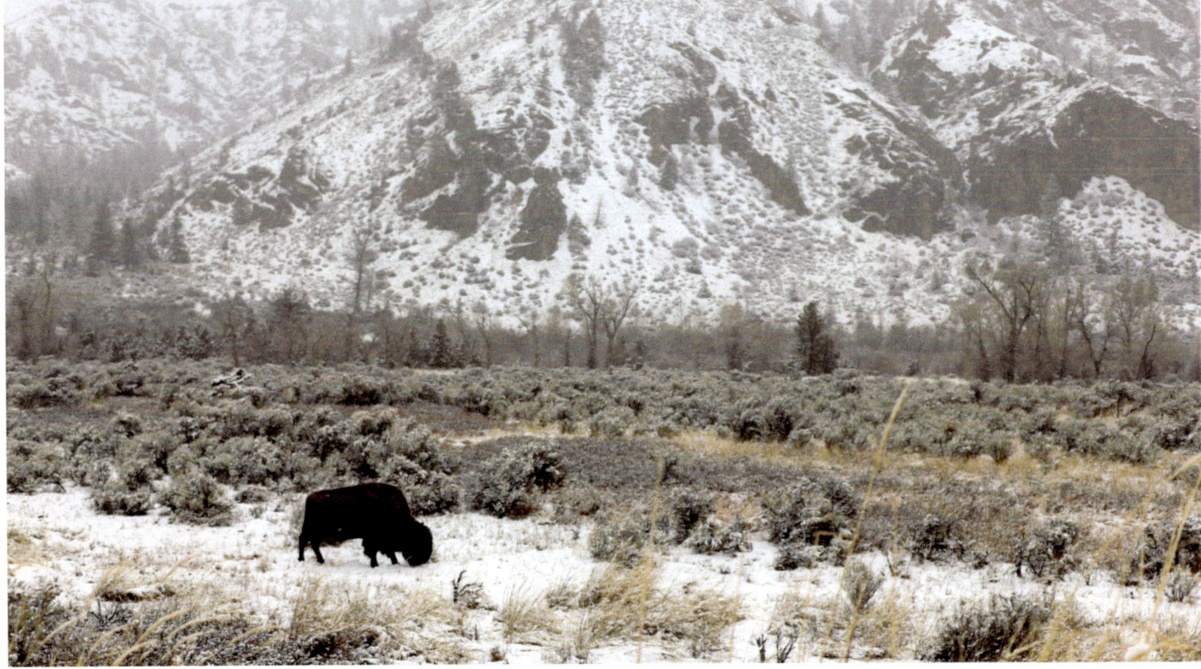

Right: Image 7X8A4607. Photograph copyright © Lochlainn Seabrook.

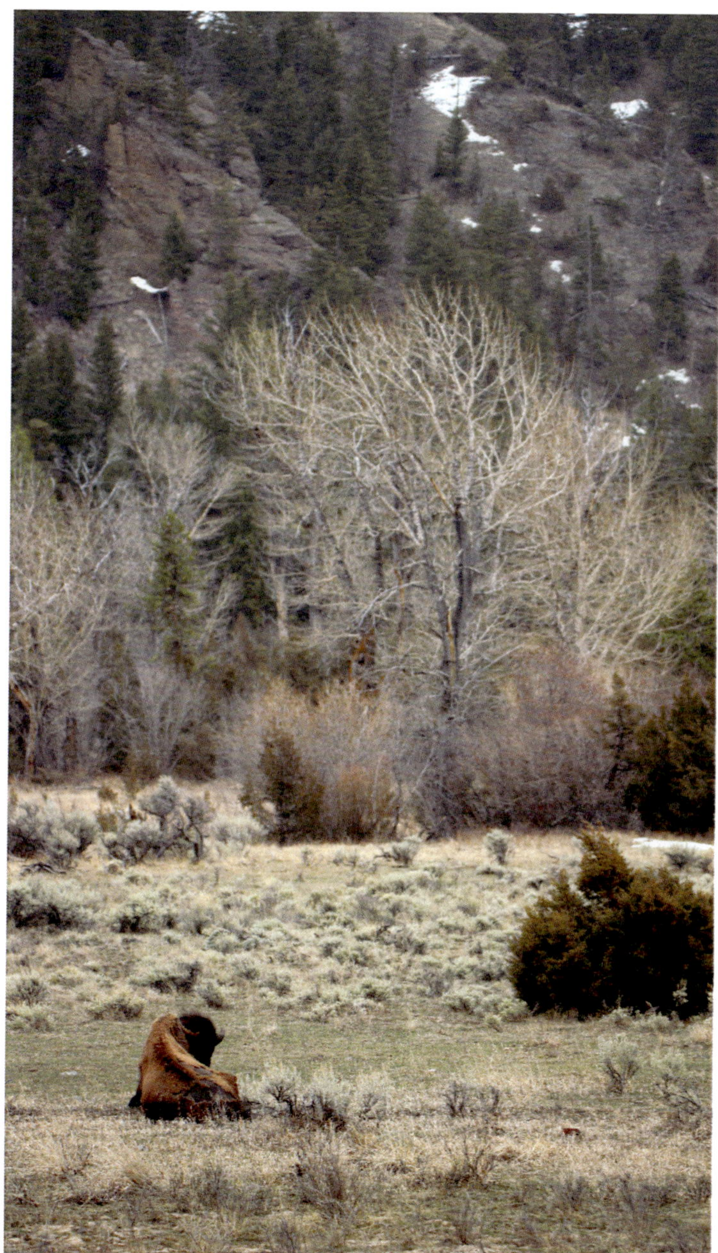

Above: Image 7X8A6492. Photograph copyright © Lochlainn Seabrook.

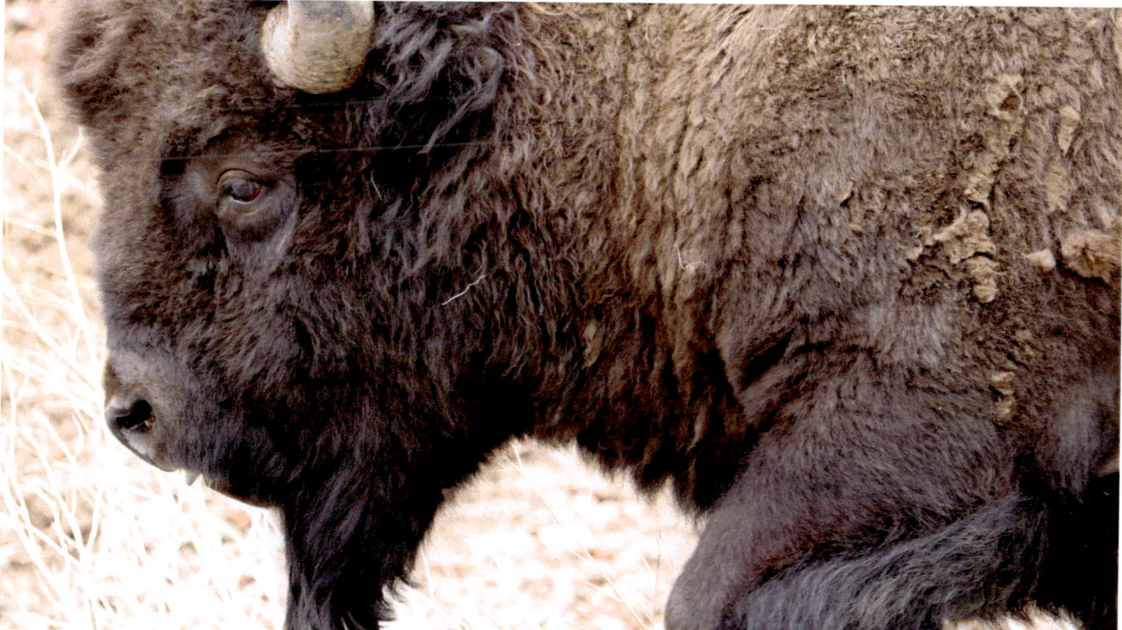

Above: Image 7X8A7919. Photograph copyright © Lochlainn Seabrook.

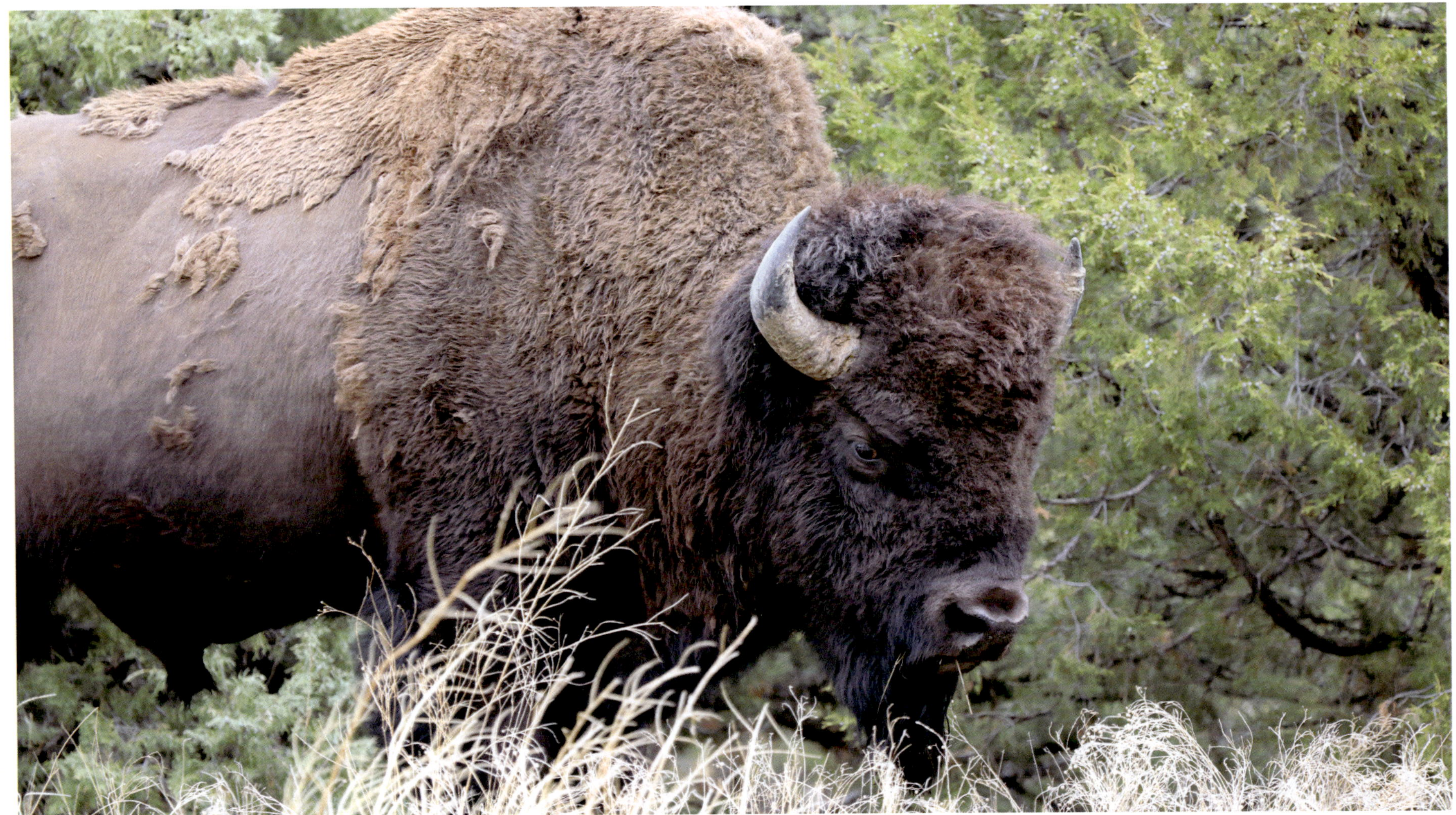

Above: Image 7X8A7863. Photograph copyright © Lochlainn Seabrook.

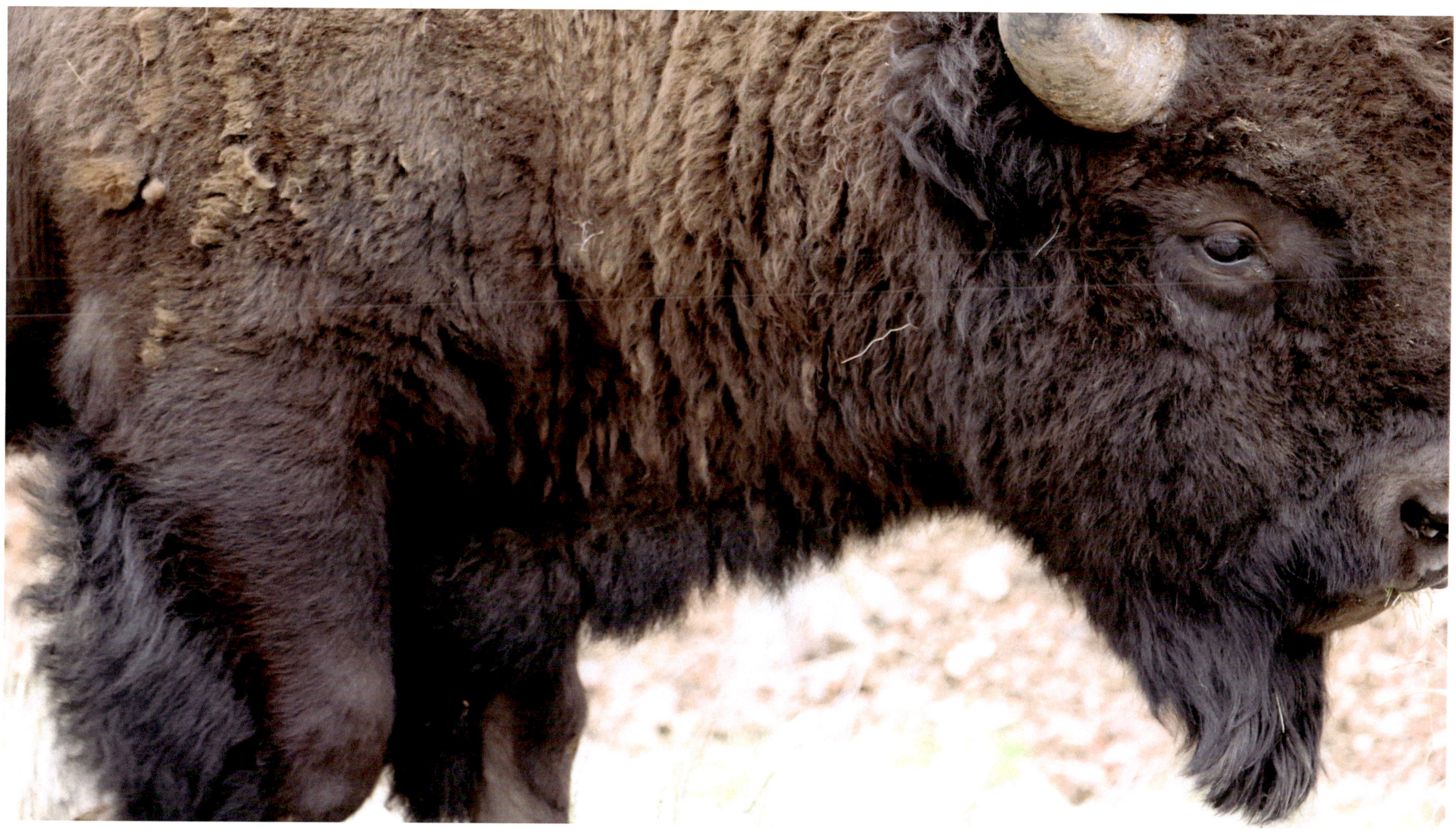

Above: Image 7X8A7917. Photograph copyright © Lochlainn Seabrook.

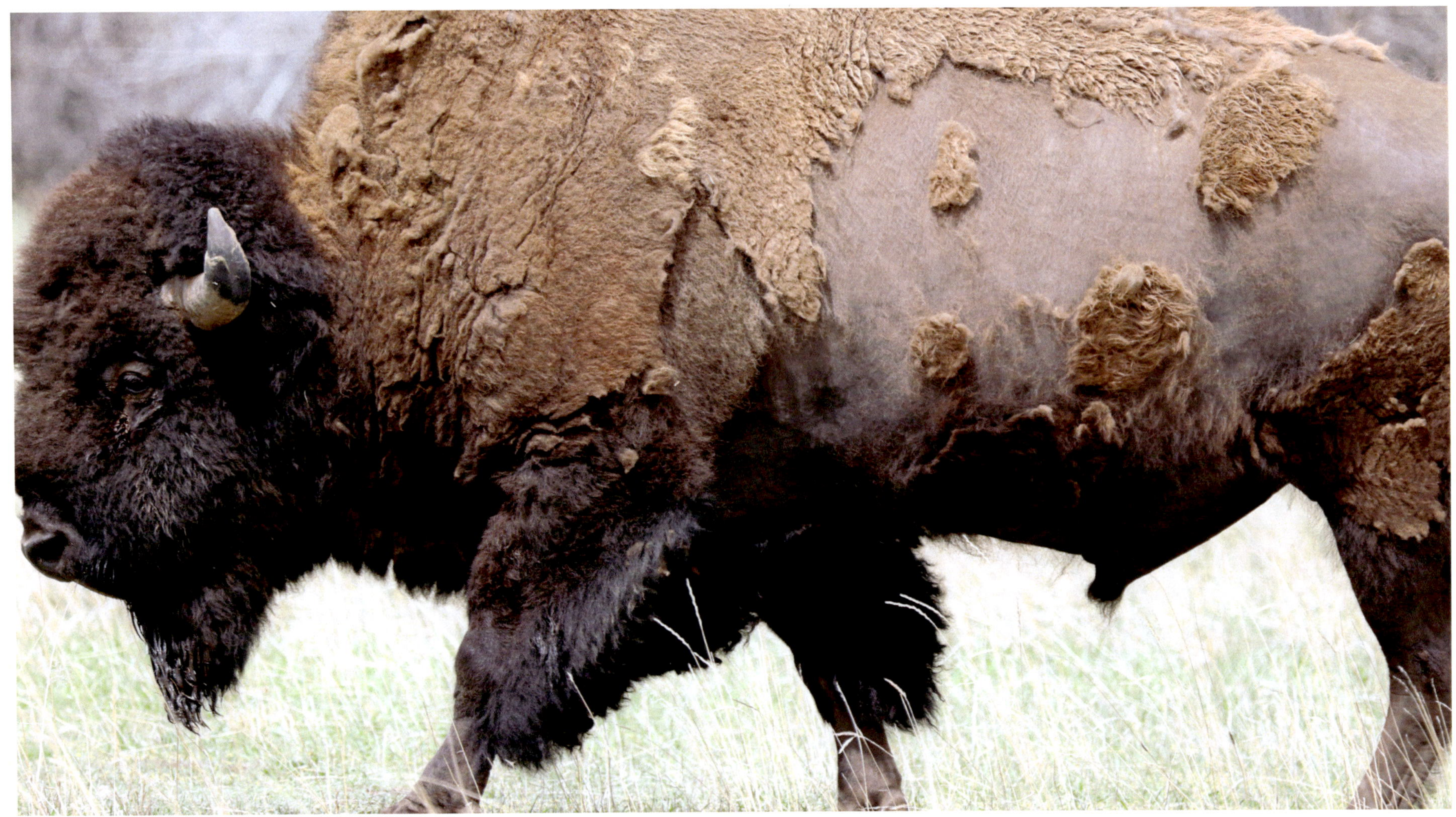

Above: Image 7X8A8210. Photograph copyright © Lochlainn Seabrook.

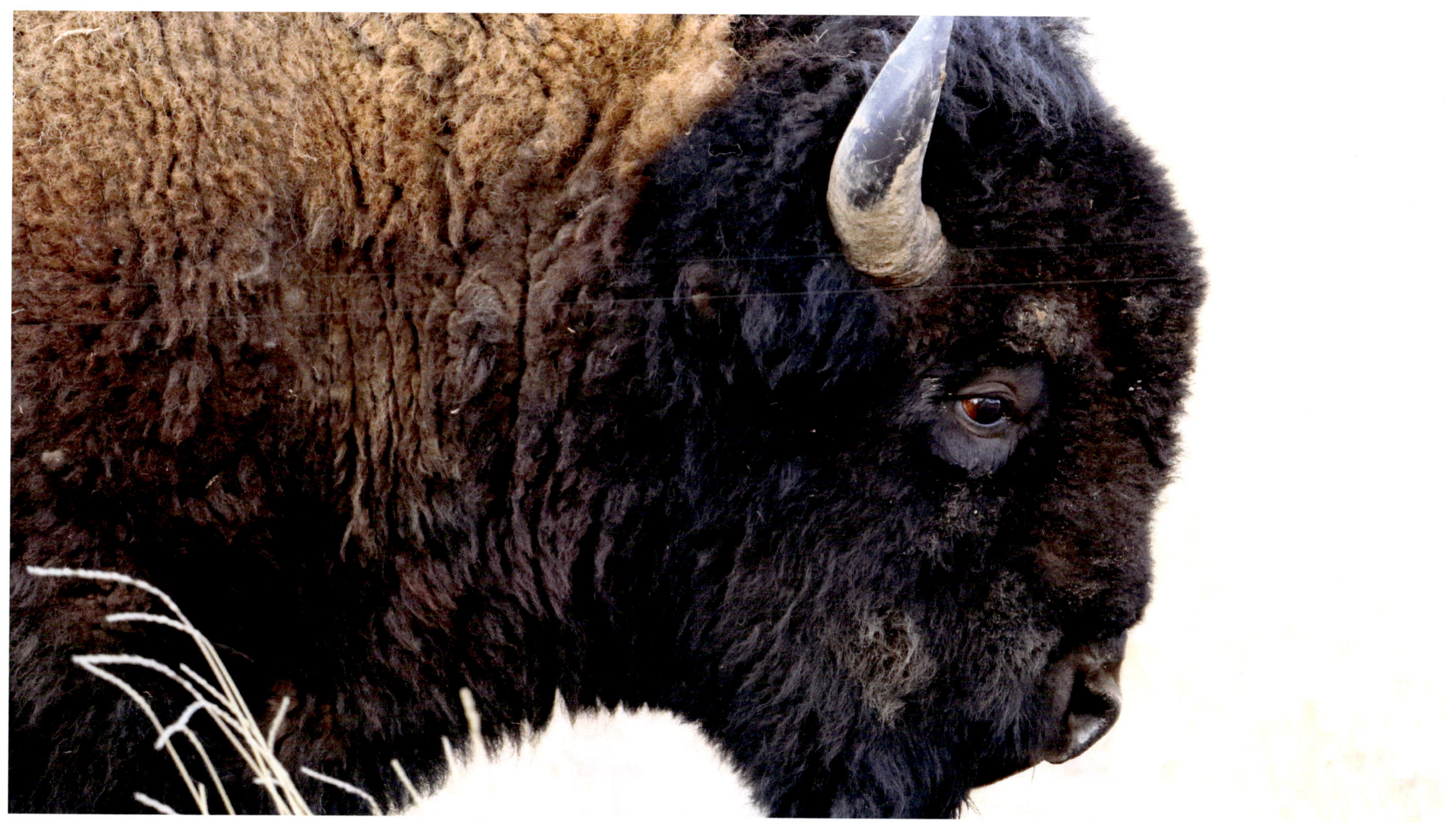

Above: Image IMG_5003. Photograph copyright © Lochlainn Seabrook.

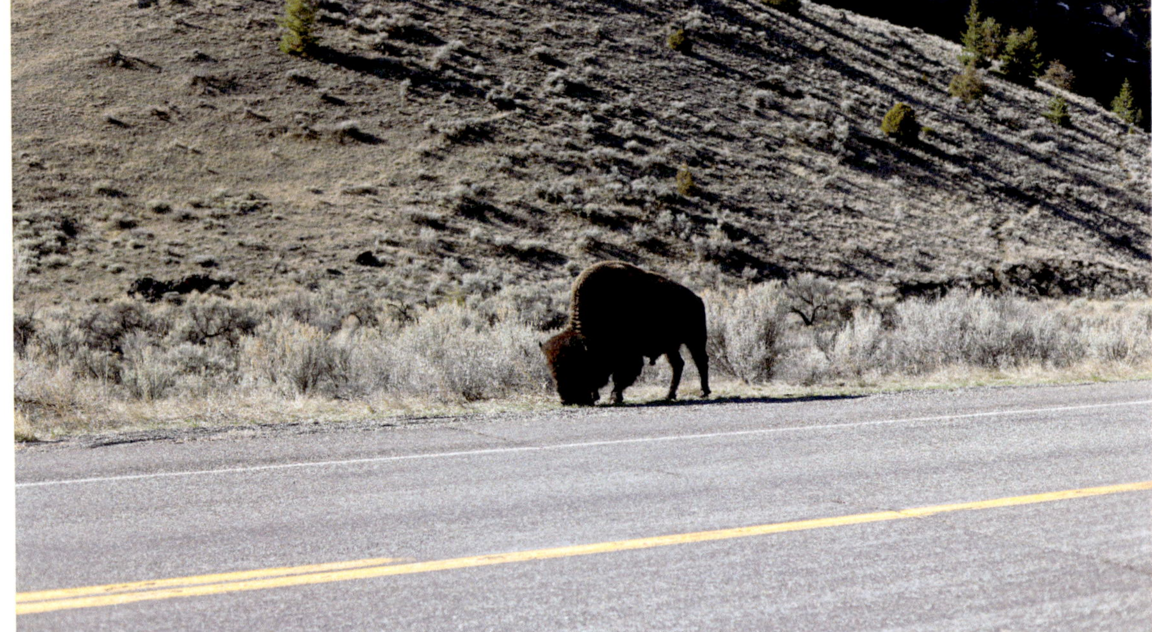

Right: Image 7X8A06939. Photograph copyright © Lochlainn Seabrook.

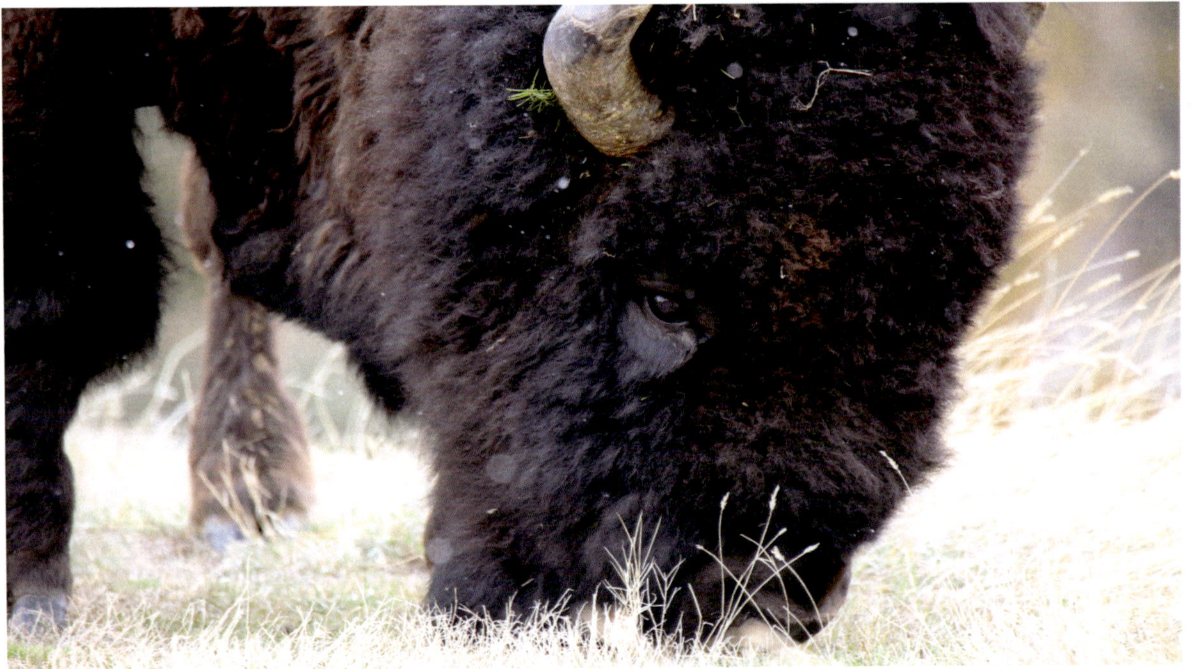

Left: Image 7X8A6605. Photograph copyright © Lochlainn Seabrook.

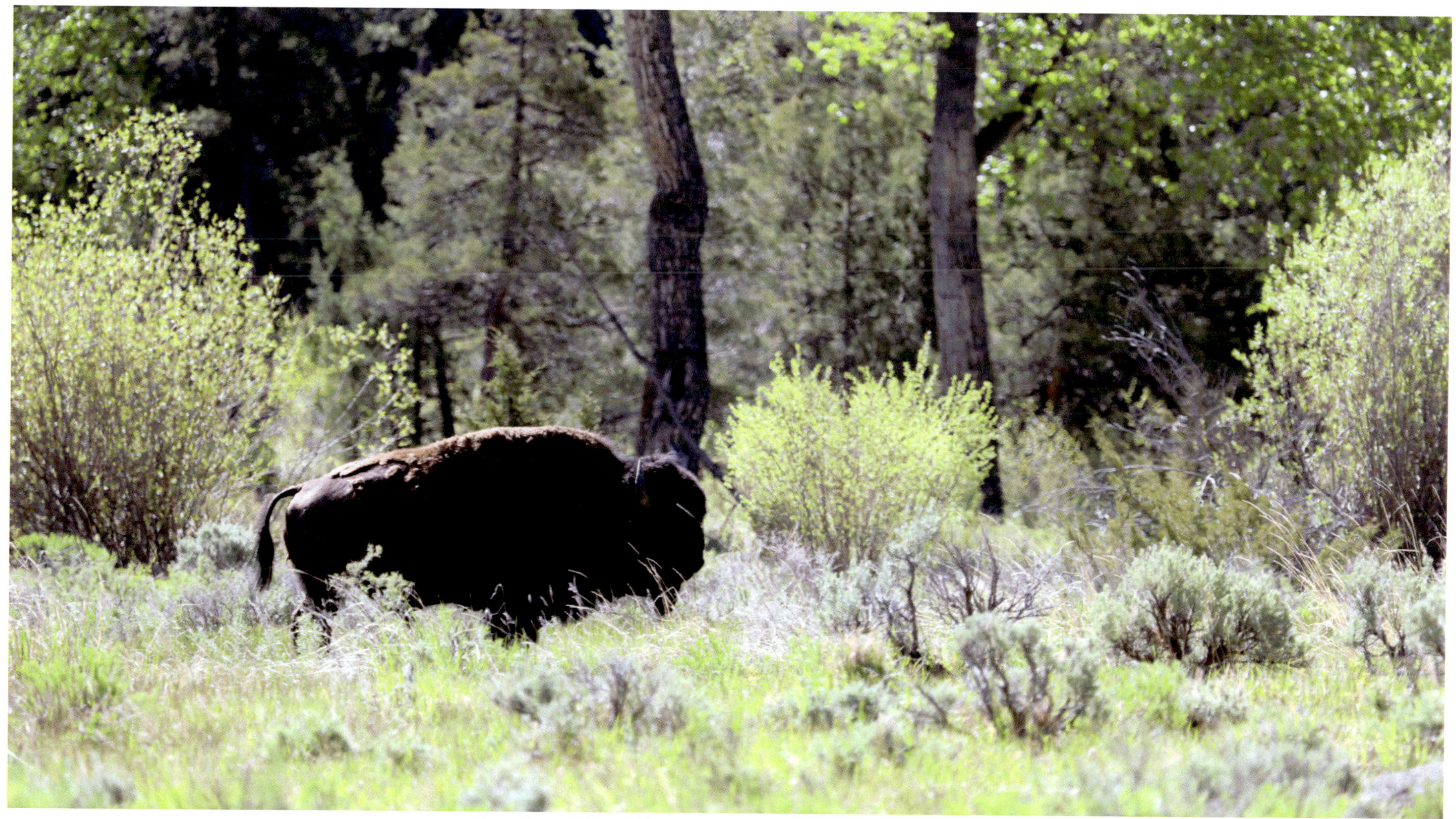

Above: Image 7X8A0729. Photograph copyright © Lochlainn Seabrook.

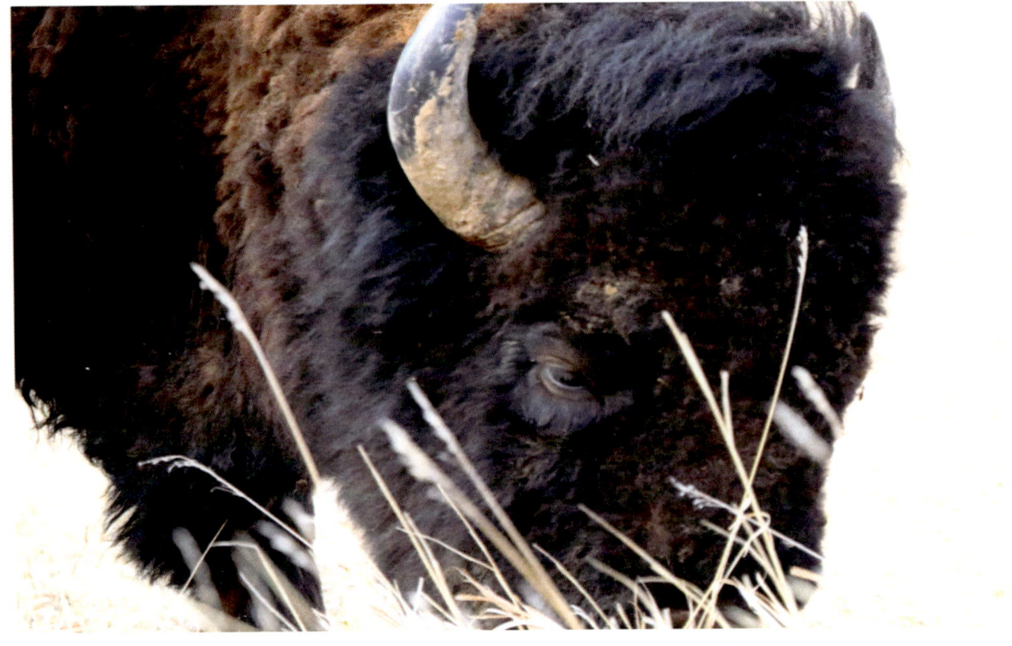

Left: Image IMG_5018. Photograph copyright © Lochlainn Seabrook.

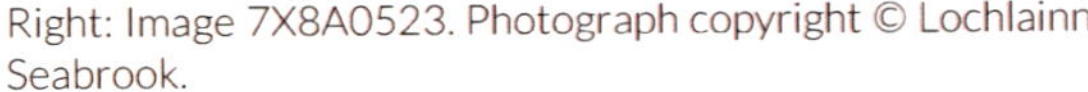

Right: Image 7X8A0523. Photograph copyright © Lochlainn Seabrook.

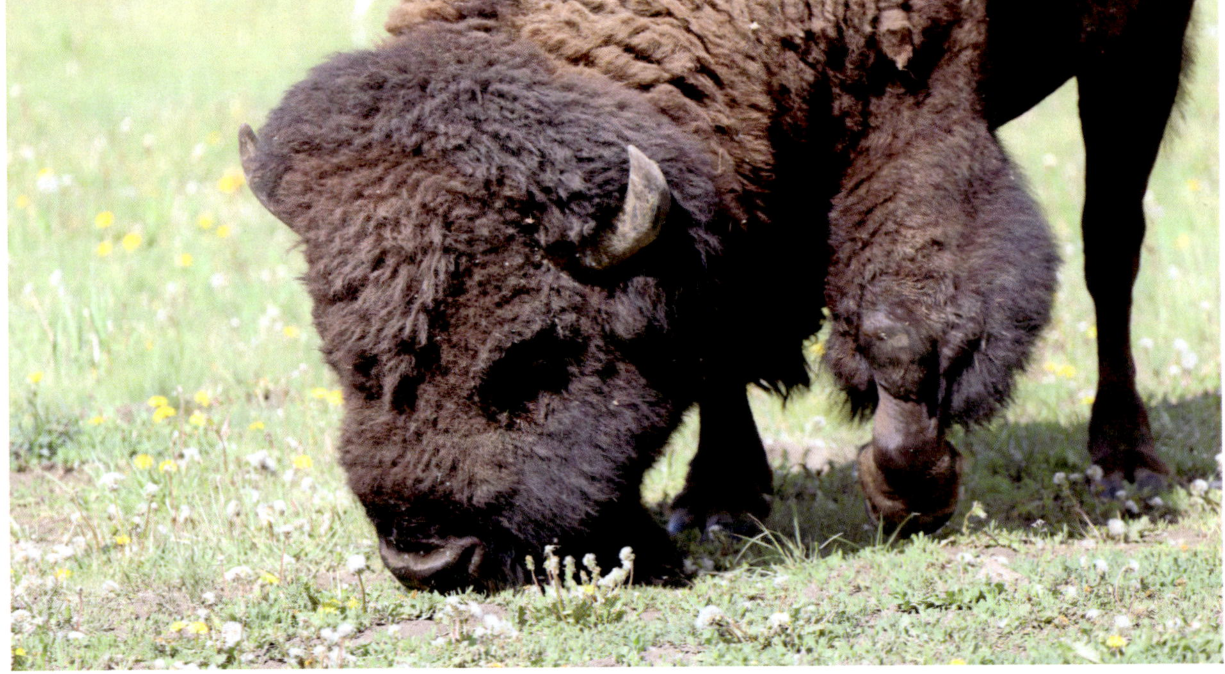

Right: Image IMG_5022. Photograph copyright © Lochlainn Seabrook.

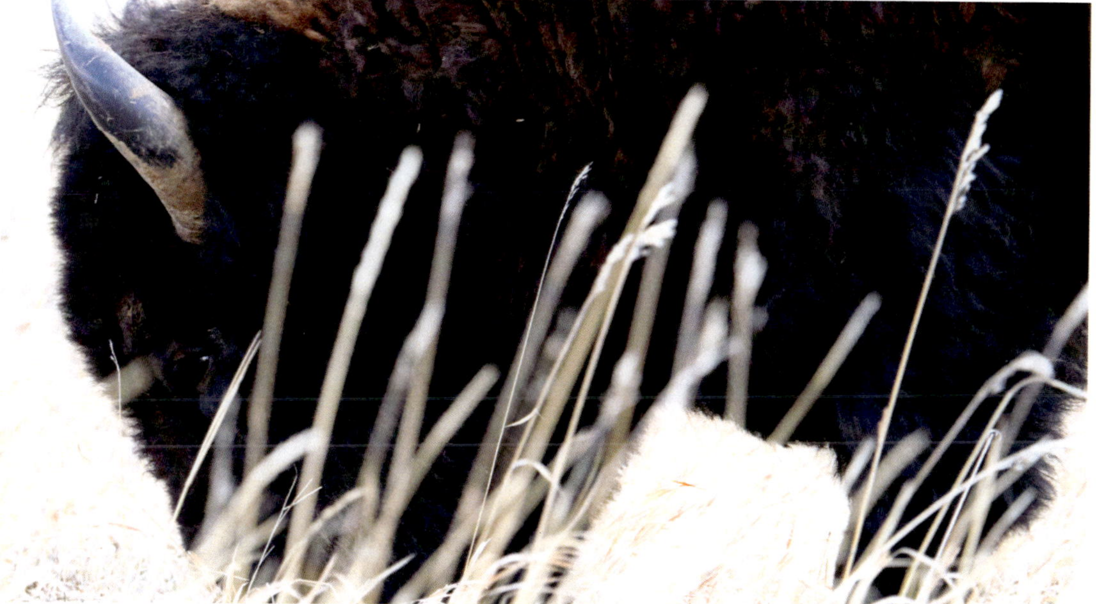

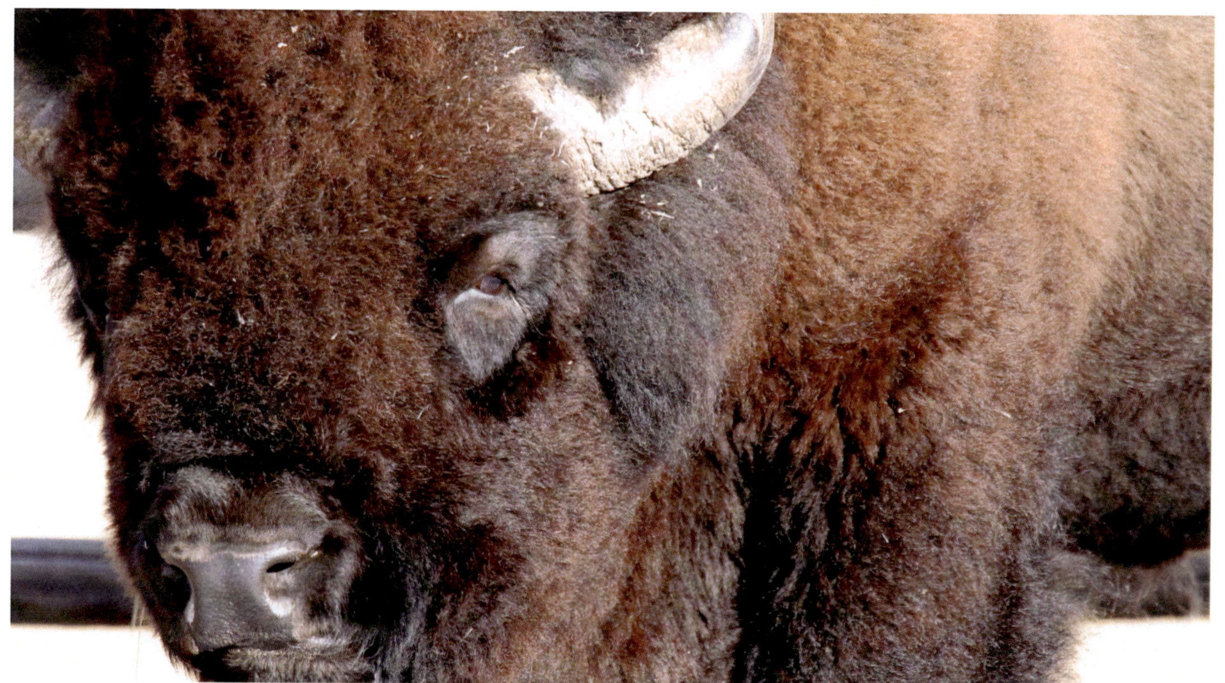

Left: Image 7X8A3388. Photograph copyright © Lochlainn Seabrook.

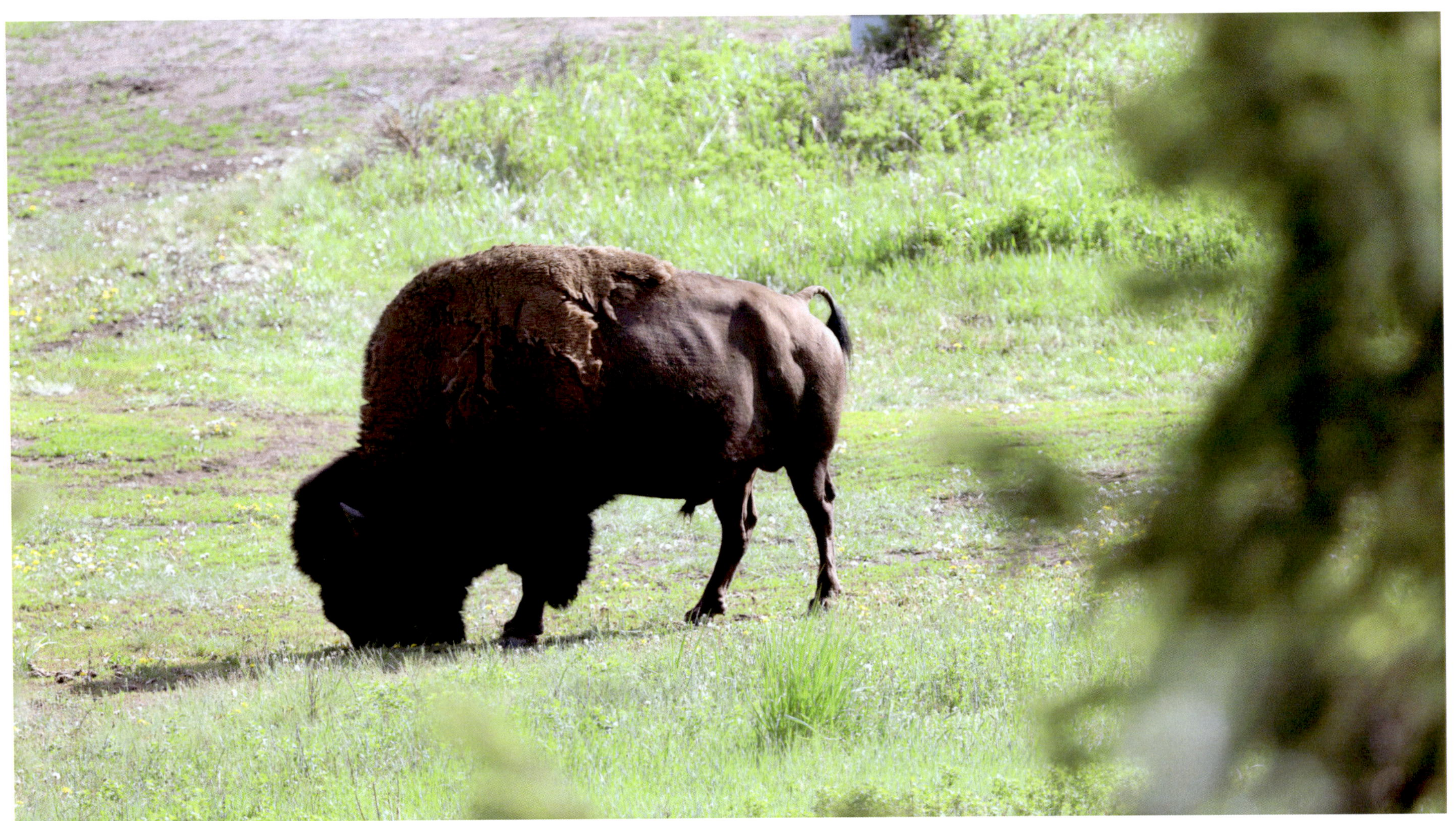

Above: Image 7X8A0494. Photograph copyright © Lochlainn Seabrook.

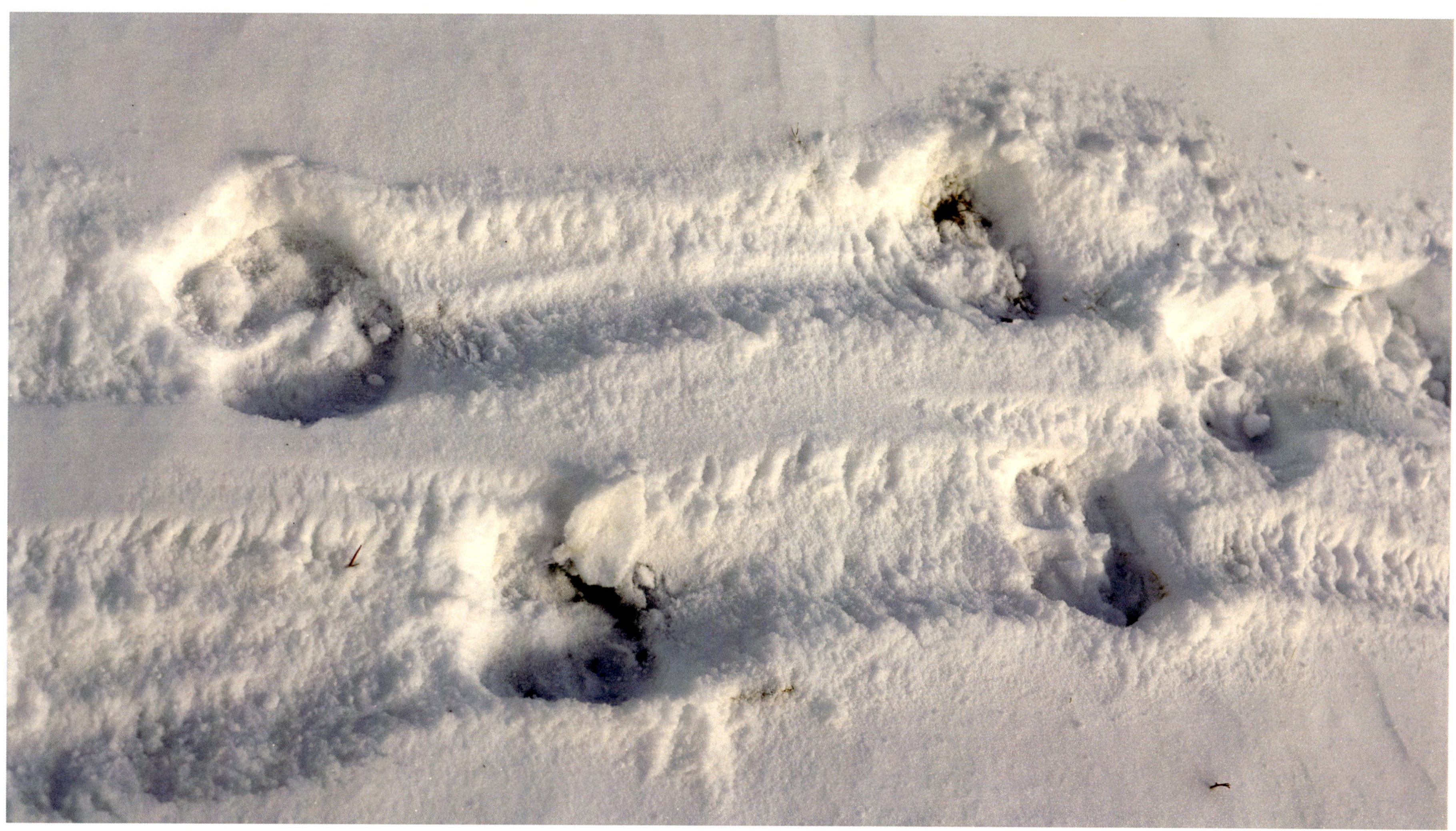

Above: Image 7X8A5296. Photograph copyright © Lochlainn Seabrook.

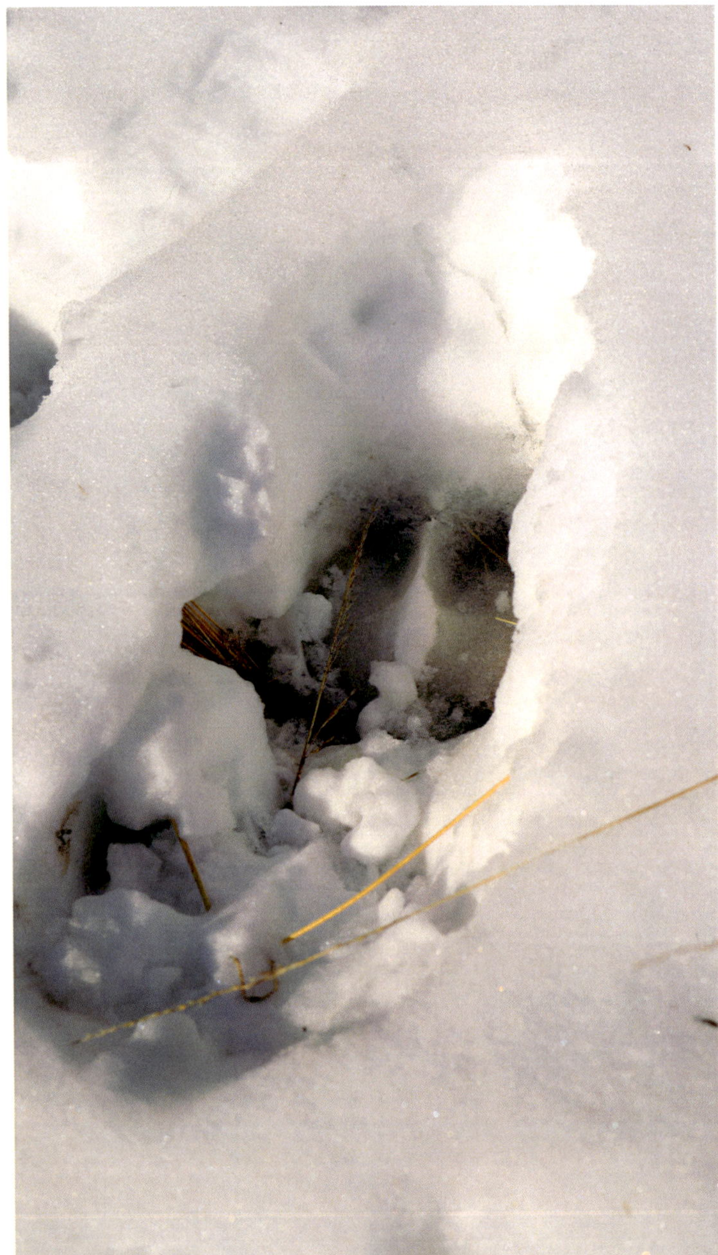

Above: Image 7X8A5604. Photograph copyright © Lochlainn Seabrook.

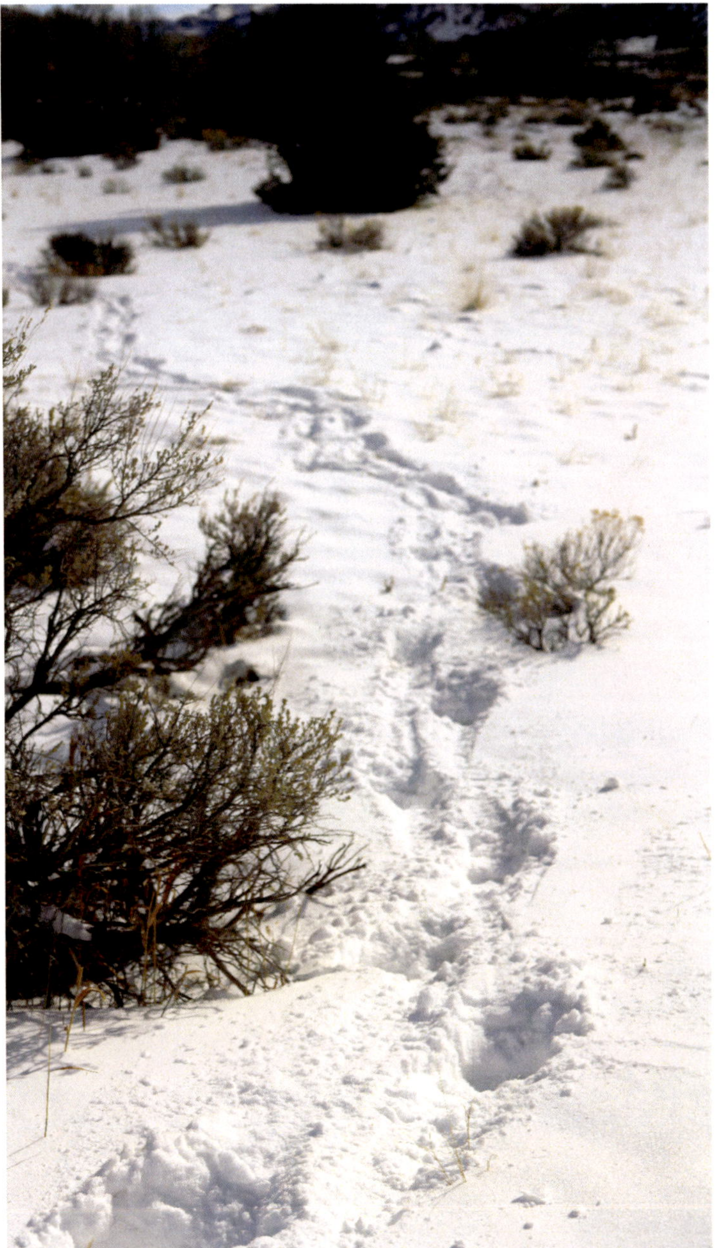

Above: Image 7X8A5297. Photograph copyright © Lochlainn Seabrook.

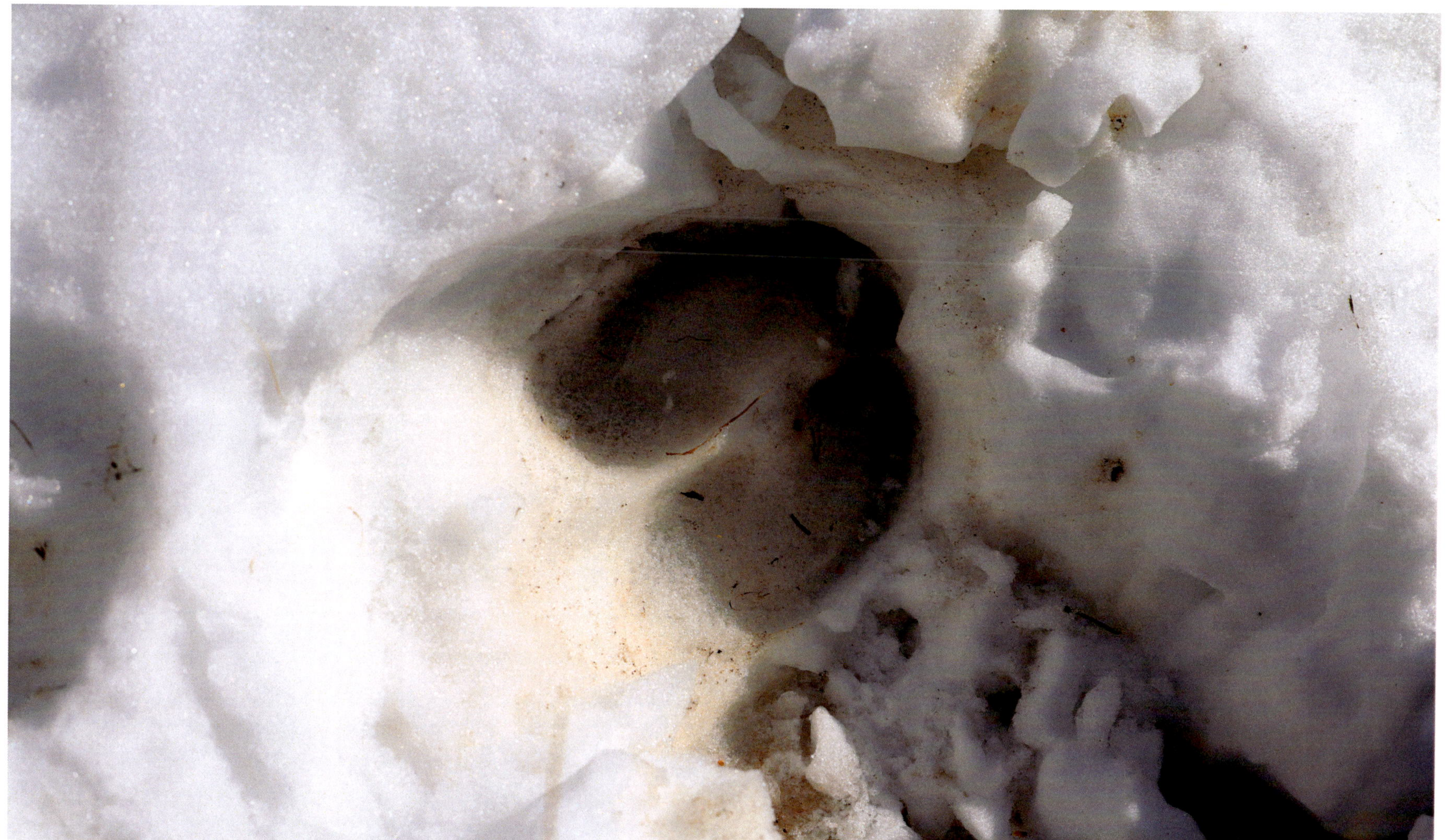

Above: Image 7X8A5605. Photograph copyright © Lochlainn Seabrook.

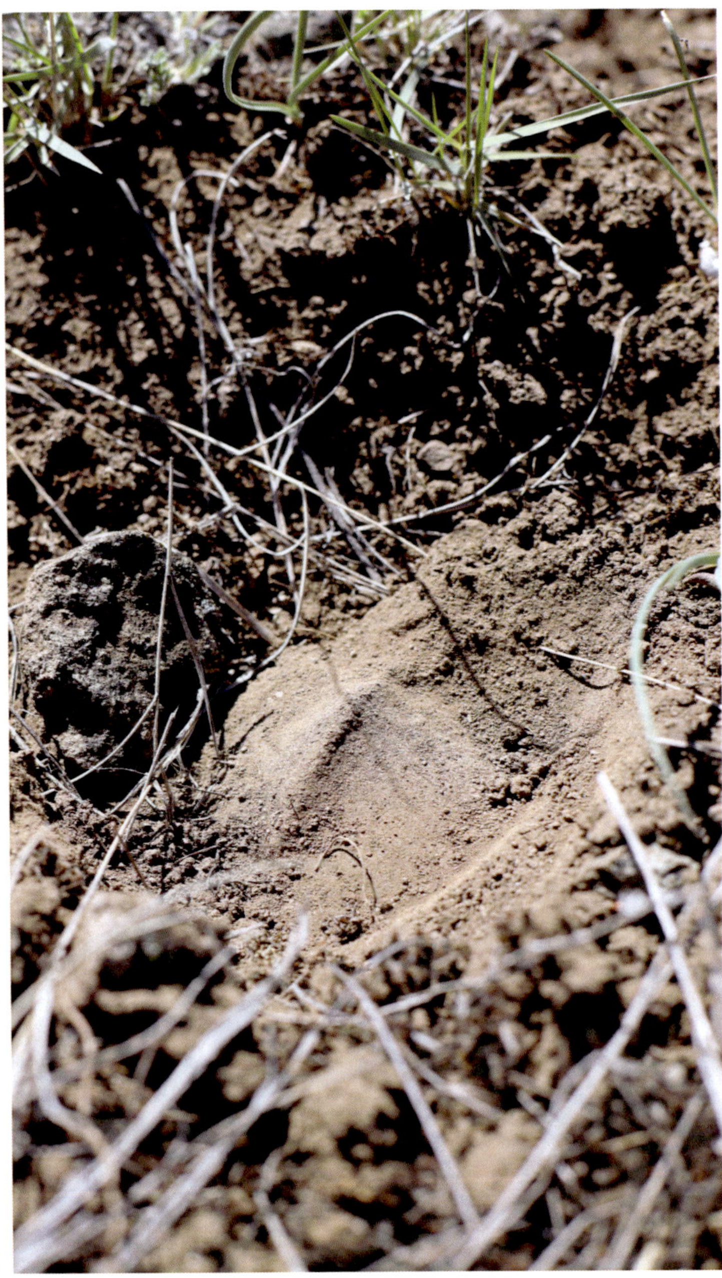
Above: Image 7X8A8635. Photograph copyright © Lochlainn Seabrook.

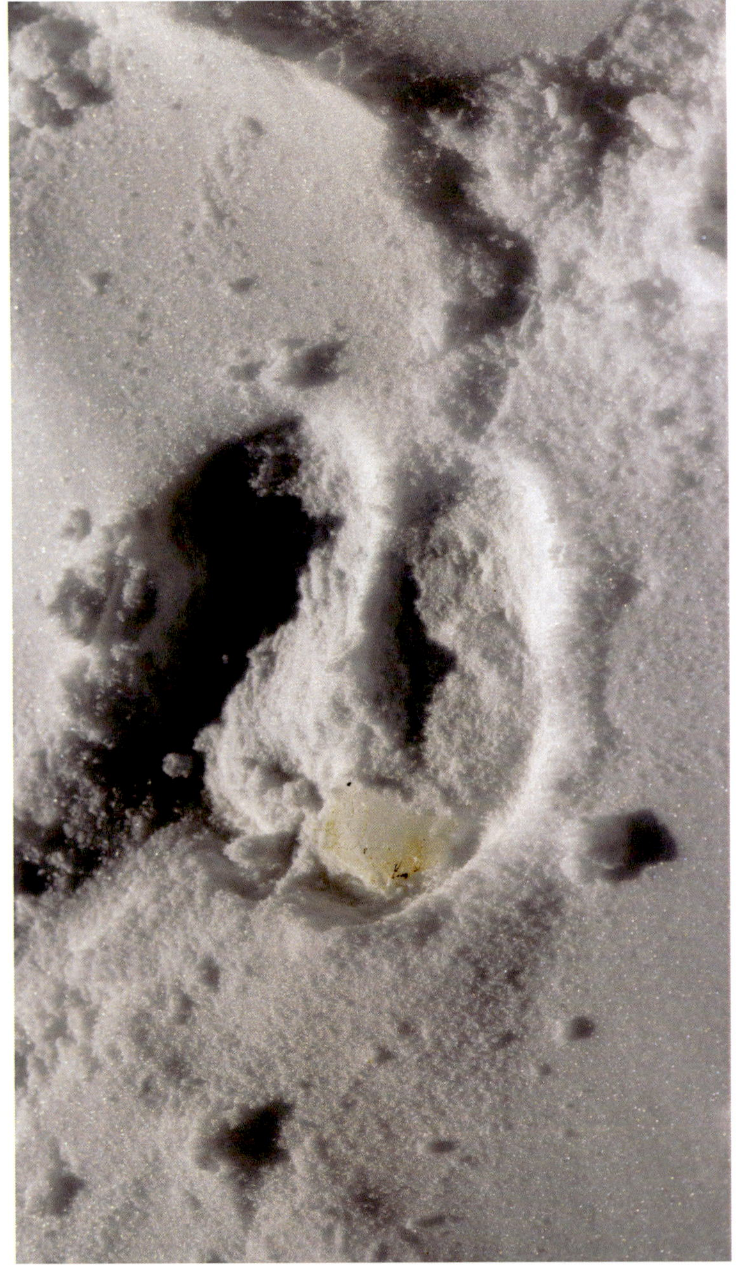
Above: Image 7X8A5300. Photograph copyright © Lochlainn Seabrook.

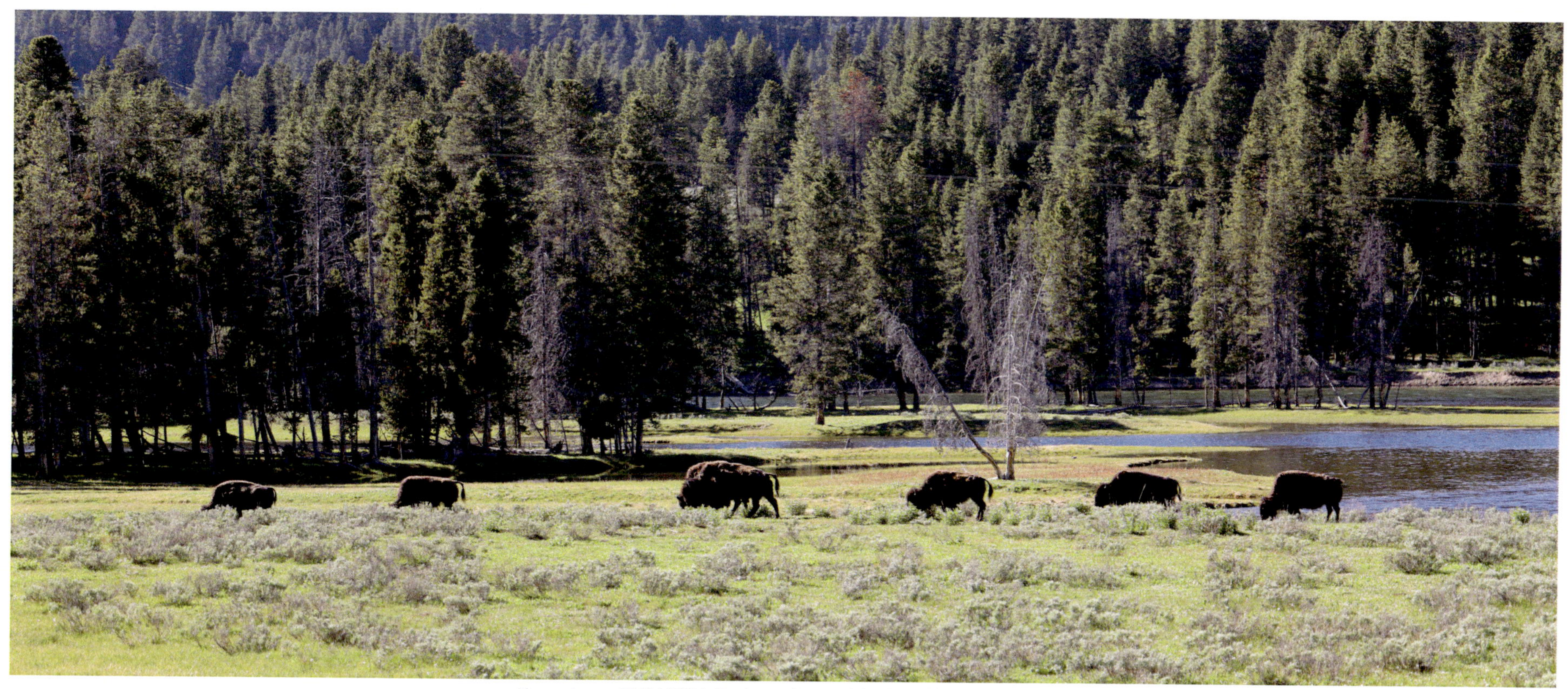

Above: Image 7X8A0804. Photograph copyright © Lochlainn Seabrook.

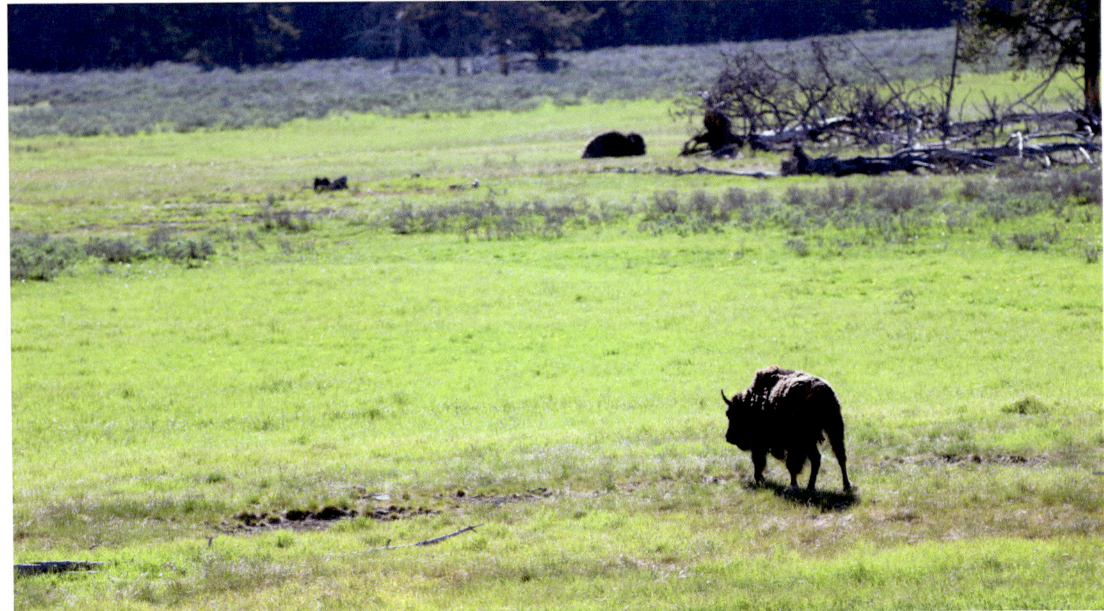

Left: Image 7X8A0801. Photograph copyright © Lochlainn Seabrook.

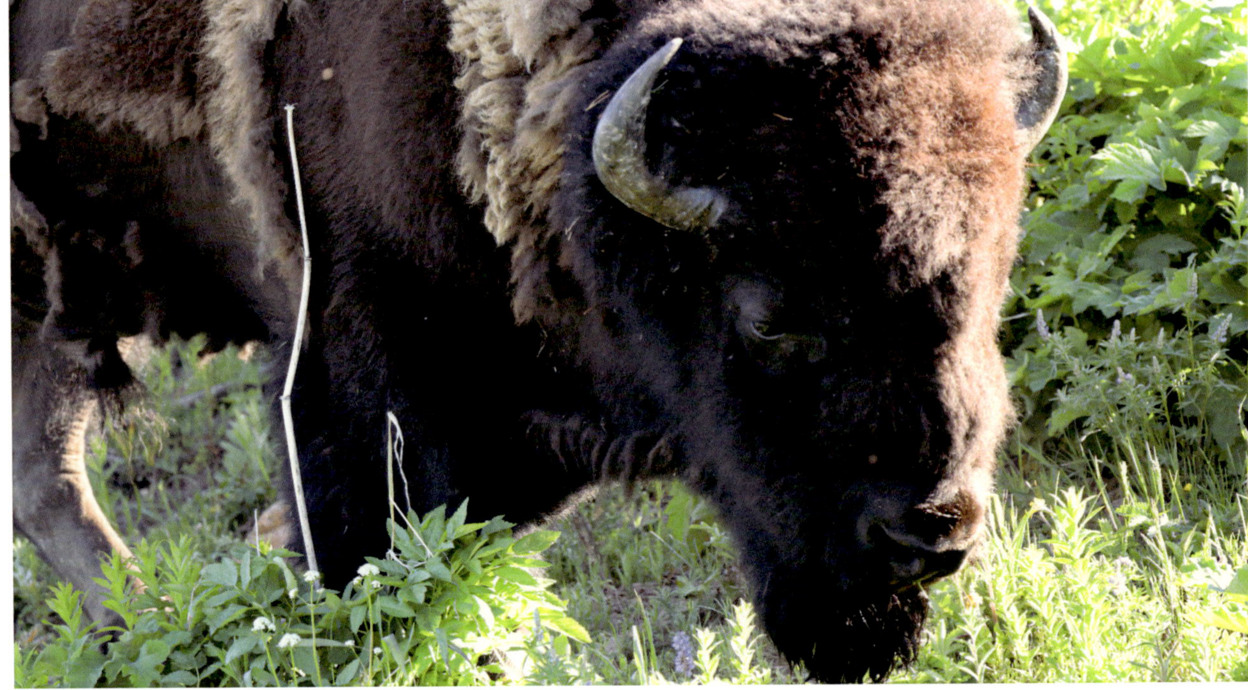

Right: Image 7X8A0691. Photograph copyright © Lochlainn Seabrook.

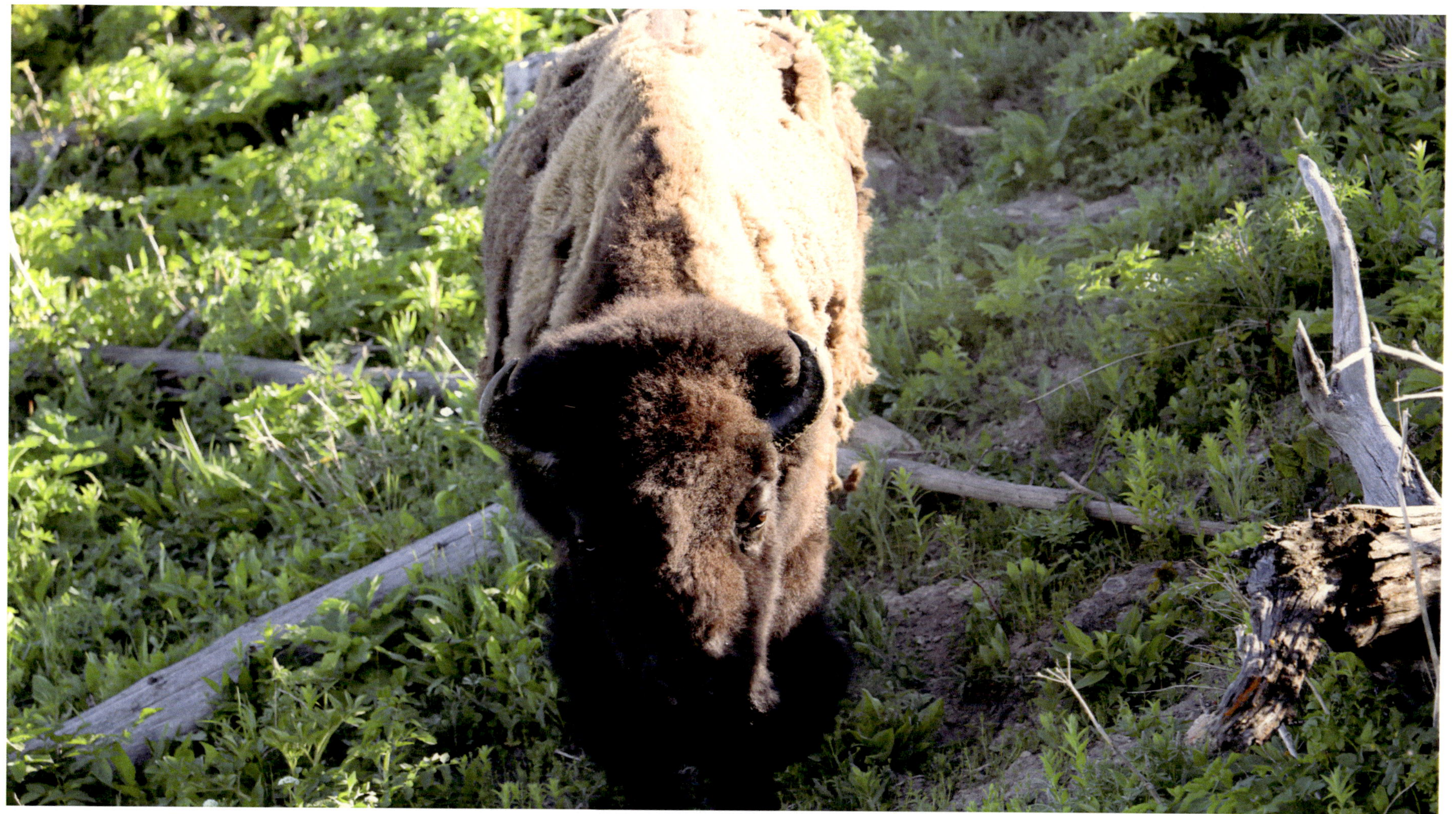

Above: Image 7X8A0680. Photograph copyright © Lochlainn Seabrook.

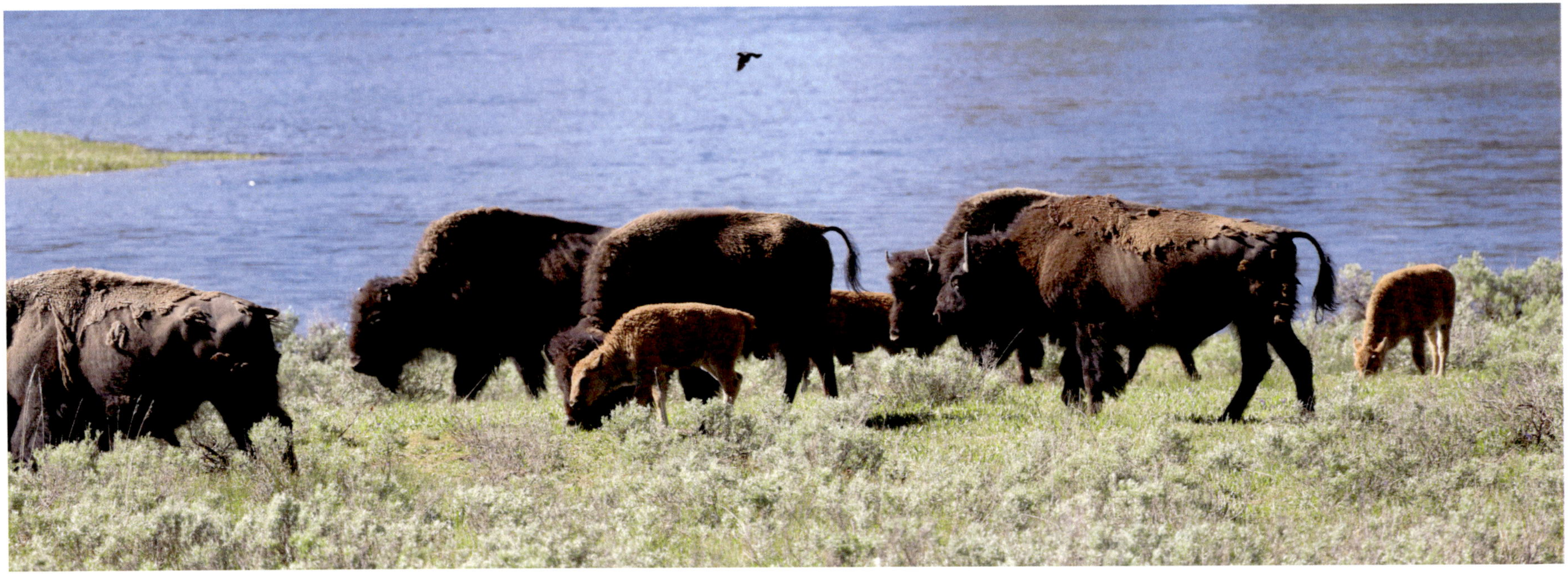

Above: Image 7X8A0820. Photograph copyright © Lochlainn Seabrook.

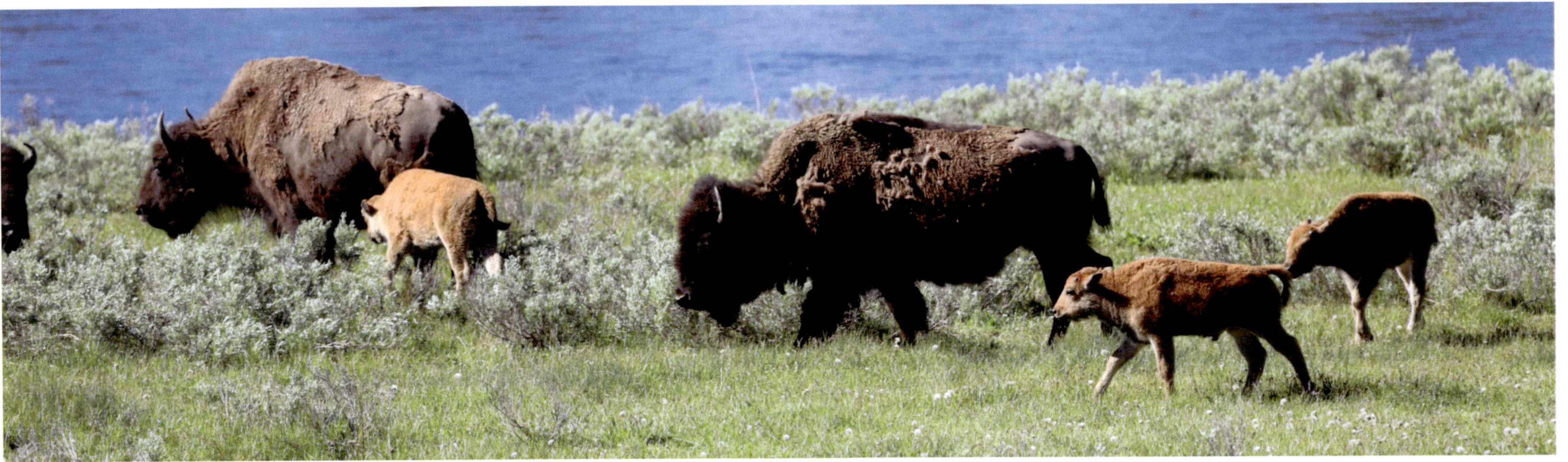

Above: Image 7X8A0847. Photograph copyright © Lochlainn Seabrook.

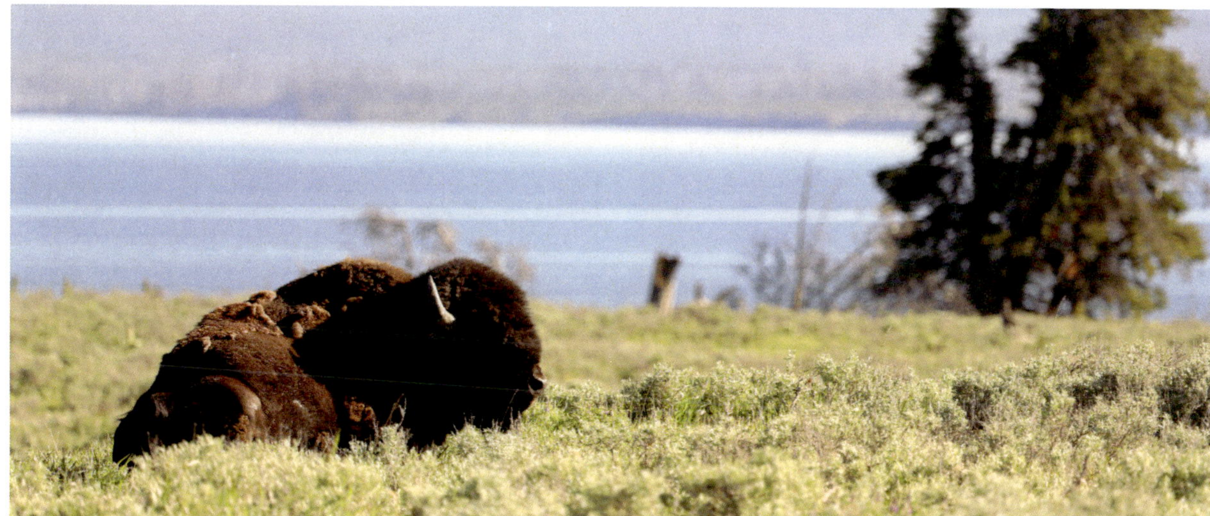

Left: Image 7X8A0732. Photograph copyright © Lochlainn Seabrook.

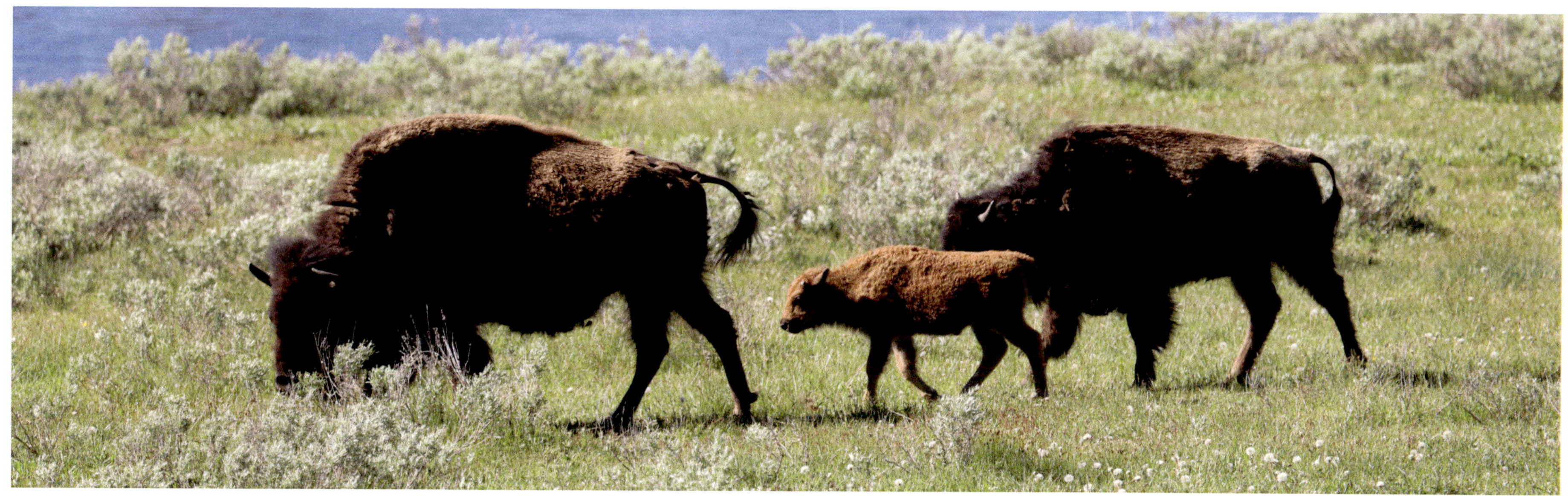

Above: Image 7X8A0881. Photograph copyright © Lochlainn Seabrook.

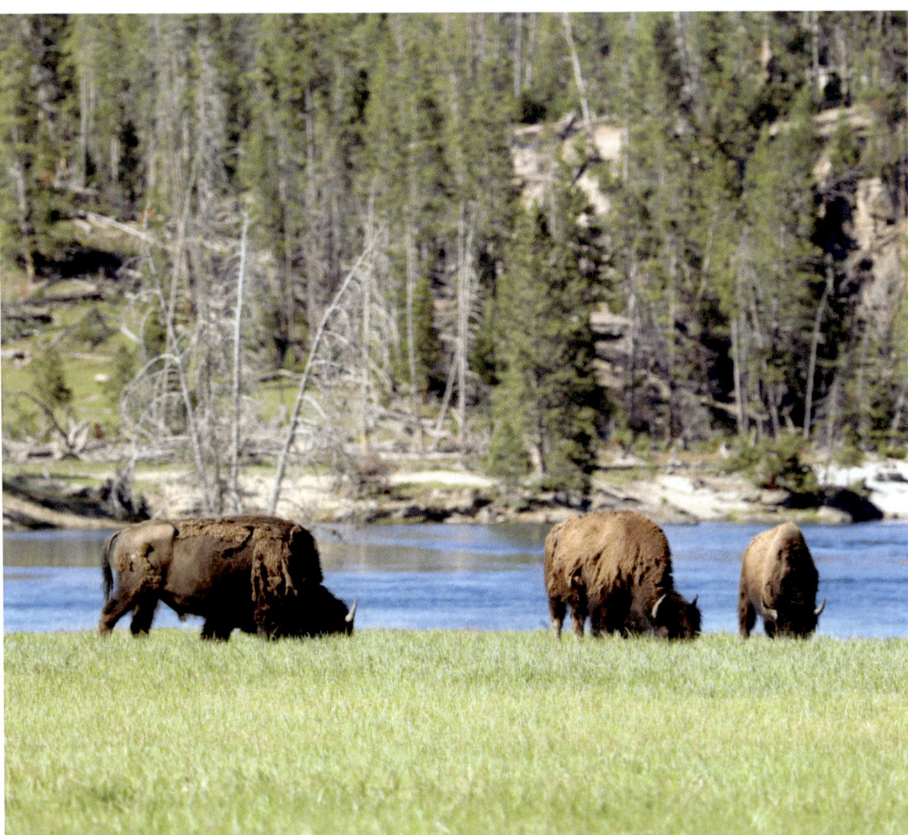

Above: Image 7X8A0788. Photograph copyright © Lochlainn Seabrook.

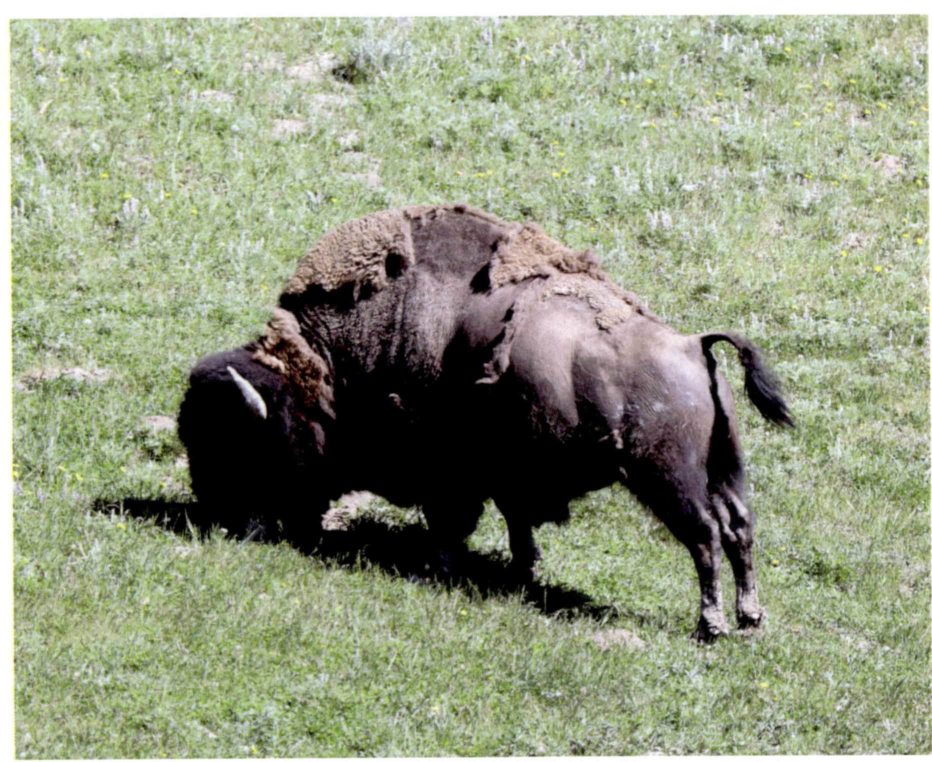

Above: Image 7X8A0898. Photograph copyright © Lochlainn Seabrook.

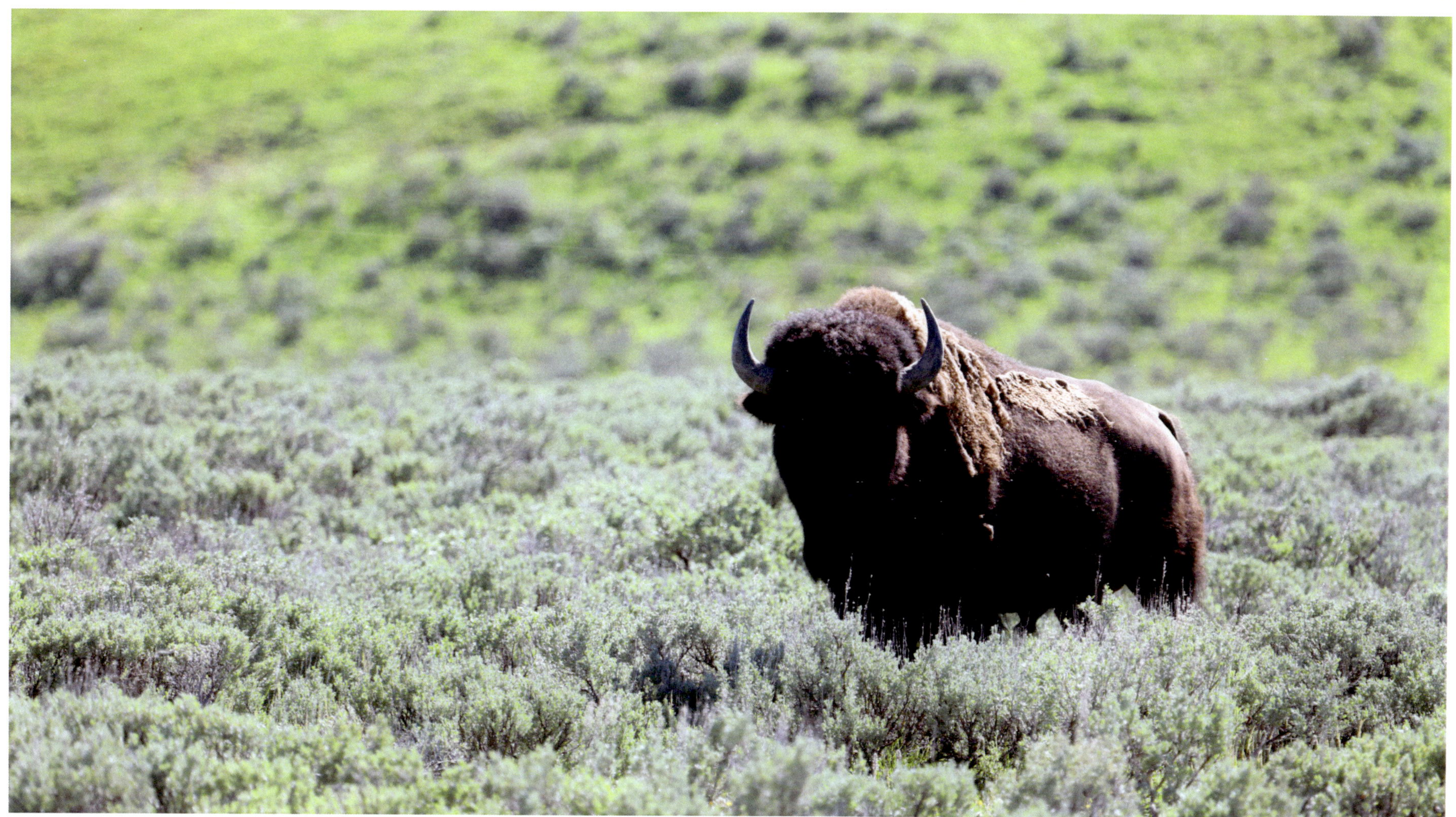

Above: Image 7X8A0945. Photograph copyright © Lochlainn Seabrook.

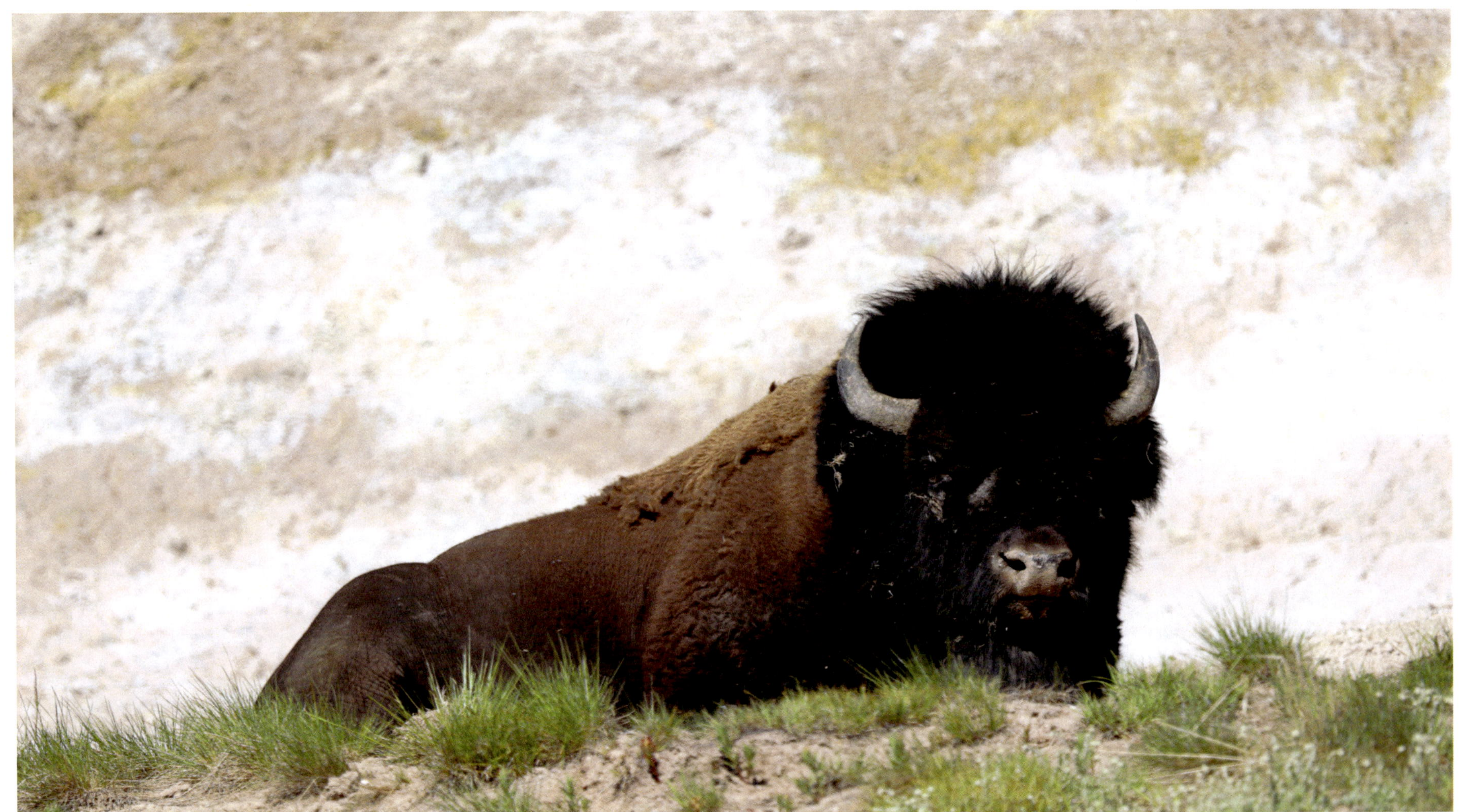

Above: Image 7X8A0900. Photograph copyright © Lochlainn Seabrook.

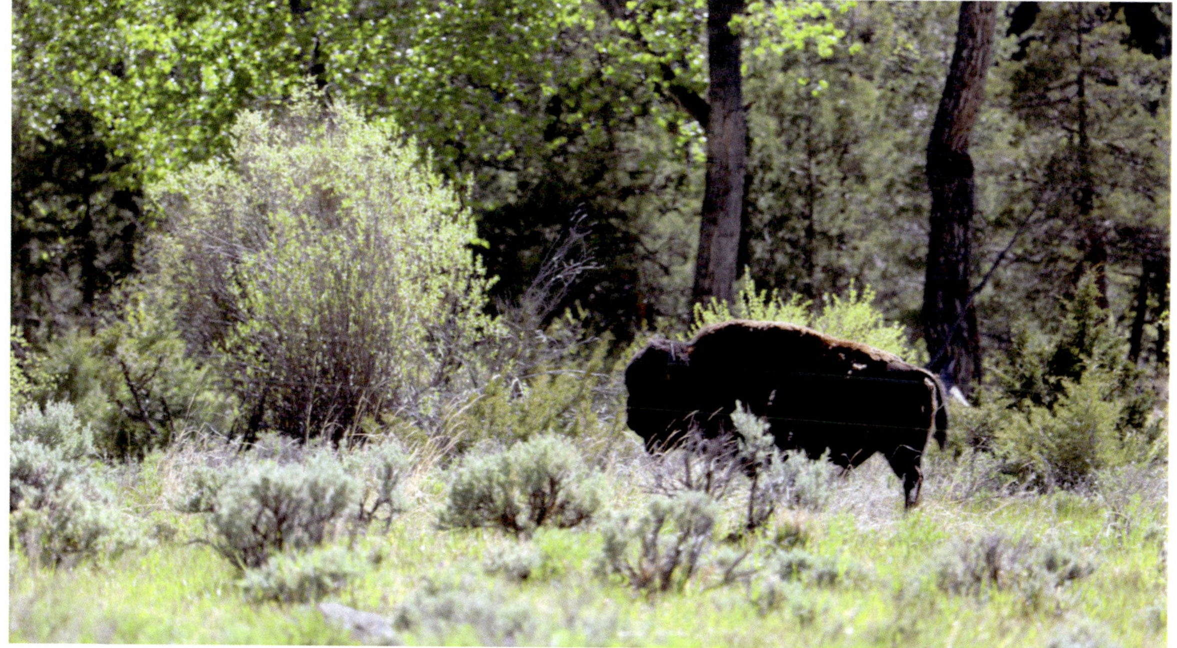

Left: Image 7X8A0265. Photograph copyright © Lochlainn Seabrook.

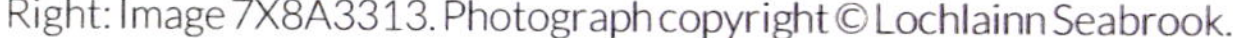

Right: Image 7X8A3313. Photograph copyright © Lochlainn Seabrook.

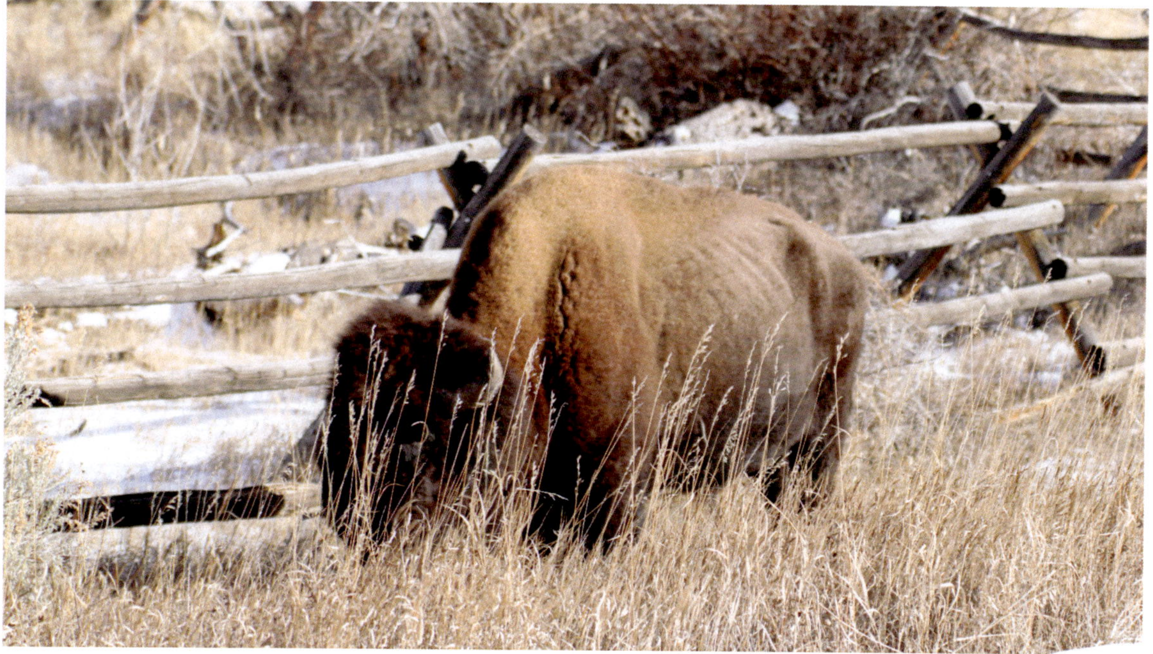

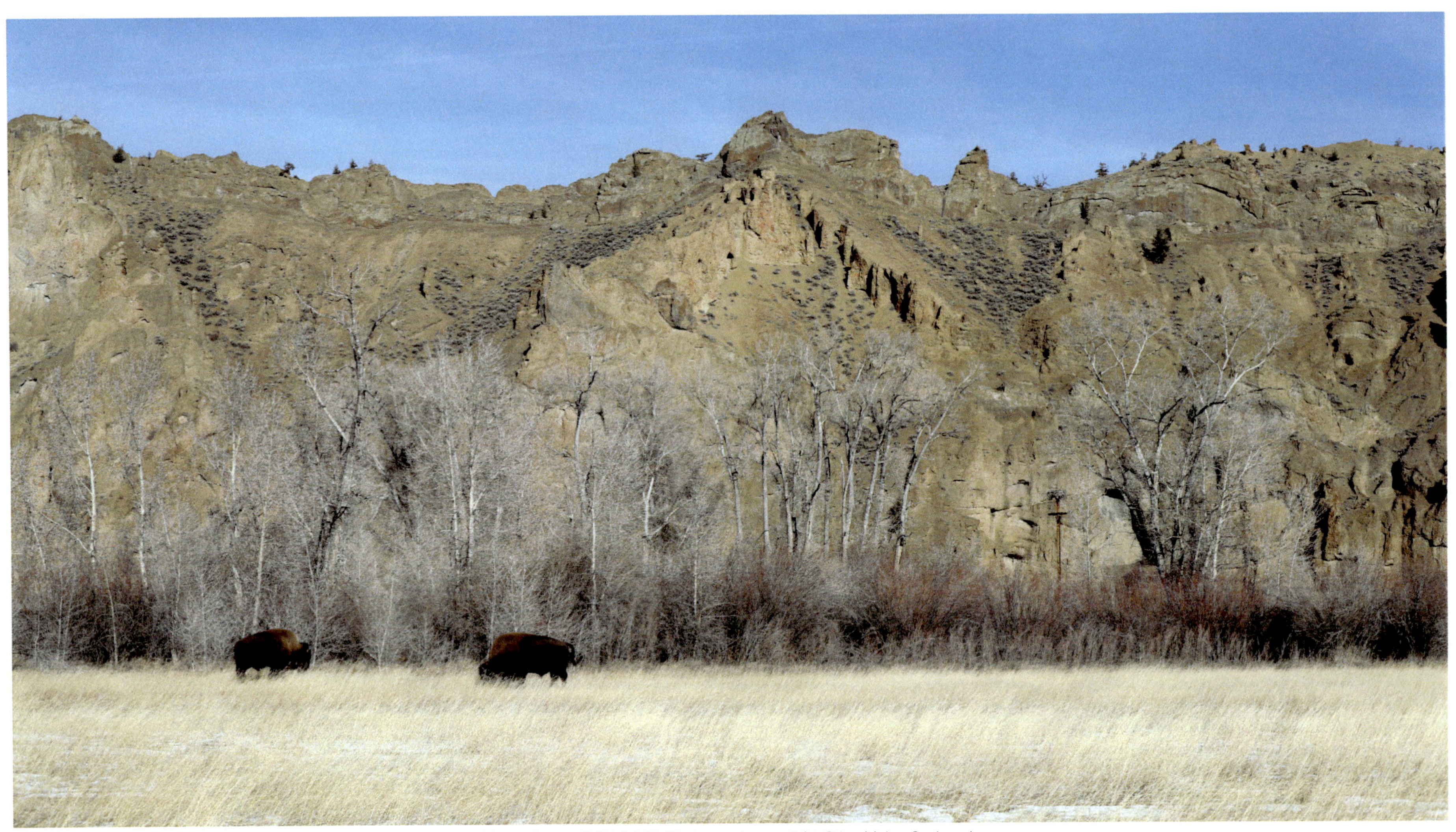

Above: Image 7X8A3469. Photograph copyright © Lochlainn Seabrook.

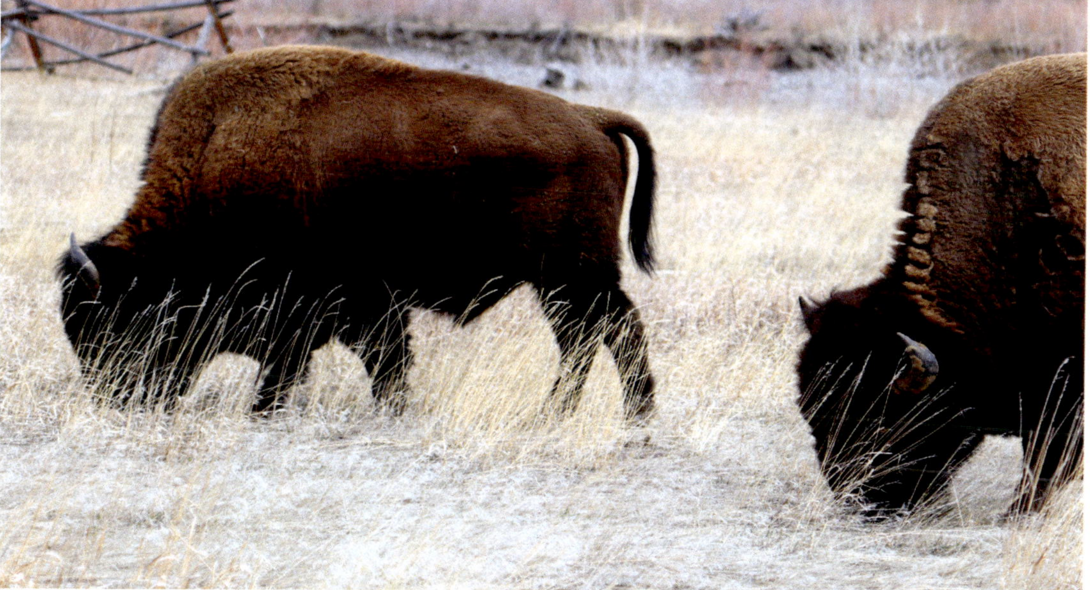

Right: Image IMG_4987. Photograph copyright © Lochlainn Seabrook.

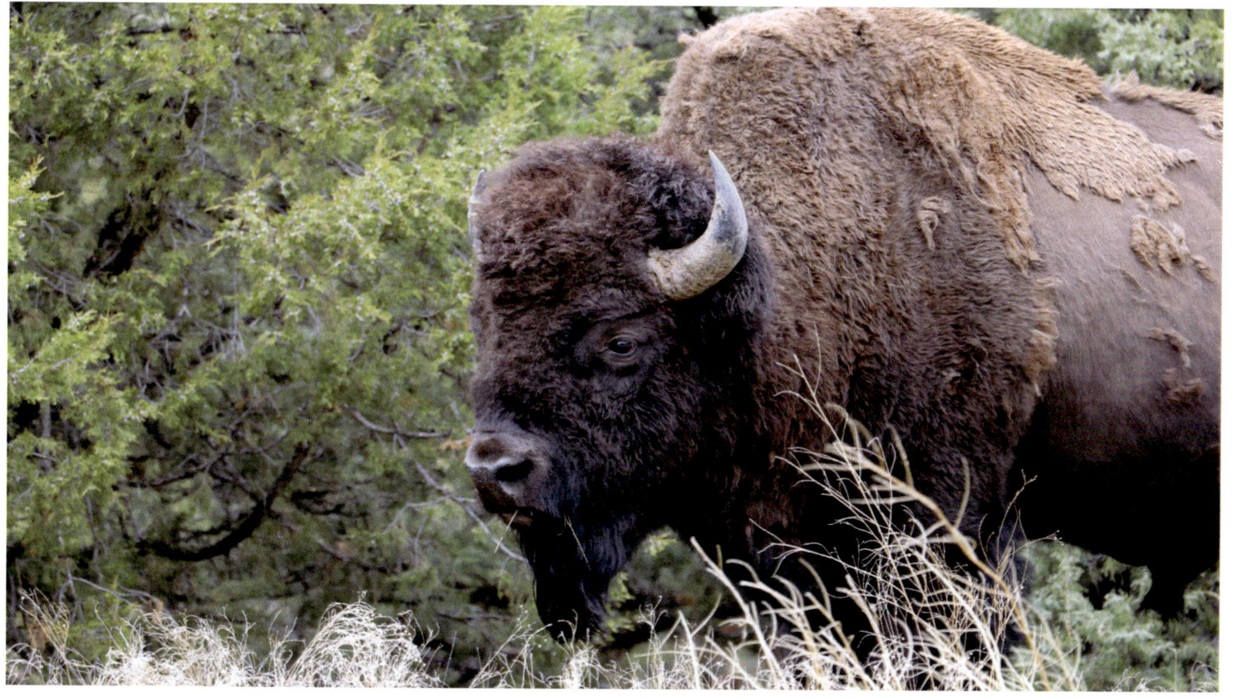

Left: Image 7X8A7860. Photograph copyright © Lochlainn Seabrook.

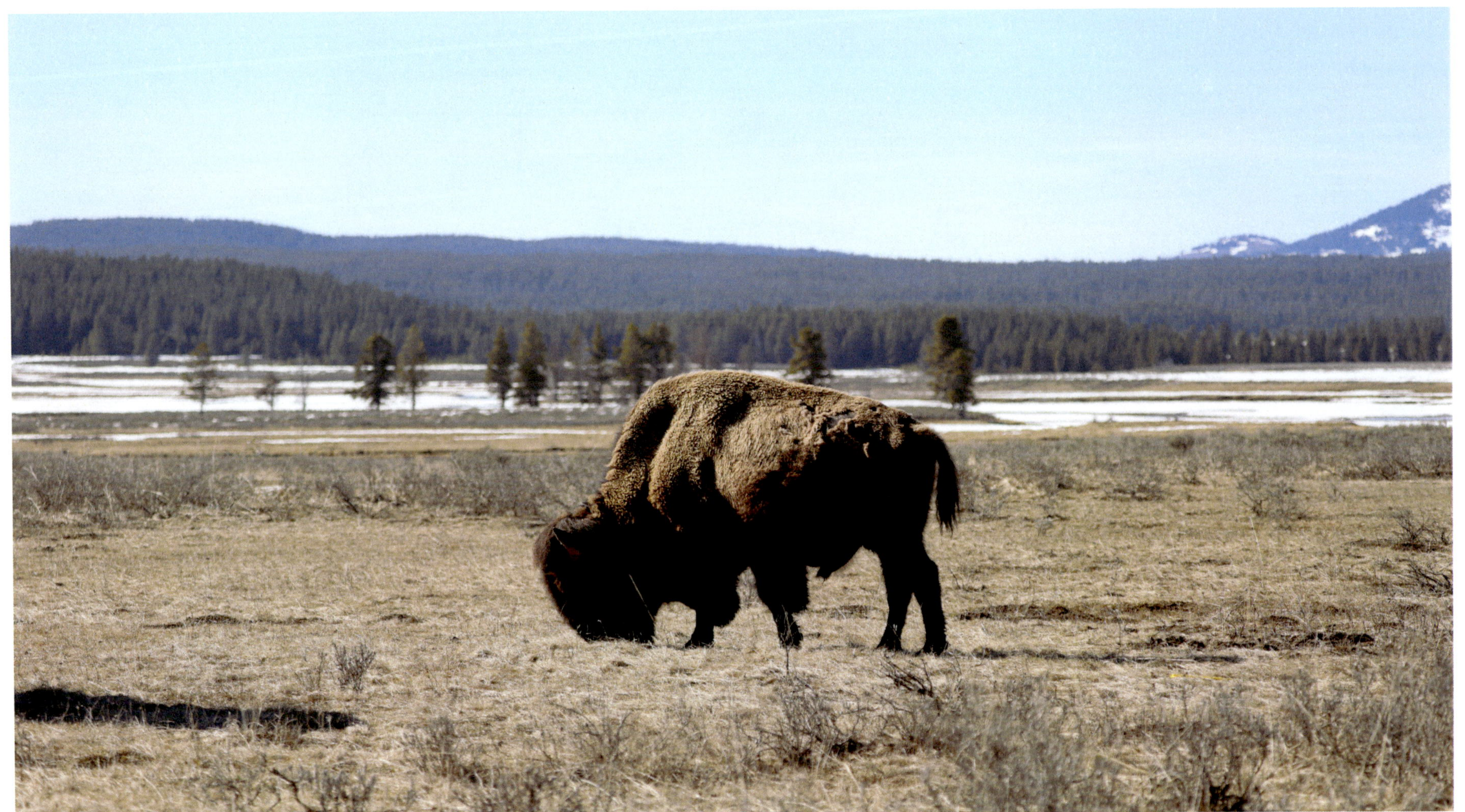

Above: Image 7X8A8938. Photograph copyright © Lochlainn Seabrook.

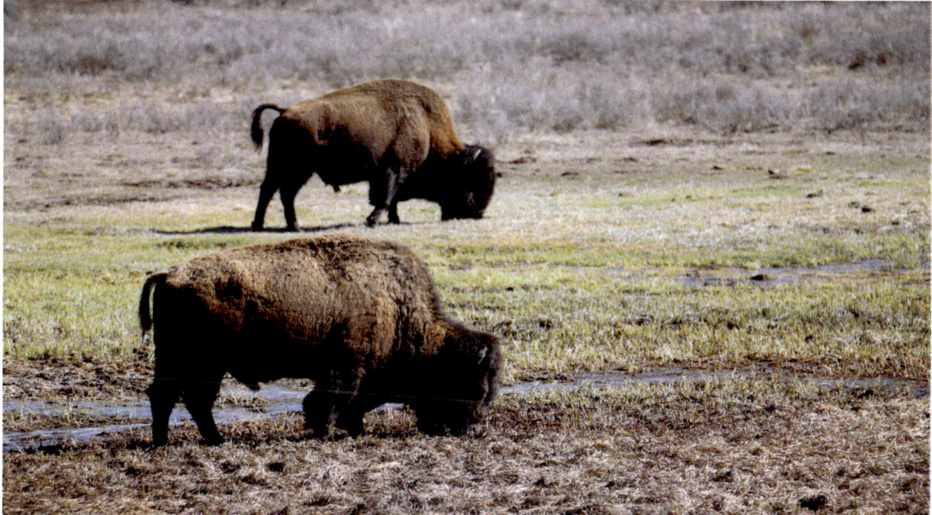

Above: Image 7X8A8972. Photograph copyright © Lochlainn Seabrook.

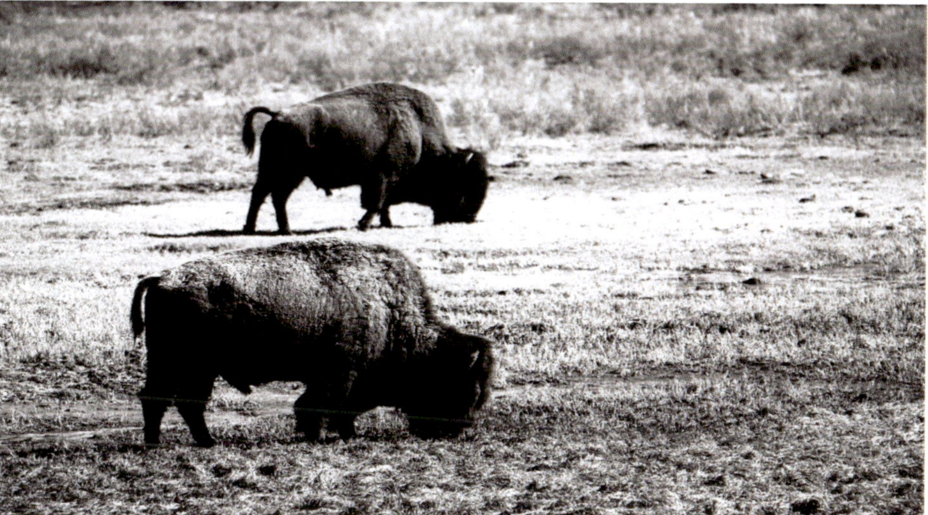

Above: Image 7X8A8972_BW. Photograph copyright © Lochlainn Seabrook.

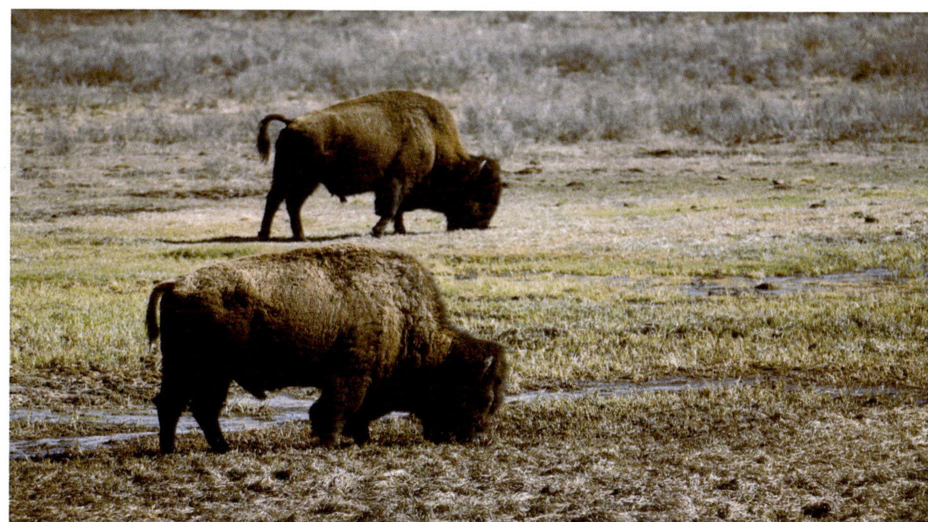

Above: Image 7X8A8972_VINTAGE. Photograph copyright © Lochlainn Seabrook.

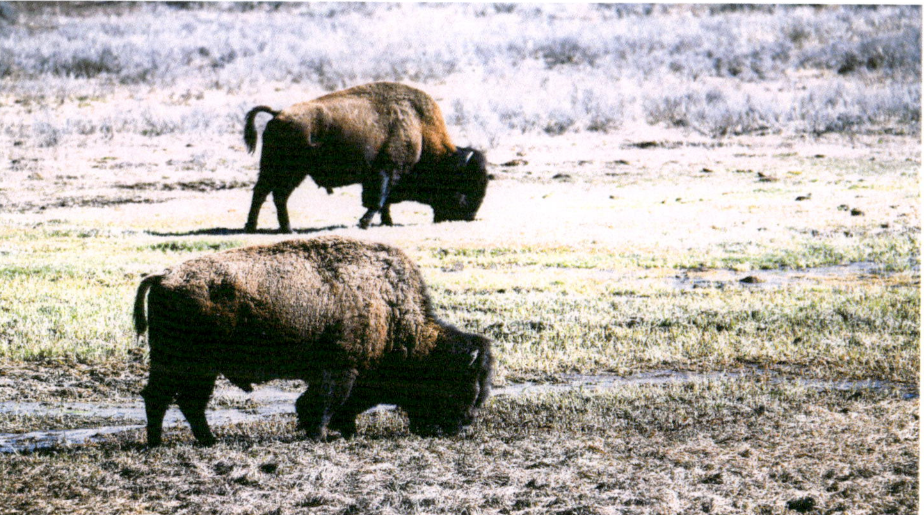

Above: Image 7X8A8972_FILM. Photograph copyright © Lochlainn Seabrook.

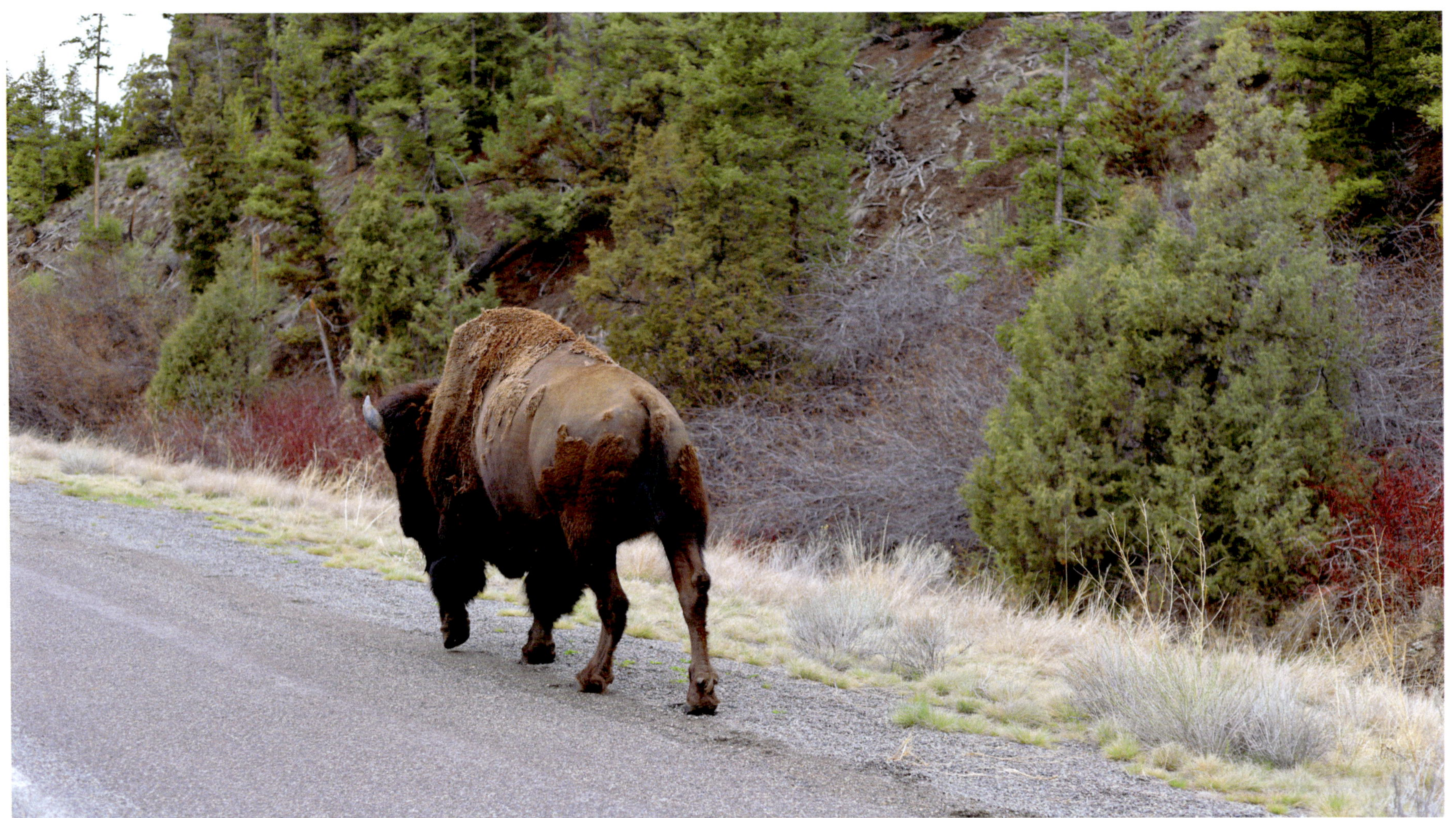
Above: Image 7X8A7846. Photograph copyright © Lochlainn Seabrook.

An Deireadh

BIBLIOGRAPHY

And Suggested Reading

A Guide to the Cave of Altamira and the Town of Santillana Del Mar. Madrid, Spain: Junta Protectora de la Cuevade Altamira, 1927.

Allen, Joel Asaph. *The American Bisons, Living and Extinct*. Cambridge, MA: Cambridge University Press, 1876.

——. *History of the American Bison: Bison Americanus*. Washington, D.C.: U.S. Government Printing Office, 1877.

Anthony, Harold Elmer. *Field Book of North American Mammals*. New York: G. P. Putnam's Sons, 1928.

Bailey, Liberty Hyde. *Cyclopedia of American Agriculture*. 4 vols. New York: Macmillan Co., 1908.

Catlin, George. *Letters and Notes on the Manners, Customs, and Condition of the North American Indians: Written During Eight Years' Travel Amongst the Wildest Tribes of Indians in North America*. 2 vols. London, UK: self-published, 1841.

Hay, Oliver P. *The Extinct Bisons of North America; with Description of One New Species, Bison Regius*. Washington, D.C.: U.S. Government Printing Office, 1913.

——. *The Pleistocene of North America and its Vertebrated Animals*. Washington, D.C.: Carnegie Institution of Washington, 1923.

Journal of Mammalogy. Vol. 1., No. 1, November 1919. Baltimore, MD: Williams and Wilkins Co., 1919.

Miller, Gerrit S., Jr. *List of North American Recent Mammals 1923*. Washington, D.C.: U.S. Government Printing Office, 1924.

Parkyn, Ernest A. *An Introduction to the Study of Prehistoric Art*. London, UK: Longmans, Green and Co., 1915.

Seabrook, Lochlainn. *The Concise Book of Owls: A Guide to Nature's Most Mysterious Birds*. Springhill, TN: Sea Raven Press, 2019.

——. *North America's Amazing Mammals: An Encyclopedia for the Whole Family*. Springhill, TN: Sea Raven Press, 2020.

——. *The Concise Book of Tigers: A Guide to Nature's Most Remarkable Cats*. Springhill, TN: Sea Raven Press, 2020.

——. *Rocky Mountain Equines: A Photographic Collection of Horses, Donkeys, and Mules of the American West*. Cody, WY: Sea Raven Press, 2024.

The Canadian Field-Naturalist. Vol. 38, No. 1, January 1924. Ottawa, CAN: Ottawa Field-Naturalists' Club, 1924.

Vasey, George. *A Monograph of the Genus Bos: The Natural History of Bulls, Bisons, and Buffaloes*. London, UK: John Russell Smith, 1851.

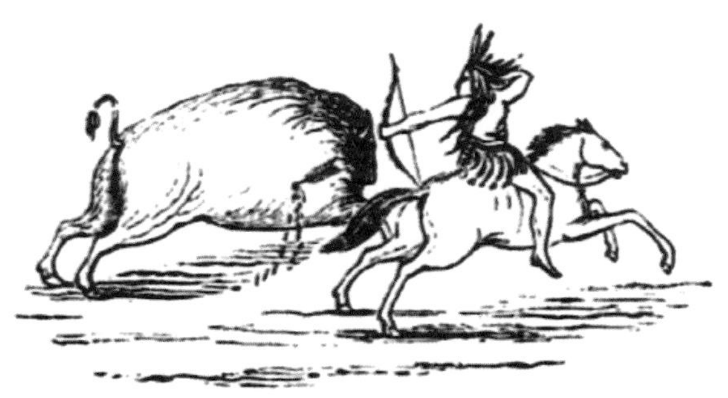

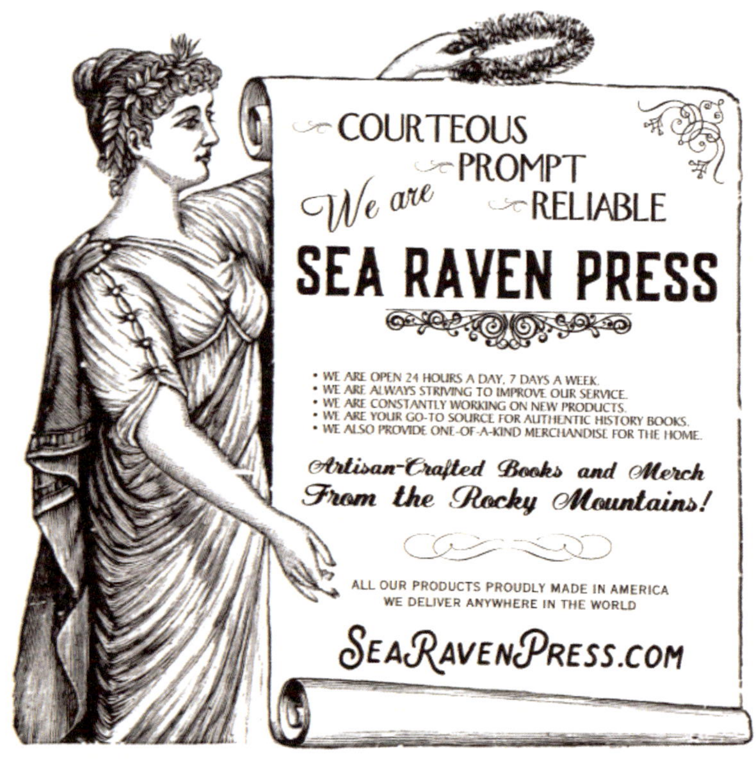

COURTEOUS
We are PROMPT
RELIABLE
SEA RAVEN PRESS
• WE ARE OPEN 24 HOURS A DAY, 7 DAYS A WEEK.
• WE ARE ALWAYS STRIVING TO IMPROVE OUR SERVICE.
• WE ARE CONSTANTLY WORKING ON NEW PRODUCTS.
• WE ARE YOUR GO-TO SOURCE FOR AUTHENTIC HISTORY BOOKS.
• WE ALSO PROVIDE ONE-OF-A-KIND MERCHANDISE FOR THE HOME.
Artisan-Crafted Books and Merch
From the Rocky Mountains!
ALL OUR PRODUCTS PROUDLY MADE IN AMERICA
WE DELIVER ANYWHERE IN THE WORLD
SEARAVENPRESS.COM

Praise for Author-Historian-Photographer

Lochlainn Seabrook

Comments from Sea Raven Press readers around the world

✯ "Lochlainn Seabrook is a genius writer!" — STEVEN WARD

✯ "I have a new favorite author and his name is Lochlainn Seabrook." — J. EWING

✯ "We get asked a lot what books we use and read. We don't do many modern historians, but we make an exception for some, and Lochlainn Seabrook is one of them. His works are completely well researched from original documents, and heavily footnoted and documented." — SOUTHERN HISTORICAL SOCIETY

✯ "Looking forward to more Lochlainn Seabrook books, my favourite historian!" — ALBERTO IGLESIAS

✯ "Lochlainn Seabrook is one of the finest authors on true history in this century. His books should be on every student's desk." — RONDA SAMMONS RENO

✯ "All of Col. Seabrook's books are great. I have bought most of them and want to end up buying them all." — DAVID VAUGHN

✯ "Lochlainn pulls together such arcane facts with relative ease, compiling these into ordinary prose that strike to the heart with substance, no fluff-speak. I am awestruck! Really. He is an inspiration to me." — JAY KRUIZENGA

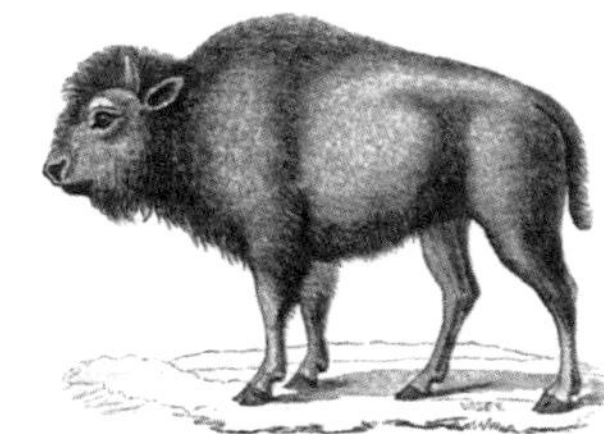

✯ "Mr. Lochlainn Seabrook is . . . the most well researched and heavily documented author I've ever read. His books are must haves. Everything he writes should be required reading! I assure you, you won't be disappointed. One simply cannot go wrong with his books. Mr. Seabrook is awesome! . . . I have never read any other author as well researched and footnoted as him. I've been in love with Mr. Seabrook for almost 5 years now. His quick wit and logic is enough reason to purchase his books. But the mere fact that he's so extensively researched is icing on the cake. Mr. Seabrook is my favorite, hands down." — LANI BURNETTE RINKEL

✯ "Best author ever." — EMILY

✯ "Lochlainn Seabrook is an incredible writer and I love all of his books on the South. . . . His writing is brilliant. . . . I look forward to reading more of his masterpieces. Thank you." — JOEY

✯ "Mr. Seabrook, thank you ever so much for blessing us with your most enlightening works." — LAURENCE DRURY

✯ "It's hard to choose just one of Lochlainn's books!" — ROSANNE STEELE

✯ "I recommend anything written by Lochlainn Seabrook." — HOTRODMOB

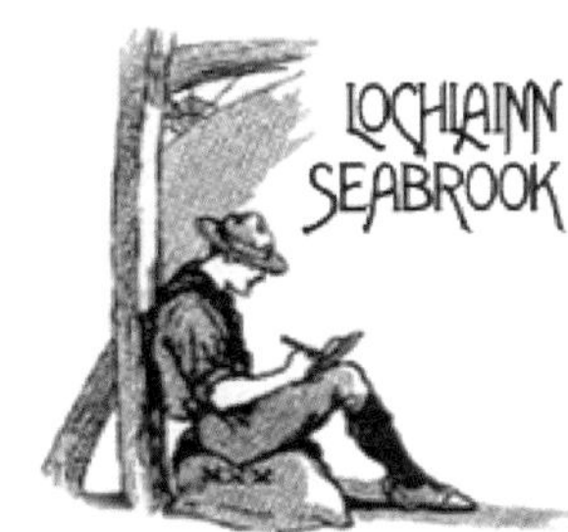

☆ "I love Lochlainn Seabrook's style and approach. It's not the 'norm.' What a miracle his books are. . . . He is a literal life changing author! Amazing books!" — KEITH PARISH

☆ "I adore Mr. Seabrook's style and I love his books. I love an author that does proper research, and still finds a way to engage the reader. Mr. Seabrook does an admirable job of both." — DONALD CAUL

☆ "Lochlainn Seabrook's books are much more well researched and authoritative than those eminently celebrated as being the authorities on the subjects he writes on. You can always trust to find the truth in his writings. . . . He does not rewrite history, but instead shows it as it is." — GARY STIER

☆ "I love all of Colonel Seabrook's books. They are informative and enlightening, and his warm Southern hospitality writing style makes you feel right at home." — KEITH CRAVEN

☆ "Lochlainn Seabrook's work is an absolute treasure of scholarship and historic scope." — MARK WAYNE CUNNINGHAM

☆ "Mr. Seabrook's command of . . . history is breathtaking. . . . He deserves great renown—check out his books!" — MARGARET SIMMONS

☆ "I love Seabrook's writings. LOVE!!! . . . So grateful to know the truth! Keep writing Lochlainn!!!" — REBECCA DALRYMPLE

☆ "Lochlainn Seabrook . . . [has] probably [written] the best book on mental science in existence by a living author. Along with Thomas Troward, Emmet Fox, and Jack Addington, Mr. Seabrook is one of the top four mental science authors of all time, since biblical times." - IAN BARTON STEWART

☆ "Glad I discovered Mr. Seabrook! . . . He writes eye opening books! Unbelievable the facts he unearths - and he backs it all up with truth, notes, footnotes, and bibliography! . . . He always amazes me! His books always see the whole picture. His timelines and bibliographies are incredible. He always provides carefully reasoned arguments! He's the best. To me I think he's better than the late great Shelby Foote! America needs more like Lochlainn Seabrook. I can't wait to own all of his books on the war [between the states] someday. Everyone who wants the Truth, who seeks the Truth and wants the full story, should read his books." — JOHN BULL BADER

☆ "I love all of Colonel Seabrook's books!" — DEBBIE SIDLE

☆ "Lochlainn Seabrook is well educated and versed in what he writes and I'm impressed with the delivery." — THOMAS L. WHITE

☆ "Thank you Lochlainn Seabrook for your wonderful books! You are the real deal! You are an amazing author and I love your books!!" — SOPHIA MEOW CELLIST

☆ "I really enjoy Mr. Seabrook's books! His knowledge is beyond belief!" — SANDRA FISH

☆ "Love Lochlainn Seabrook. Awesome!!" — ROBIN HENDERSON ARISTIDES

☆ "Kudos to Lochlainn Seabrook who is a very good and informative professional truthful historian. We need more like him!" — AMY VACHON

MEET THE AUTHOR-PHOTOGRAPHER

Lochlainn Seabrook is a lifelong writer, historian, naturalist, and award-winning multi-genre author and editor of 100 books ranging in topic from nature and science to history and religion. He wrote his first natural history composition at age nine, an essay on the fisher (*Martes pennanti*).

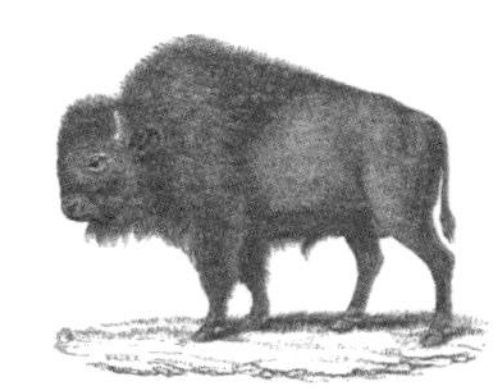

His love of animals, natural history, and the great outdoors has taken him to nearly every corner of the U.S., from working as a personal hunting guide in the Rocky Mountains to ranch hand on the Great Plains, from farrier assistant in the Northeast to stableman in the Southwest, from wrangler in the Midwest to fish farmer in the Deep South.

A nature, wildlife, and landscape photographer and videographer, a Kentucky Colonel, and a 17th-generation Southerner of Appalachian heritage (who spent much of his childhood in the mountainous regions of Wyoming, Utah, and Colorado), he has also worked as a zookeeper and animal handler caring for the following fauna: birds of prey (owl, hawk, eagle, vulture); reptiles (alligator, snake, turtle); small mammals (mouse, rat, chipmunk); medium-sized mammals (rabbit, skunk, prairie dog, otter); large mammals (bear, deer, horse); canids (fox, coyote); medium-sized cats (bobcat, lynx, margay); large cats (Amur tiger, mountain lion, jaguar).

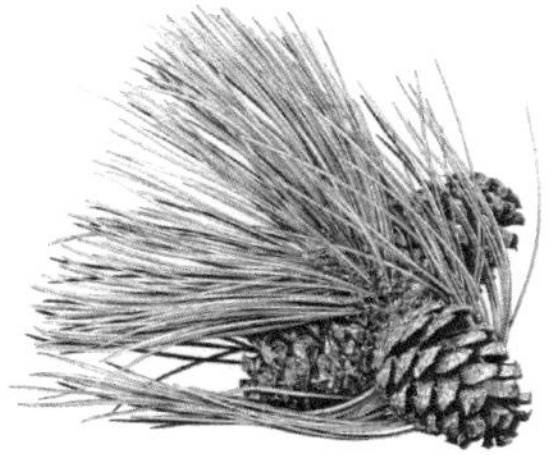

In addition to both *Rocky Mountain Equines*—the first volume in his American West Nature Series—and *Rocky Mountain Bison*, Colonel Seabrook is also the author of the bestseller, *The Concise Book of Owls: A Guide to Nature's Most Mysterious Birds* (endorsed by the World Bird Sanctuary), *The Concise Book of Tigers: A Guide to Nature's Most Remarkable Cats*, and the monumental work, *North America's Amazing Mammals: An Encyclopedia for the Whole Family*—the world's first scientific animal guide to include an entry on Sasquatch.

Seabrook has traveled the U.S. from coast to coast shooting fine art photos for his books, commercial prints, and posters, as well as recording live shots for his online nature-oriented video channel "Ambiance Gone Wild." A constitutionalist, avid outdoorsman, and gun rights advocate, he lives with his wife and family in the Rocky Mountains, heart of the American West, where you will find him hiking, filming, and writing.

For more info visit

LochlainnSeabrook.com

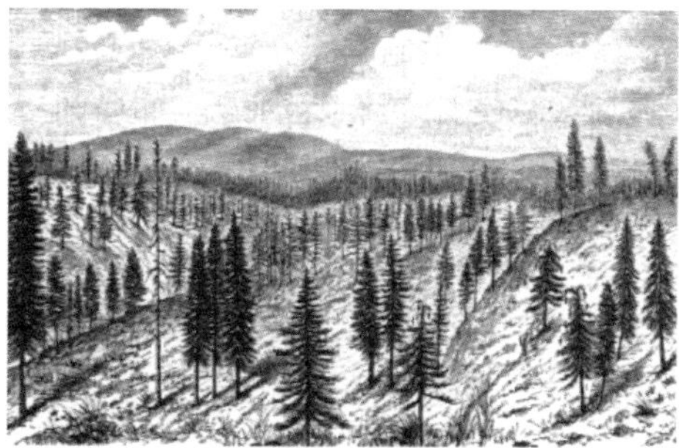

www.ingramcontent.com/pod-product-compliance
Lightning Source LLC
LaVergne TN
LVRC080420110826
845147LV00010B/739

* 9 7 8 1 9 5 5 3 5 1 5 5 3 *